Glencoe
Literature
The Reader's Choice

Active Learning and Note Taking Guide
British Literature

 Glencoe

New York, New York   Columbus, Ohio   Chicago, Illinois   Peoria, Illinois   Woodland Hills, California

Acknowledgments
Grateful acknowledgment is given to authors, publishers, photographers, museums, and agents for permission to reprint the following copyrighted material. Every effort has been made to determine copyright owners. In case of any omissions, the Publisher will be pleased to make suitable acknowledgments in future editions.

TIME © Time, Inc. TIME and the red border design are trademarks of TIME, Inc. used under license.

The McGraw·Hill Companies

Send all inquiries to:
Glencoe/McGraw-Hill
8787 Orion Place
Columbus, OH 43240-4027

ISBN-13: 9780078763960
ISBN-10: 0078763967

Printed in the United States of America.
  2 3 4 5 6 7 8 9 024-BA 12 11 10 09 08 07

Table of Contents

UNIT 1

UNIT 2

UNIT 5

UNIT 6

UNIT 7

To Students and Parents

Welcome to the *Active Learning and Note Taking Guide*. This portable book is designed for you to write in. It is **interactive**: the book prompts, and you respond. The *Guide* encourages, questions, provides space for notes, and invites you to jot down your thoughts and ideas. You can use it to circle and underline words and phrases you think are important, and to write questions that will guide your reading. Also, the *Guide* provides more support in earlier lessons than in later ones to reflect your growing skill development.

The *Active Learning and Note Taking Guide* helps you develop skills for reading **informational** text—skills such as identifying main ideas, previewing, sequencing, and recognizing organizational patterns in text. Informational text is nonfiction. It presents facts, explanations, and opinions, and is often accompanied by charts, diagrams, and other graphics that make information easier to grasp. Among the types of interesting and challenging texts in this *Guide*, you'll find:

- Biographical sketches
- Memoirs
- Literary history
- Criticism
- Surveys
- Award-winning nonfiction book excerpts
- Primary source documents
- High-interest articles from *TIME* magazine

The *Active Learning and Note Taking Guide* helps you study the background articles found in the Unit and Part Introductions of your textbook, *Glencoe Literature: The Reader's Choice*. The *Guide* includes two types of lessons:

- **Note Taking on Informational Text Lessons** present a tried-and-true method of note taking—called The Cornell Note Taking System—along with prompts to help you preview, record, reduce, and summarize the introductory articles in your textbook. Using the book will help you learn this valuable note-taking method, so you can make your own Cornell notes whenever you study.

- **Active Reading of Informational Text Lessons** are lessons based on the Perspectives and *TIME* magazine articles in your anthology. In this part of the book, you'll practice identifying important passages, writing paragraphs, and completing graphic organizers—all tools that expert readers use to help them comprehend informational texts.

Note to Parents and Guardians: Ask your students to show you their work periodically, and explain how it helps them study. You might want to talk to them about how the skills they are learning cross over to other subjects.

The Cornell Note Taking System

By Douglas Fisher, Ph.D.

Are you secretly asking yourself, "Do I really have to take notes?" Are you wondering what you will write down and how you'll know if you're doing a good job of taking notes? If you are, don't worry. The note-taking lessons in this book will guide you to take good notes that will help you remember what you read. These lessons are based on the Cornell Note Taking System.

Note Taking and Active Learning

The ability to take notes can make a difference in your life. Research shows that students who take good notes perform better on tests, and note-taking skills are crucial if you plan to attend college. They are also important in a variety of jobs and careers. Notes provide an opportunity to put what you read into your own words. You can organize your notes in ways that will help you understand them, including creating diagrams and graphic organizers. When you take notes you become more actively engaged in what you read by constantly looking for main ideas, supporting details, and key relationships. Having a process for taking notes is particularly useful in understanding informational text—nonfiction that presents facts, explanations, and opinions.

Previewing the Note Taking Steps

The note-taking pages in this book are divided in two columns, one wide and one narrow. This format provides a way to organize your thinking. It is based on the Cornell Note Taking System, first developed at Cornell University to help students take more effective notes. The following list previews the steps of the Cornell Note Taking System. You'll use this system as you complete the note-taking lessons, in which you'll be taking notes on Unit Introductions, Part Introductions, and Literary Histories in your textbook, *Glencoe Literature, The Reader's Choice.*

Record First, you will **Record** notes in the right (wide) column as you read. Your notes will take a variety of forms, including summaries, bulleted lists, and graphic organizers. They will help you understand what you read and will be useful later on when you need to write an essay, read a literary selection, or study for a test.

Reduce Once you've taken notes in the Record column, you will **Reduce** your notes into key words, phrases, and questions in the left (narrow) column. This step will help you clarify meaning, find information within your notes, and trigger your memory when you study.

Recap At the end of significant parts of a Unit Introduction, such as a Genre Focus, you will use the bottom portion of the page to **Recap** what you've learned. This step helps strengthen your grasp of what you just read before you move on to the next part.

At the end of each lesson there's space to **Summarize** your notes, often by using a graphic organizer. You will also **Apply** your notes by taking a brief test.

Recite To increase your ability to recall your notes, you will cover the Record column and **Recite**—or read aloud—the facts and ideas in your notes by using the key words, phrases, and questions in the Reduce column as cues. Check to see how well you can Recite the information in your Record column from memory.

Reflect After you complete the Recite step, you will **Reflect** on your notes. Consider how your notes relate to what you already know, your other classes, and your life experiences.

Review Finally, you will **Review** your notes periodically. By following the Cornell Note Taking System you will produce valuable notes that you can refer to when you study or write.

Developing Your Note Taking Habits

Learning to take efficient notes can be hard work. One motivation to improve this skill is that good note takers do better in school. They remember more and can use that knowledge in a variety of ways. In addition, good note takers develop habits that they can use later in their life—whether during a job-related meeting or a lecture in a college class. Once you're able to complete the lessons in this book, you'll be able to use the Cornell Note Taking System when you read other books, listen to a lecture in class, attend a meeting, or even as you watch a film.

How To Use This Book: Note Taking Lessons

The note taking lessons lead you through the process of taking Cornell notes on the Unit Introductions, Part Introductions, and Literary Histories in your textbook, *Glencoe Literature: The Reader's Choice.* You'll be learning to record important information in your own words, to reduce it to key words that will help you remember your notes, and to apply your notes as you read the literature in your textbook. You'll also learn to recognize patterns of organization in informational text, use graphic organizers to take notes, and write summaries to help you remember what you read. Not only will you have a record of the ideas about the historical contexts and literary movements in which the authors wrote, but you will also be learning a note taking skill you can use in all your classes.

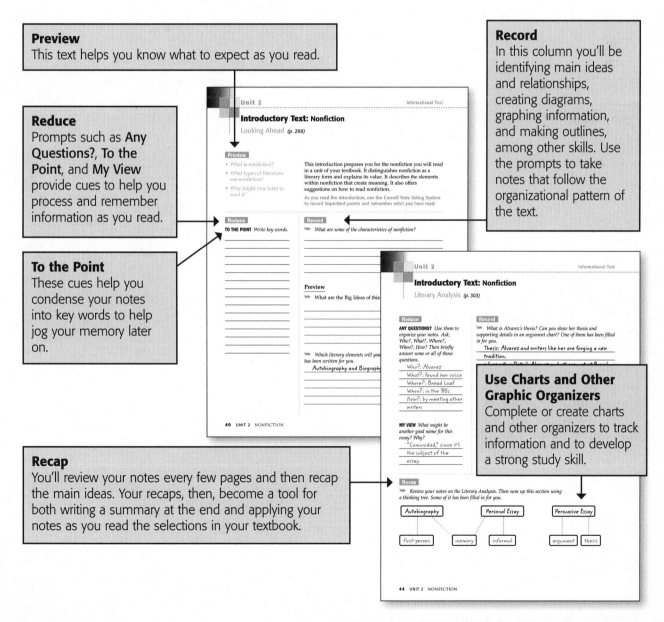

Preview
This text helps you know what to expect as you read.

Reduce
Prompts such as **Any Questions?**, **To the Point**, and **My View** provide cues to help you process and remember information as you read.

To the Point
These cues help you condense your notes into key words to help jog your memory later on.

Recap
You'll review your notes every few pages and then recap the main ideas. Your recaps, then, become a tool for both writing a summary at the end and applying your notes as you read the selections in your textbook.

Record
In this column you'll be identifying main ideas and relationships, creating diagrams, graphing information, and making outlines, among other skills. Use the prompts to take notes that follow the organizational pattern of the text.

Use Charts and Other Graphic Organizers
Complete or create charts and other organizers to track information and to develop a strong study skill.

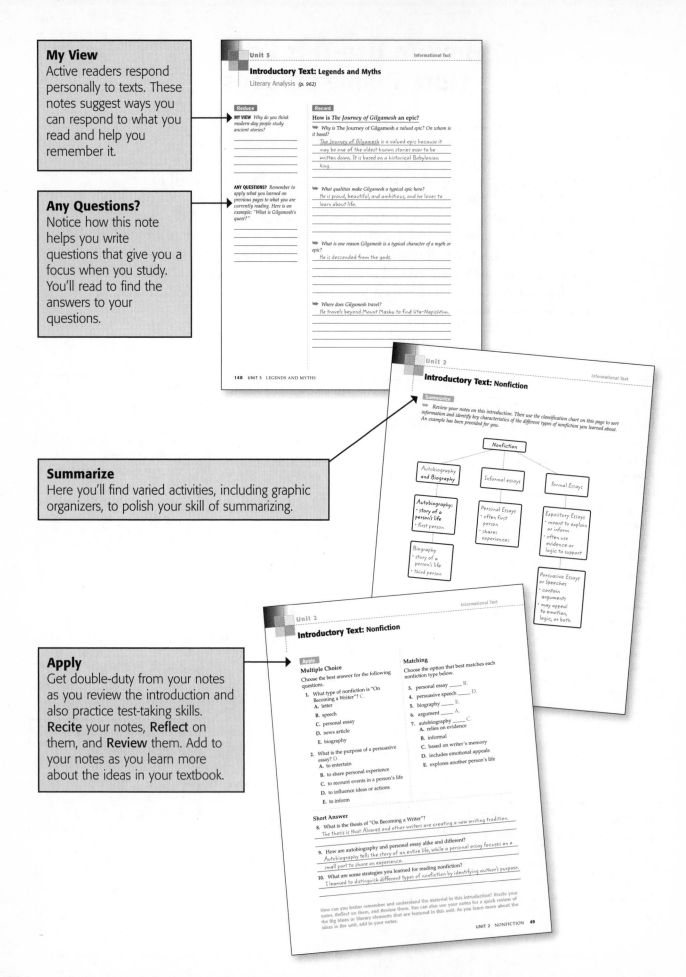

My View
Active readers respond personally to texts. These notes suggest ways you can respond to what you read and help you remember it.

Any Questions?
Notice how this note helps you write questions that give you a focus when you study. You'll read to find the answers to your questions.

Summarize
Here you'll find varied activities, including graphic organizers, to polish your skill of summarizing.

Apply
Get double-duty from your notes as you review the introduction and also practice test-taking skills. **Recite** your notes, **Reflect** on them, and **Review** them. Add to your notes as you learn more about the ideas in your textbook.

Active Reading Skills

Active reading is smart reading. When you read actively, you don't just let your eyes roll across the text and turn the page when you get to the bottom. When you read actively, you pause, reflect, ask yourself questions, and use many skills that help you understand what you read. Active reading is a part of active learning. The more you refer to the chart, the more these active reading strategies will become a natural part of the way you read.

Skill/Strategy

What Is It?	Why It's Important	How to Do It
Preview Previewing is looking over a selection before you read.	Previewing lets you begin to see what you already know and what you'll need to know. It helps you set a purpose for reading.	Look at the title, illustrations, headings, captions, and graphics. Look at how ideas are organized. Ask questions about the text.
Predict Predicting is taking an educated guess about what will happen in a selection.	Predicting gives you a reason to read. You want to find out if your prediction is verified in the selection. As you read, adjust or change your prediction if it doesn't fit what you learn.	Guess at what will be included in the text by combining what you already know about an author or subject with what you learned in your preview.

What Is It?	Why It's Important	How to Do It
Activate Prior Knowledge You have knowledge from your own experiences and from what you have read or learned in the past. That can help you understand what you are reading. When you activate this prior knowledge, you tap into it.	Activating prior knowledge draws on your own resources and helps you get the "I can do this" feeling. It also helps you connect new ideas and information to what you already know.	Pause and recall your knowledge and feelings about a topic. Ask yourself questions such as these: How does this fit my understanding? Does it agree with what I know? What part of this do I recognize?
Question Questioning is asking yourself whether information in a selection is important. Questioning is also regularly asking yourself whether you've understood what you've read.	When you ask questions as you read, you're reading strategically. As you answer your questions, you're making sure that you'll get the main ideas of a text.	Have a running conversation with yourself as you read. Keep asking questions such as these: Is this idea important? Why? Do I understand what this is about? Might this information be on a test later?
Visualize Visualizing is picturing a writer's ideas or descriptions in your mind's eye.	Visualizing is one of the best ways to understand and remember information in fiction, nonfiction, and informational text.	Carefully read how a writer describes a person, place, or thing. Ask yourself questions such as these: What would this look like? Can I see how these steps or events proceed?
Monitor Comprehension Monitoring your comprehension means thinking about whether you're understanding what you're reading.	The whole point of reading is to understand a piece of text. When you don't understand a selection, you're not really reading it.	Keep asking yourself questions about main ideas, people, and events. When you can't answer a question, review, read more slowly, or ask someone to help you.

What Is It?	Why It's Important	How to Do It
Respond Responding is telling what you like, dislike, find surprising, or find interesting in a selection.	When you react in a personal way to what you read, you'll enjoy a selection more and remember it better.	As you read, think about how you feel about the information or ideas in a selection. What's your reaction? Are you astonished? Pleased? Disgusted? Motivated to do something? What grabs your attention as you read?
Connect Connecting means linking what you read to events in your own life, to contemporary issues, or to other selections you've read.	You'll get into your reading and recall information and ideas better by connecting events, emotions, ideas, and characters to your own life and world.	Ask yourself questions such as these: Do I know someone like this? Have I ever felt this way? How is this like something I've heard about? What else have I read that is like this selection?
Review Reviewing is going back over what you've read to remember what's important and to organize ideas so you'll recall them later.	Reviewing is especially important when you have new ideas and a lot of information to remember.	Filling in a graphic organizer, such as a chart or a diagram, as you read helps you organize information. These study aids will help you review later.
Interpret Interpreting is when you use your own understanding of the world to decide what the events or ideas in a selection mean.	Every reader constructs meaning on the basis of what he or she understands about the world. Finding meaning as you read is all about you interacting with the text.	Think about what you already know about yourself and the world. Ask yourself questions such as these: What is the author really trying to say here? What larger idea might these events be about?

What Is It?	Why It's Important	How to Do It
Analyze Analyzing is looking at separate parts of a selection in order to understand the entire selection.	Analyzing helps you look critically at a piece of writing. When you analyze a selection, you'll discover its theme or message, and you'll learn the author's purpose for writing. Your analysis becomes a tool for your evaluation of the text.	To analyze any piece of writing, look carefully at its parts. Where does the introduction end? Find the parts that make up the middle. Recognize the ending. Identify the main idea, and supporting details. Examine each step in a process or each event that leads to an outcome.
Evaluate Evaluating is making a judgment or forming an opinion about something you read. Is the text reliable? Accurate? Persuasive? The answers to such questions are examples of judgments.	Evaluating helps you become a wise reader. For example, when you judge whether an author is qualified to speak about a topic or whether the author's points make sense, you can avoid being misled by what you read.	As you read, ask yourself questions such as these: Is this realistic and believable? Is this author qualified to write on this subject? Is this author biased? Does this author present opinions as facts?

How To Use This Book:
Active Reading Lessons

The notes and features in the active reading lessons will direct you through the process of reading and making meaning from each selection. As you use these notes and features, you'll be practicing and mastering the skills and strategies that good readers use whenever they read.

Get Set to Read

Building Background
Read to learn about the author and the cultural and historical events that shaped the selection. Building Background will help you become a more knowledgeable reader.

Setting Purposes for Reading
What will you learn from reading the selection? This feature will help you connect your own experiences to the selection. It will also help you determine your reasons for reading.

Reading Strategy
This feature will improve your understanding of the reading strategies taught in your textbook.

Active Reading Focus
Active reading strategies improve your ability to comprehend and appreciate each selection.

Literary Element
Learn about a literary element important to this selection before you begin reading.

Big Idea
Read about one of the Big Ideas from your textbook to better understand how each selection relates to a broader historical or literary topic.

Vocabulary
Here you'll preview the selection vocabulary words and vocabulary skill. Each word is highlighted and defined again in the selection.

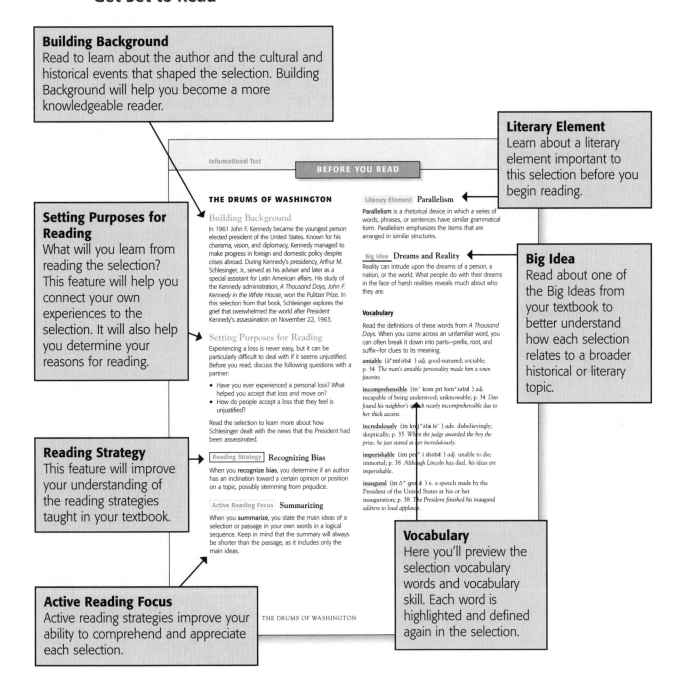

Informational Text

BEFORE YOU READ

THE DRUMS OF WASHINGTON

Building Background

In 1961 John F. Kennedy became the youngest person elected president of the United States. Known for his charisma, vision, and diplomacy, Kennedy managed to make progress in foreign and domestic policy despite crises abroad. During Kennedy's presidency, Arthur M. Schlesinger, Jr., served as his adviser and later as a special assistant for Latin American affairs. His study of the Kennedy administration, *A Thousand Days, John F. Kennedy in the White House*, won the Pulitzer Prize. In this selection from that book, Schlesinger explores the grief that overwhelmed the world after President Kennedy's assassination on November 22, 1963.

Setting Purposes for Reading

Experiencing a loss is never easy, but it can be particularly difficult to deal with if it seems unjustified. Before you read, discuss the following questions with a partner:

- Have you ever experienced a personal loss? What helped you accept that loss and move on?
- How do people accept a loss that they feel is unjustified?

Read the selection to learn more about how Schlesinger dealt with the news that the President had been assassinated.

Reading Strategy **Recognizing Bias**

When you **recognize bias**, you determine if an author has an inclination toward a certain opinion or position on a topic, possibly stemming from prejudice.

Active Reading Focus **Summarizing**

When you **summarize**, you state the main ideas of a selection or passage in your own words in a logical sequence. Keep in mind that the summary will always be shorter than the passage, as it includes only the main ideas.

Literary Element **Parallelism**

Parallelism is a rhetorical device in which a series of words, phrases, or sentences have similar grammatical form. Parallelism emphasizes the items that are arranged in similar structures.

Big Idea **Dreams and Reality**

Reality can intrude upon the dreams of a person, a nation, or the world. What people do with their dreams in the face of harsh realities reveals much about who they are.

Vocabulary

Read the definitions of these words from *A Thousand Days*. When you come across an unfamiliar word, you can often break it down into parts—prefix, root, and suffix—for clues to its meaning.

amiable (ā′ mē ə bəl) *adj.* good-natured; sociable; p. 34 *The man's amiable personality made him a town favorite.*

incomprehensible (in′ kom pri hen′ səbəl) *adj.* incapable of being understood; unknowable; p. 34 *Dan found his neighbor's speech nearly incomprehensible due to her thick accent.*

incredulously (in krej′ ələ lē¯) *adv.* disbelievingly; skeptically; p. 35 *When the judge awarded the boy the prize, he just stared at her incredulously.*

imperishable (im per′ i shəbəl) *adj.* unable to die; immortal; p. 38 *Although Lincoln has died, his ideas are imperishable.*

inaugural (in ô′ gyər əl) *n.* a speech made by the President of the United States at his or her inauguration; p. 38 *The President finished his inaugural address to loud applause.*

THE DRUMS OF WASHINGTON

Read, Respond, Interpret

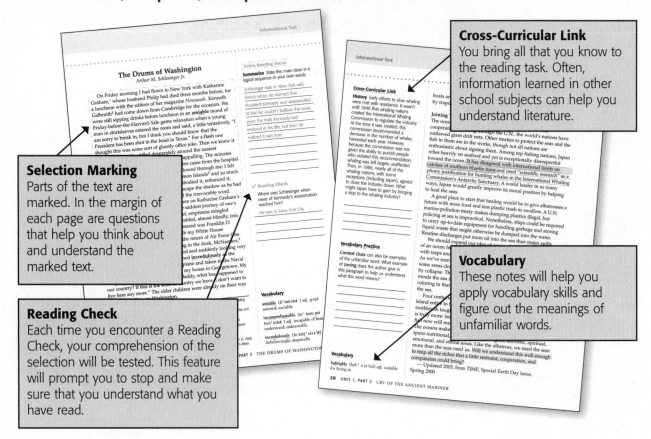

Cross-Curricular Link
You bring all that you know to the reading task. Often, information learned in other school subjects can help you understand literature.

Selection Marking
Parts of the text are marked. In the margin of each page are questions that help you think about and understand the marked text.

Reading Check
Each time you encounter a Reading Check, your comprehension of the selection will be tested. This feature will prompt you to stop and make sure that you understand what you have read.

Vocabulary
These notes will help you apply vocabulary skills and figure out the meanings of unfamiliar words.

Show What You Know

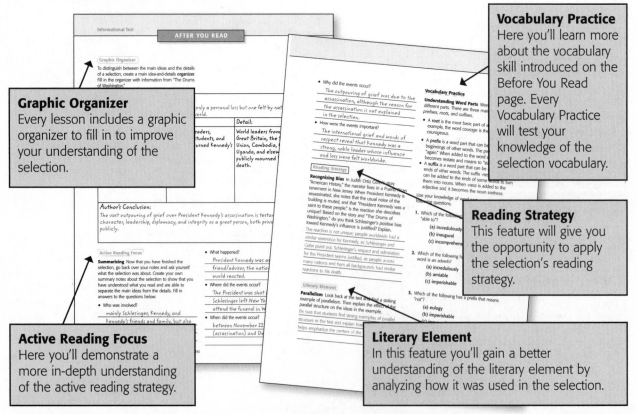

Vocabulary Practice
Here you'll learn more about the vocabulary skill introduced on the Before You Read page. Every Vocabulary Practice will test your knowledge of the selection vocabulary.

Graphic Organizer
Every lesson includes a graphic organizer to fill in to improve your understanding of the selection.

Reading Strategy
This feature will give you the opportunity to apply the selection's reading strategy.

Active Reading Focus
Here you'll demonstrate a more in-depth understanding of the active reading strategy.

Literary Element
In this feature you'll gain a better understanding of the literary element by analyzing how it was used in the selection.

To the Teacher

Introducing the *Active Learning and Note Taking Guide*

This workbook responds to a growing desire for informational text keyed to both literary content and core literacy skills. What is the role of informational text in the literature curriculum? In *Glencoe Literature: The Reader's Choice* it appears as Unit Introductions, Part Introductions (for grades 9 and 10), Literary History articles, and nonfiction features that provide a variety of background on literary selections. This information-rich material shows students the relevance of literature and connects it to historical and contemporary issues. Beyond literary context and motivation to read, the informational text in *The Reader's Choice* provides an opportunity for students to improve reading literacy skills.

What can you do with these texts beyond assigning them as background reading? Through scaffolded, interactive activities, the *Active Learning and Note Taking Guide (ALNTG)* expands your students' experience with the informational text in their literature anthology and addresses the need for differentiated instruction with 4 leveled books: *Grade-level, Enriched, Adapted,* and *ELL*. In the ANLTG, students analyze organizational patterns in text, take effective notes, and realize the power of annotating text as they read. The lessons in this workbook develop students' ability to read, write, and discuss literature while teaching skills that apply to real-world informational texts.

Informational Text

Supporting the literature curriculum with real-world skills

Years from now we may call this period the "Information Age." The presence of the Internet and the proliferation of Web sites covering innumerable topics have changed the way this generation of students view their world. They use the Internet to keep up with current events, talk to friends, and learn about the past. They search newspapers, encyclopedias, maps, and schedules on-line. Informational text—such as newspapers, magazines, and textbooks—has been adapting to our multimedia world. One key response has been an increasing number of access points and smaller chunks of information, such as sidebars, graphics, and imagery.

The Decline of Informational Skills While informational text and the technology used to disseminate information have been evolving at ever-increasing speed, the reading and writing skills of today's students have been deteriorating. According to a U.S. Department of Education study reported in 2003, more than eight million students in grades 4–12 lack the ability to read properly. Declines in test scores, graduation rates, and the writing skills of the American work force reflect this problem. As basic comprehension skills have declined, new pressure has been placed on high-school English programs to help students gain the reading skills they need to succeed in school and in their careers.

Range of Informational Texts Most of a student's classes, including social studies, science, and math, are based on informational texts. Beyond the informational texts that students are exposed to in school, they will encounter another range of texts in the real world for which they will need to employ similar reading strategies. Whatever their backgrounds and goals, students need to know how to understand *public documents*, from bus schedules to government warnings; *workplace documents*, from job applications to business memos; *technical instructions*, from computer manuals to cookbooks; and *product information*, from over-the-counter drug labels to credit-card applications. In fact, most of the reading and writing that adults do is nonfiction, and much of it is informational.

Improving Informational Skills The *Active Learning and Note Taking Guide* provides your classroom with a collection of material that prompts students to discover the power of reading actively. This workbook shows the student how to use the Cornell Note Taking System and mentors them to interact with the Perspectives features and *Time* articles in *Glencoe Literature: The Reader's Choice.* The *ALNTG* bolsters fundamental literacy skills, empowers students to be independent thinkers, and prepares them for reading they will have to do in the real world—timely skills for today's literature curriculum.

Note Taking

Organizing information in the classroom and beyond

Many students feel that education is a complex, puzzling game for which everyone seems to understand the rules except them. One of the most important roles of the teacher is to demystify the process of learning, to show students that its "rules" are not secrets known to a privileged few, but instead are common-sense strategies available to everyone willing to make the effort to grasp them. Efficient note taking is one of the most valuable of these success strategies.

The Cornell System According to a number of studies, a two-column note-taking format, such as the Cornell Note Taking System, is effective (Fisher 2001). In this format, students take notes on the right side of the page and they reduce their notes into key words and questions on the left side. They continually recap their notes and recite, reflect, and review them. This system provides a method to improve comprehension and test scores. Based on the Cornell model, the note-taking lessons in this workbook will guide your students to master this effective learning and organizational skill, which was developed at Cornell University by Walter Pauk.

Making Sense of Information In reading their textbooks, listening to lectures, doing library research, watching instructional videos, and pursuing other learning activities, students are deluged with information. One of the key elements of the learning process is sifting out what is most valuable from this flood of data. Students who attend college will likely find themselves as freshman in large lecture halls where they'll be on their own to take good notes. Their ability to take notes in large measure determines how well they perform in college (Pauk 1974). Good notes do two things: they condense main ideas and important details, and they show relationships between ideas and details. Note taking helps students organize ideas into patterns that are easier to remember than isolated facts. This helps students move away from simply trying to memorize facts and toward more fully understanding them.

Keeping Focused Everyone has experienced the challenge of maintaining attention while reading or listening to a lecture. This can be a particular problem for young people. Information gathered in a passive state lacks clarity and meaning to the reader or listener. Sharpening one's focus on a task is an immediate benefit of taking notes. Notes also help students to increase their recall of material they have listened to or read. Note taking encourages them to be active readers and listeners who ask questions about points they don't understand and relate the material to what they have learned in other classes and to their lives outside of school.

One good way to test whether we understand something we read is to paraphrase it. In writing their notes, students rephrase in their own words what they are hearing or reading. Though this process students make the information their own by processing and recording it in a way that makes sense to them. They shape the information and apply their own identity and learning style to their understanding of it, as when they convert information from a paragraph into a graphic organizer. The product of students' note taking is a concise record of main ideas and supporting details that they can review to recall information, use to complete classroom assignments, or prepare for exams.

Beyond the Classroom Note taking isn't just an academic skill. The ability to take good notes is an application of the familiar business advice that, to get ahead, it is more important to work smarter than to work harder. Real-life tests that professionals take for certification in fields such as civil service, engineering, law, and medicine, or to qualify as journeyman or master in a trade union, require people to learn and remember a body of knowledge. On the job, workers need to take good notes during briefings, training sessions, in meetings, and at conventions.

People often describe the mind as a sieve. The trick to excelling in any number of pursuits is to capture information. Professionals are expected to apply information from their training when they are left alone to work. A critical moment in Mark Twain's *Life on the Mississippi* occurs early in the narrator's training to be a riverboat pilot. Given a pop quiz on features of the river by the pilot who has been instructing him, the narrator is forced to confess he has remembered nothing of what he has been told. After vividly cursing for a time, the pilot calms down and advises the narrator, "'My boy, you must get a little memorandum book, and every time I tell you a thing, put it down right away. There's only one way to be a pilot, and that is to get this entire river by heart. You have to know it just like A B C.'" This is good advice in any type of learning, in school or at work.

Active Reading

Empowering students to discover meaning

The effects and rewards of reading—indeed of all learning—are largely in proportion to the aggressiveness of the reader. As one of the earliest advocates of the value of active learning, the Chinese thinker Confucius observed, "Learn as if you were following someone whom you could not catch up, as though it were someone you were frightened of losing." An unengaged reader absorbs little and is probably bored. An active reader is much more likely to both enjoy reading and grasp what he or she reads, retain what is read, and apply it to future reading and writing. This workbook gives students practice with a variety of the skills and strategies that good readers use whenever they read.

Interacting with Texts Suggest that students consider how they learn things outside of the classroom, such as playing a sport, a musical instrument, or a video game. For good readers, reading is an *activity*, something they *do*. When they read something they don't simply run their eyes over it, they *interact* with it. Effective readers get involved with what they read; they have conversations with themselves about the text. They summarize information, predict what's coming next, make connections between their lives and the text, question the information in the text and the author of the text, clarify information and ideas, visualize what the text has to say, and make inferences or draw conclusions from facts and ideas (Harvey & Goudvis 2000). To conclude, for a good reader, a text is alive, it speaks.

The *ALNTG* Experience The *ALNTG* provides call-outs and interactive exercises that show students how to participate more deeply in their reading. These active-reading lessons are keyed to the Perspectives features and *Time* articles in *Glencoe Literature: The Reader's Choice*. Each selection in this workbook expands on the reading strategy presented in *The Reader's Choice* and shows the student at point-of-use how to apply the skill. The version of these selections printed in this workbook also includes an Active Reading Focus, which furthers the student's interaction with the text, plus new features on literary elements, the Big Ideas, vocabulary, and cross-curricular subjects. These focal points draw students into the selections and guide them to read actively. Contrary to their use of *The Reader's Choice*, students are invited to mark the text and write in the *ALNTG*—to interact with it.

An array of research supports this method, including the 2004 report *Reading Next* from the Alliance for Excellent Education. This report highlights the benefit of literacy instruction in high school, including "direct, explicit comprehension instruction." Research also shows that most high school readers are proficient decoders—they are able to sound out words. The key problem these readers face is organizing what they read into a meaningful framework. They need help conceptualizing what they read and connecting it to their own knowledge and experiences. Using this workbook is one way to mentor your students in building both content knowledge and the skills to understand and retain it.

The *ALNTG* is a good place to develop these skills because it connects to an authentic reading purpose. The active-reading selections in this workbook provide the student with knowledge to understand both the literary selections and Big Ideas in *Glencoe Literature: The Reader's Choice.* This focus is keyed to the inquiry-based instruction that guides *The Reader's Choice* program and that takes shape in the Big Ideas. Inquiry is a research-based approach that gives students significant reasons or purposes for reading. It also offers an array of benefits to reading, writing, and classroom activities (Hillocks 1999). In additional, these lessons make the literary selections in *The Reader's Choice* come alive by explaining behind-the-scenes information about writers, their inspirations, and their connections to real-world events. The experience is designed to be both satisfying and productive.

Differentiated Instruction

Using leveled books to motivate all students

"One-size-fits-all" curriculum is becoming less and less realistic in today's classroom. By differentiating instruction we acknowledge that there are underlying skills and experiences that students gain from class beyond a standard coverage of content. The four levels of the *Active Learning and Note Taking Guide—Grade-level, Enriched, Adapted,* and *ELL*—allow each student to take risks and progress at a manageable pace.

Scaffolding and Gradual Release The four levels of the *ALNTG* cover the same content from *Glencoe Literature: The Reader's Choice.*; the differentiation lies in the process the student uses to engage the material and the products they create to put the material into their own words. Each level contains distinct activities and scaffolding that are written with students of a particular level in mind. Each book incorporates a gradual release of scaffolding. This means that in the first few lessons student receive more guidance and, as they progress, they receive less guidance and are allowed to take more responsibility. The pace of the gradual release is designed at each level to match students' ability and increasing mastery of the skills required in note taking and active reading.

Grade-level is for students reading at grade level. The difficulty of the activities, degree of scaffolding, and the pace of gradual release are geared toward the grade-level student.

Enriched is for students who need more challenge to be motivated. Students will find less scaffolding, more activities that guide them toward synthesis, and more opportunities to express themselves creatively. Gradual release is quicker in the Enriched version.

Adapted is for students up to two years below grade level. Here more scaffolding and structure are provided, the instructional language is simpler, and gradual release is slower.

ELL is for English language learners. This book features English Language Coach items, which fortify English learners' vocabulary development. Gradual release is taken slowly.

Classroom Management While students will be working with the same selections and using similar procedures, you might divide students into four literary circles to match these four levels. This can help you manage a classroom in which students are using four versions of the same book. Groups can be assigned or be allowed to create a name, color, and so on to identify themselves. Students in the same group can compare notes and share questions and inspirations they have as they complete the exercises in the workbook. Each group can also review together and then share their group's findings with the class as a whole.

One way to give students in each group a different task is to divide the note-taking lessons into parts and the active-reading lessons into skills. Then each group can report to the class on a distinct topic. For a note-taking lesson, you might have students working with the Adapted book prepare a report on the Looking Ahead section of a Unit Introduction and have students working with the Enriched book prepare a report on a Literary Analysis model. For an active-reading lesson, you might have English learners prepare a report on their work with an Active Reading Focus and Grade-level students prepare a report on their work with a Reading Strategy.

Another option is to have students from different levels review in partner activities. This allows able students to serve as mentors and struggling readers to express questions they have about their reading. Among others, these methods foster a collaborative environment that brings together students of different abilities. Difference is an asset and resource in the classroom when these ideas are employed because students who use different strategies and apply different ideas can make valuable contributions to the group (Wilhelm 2006).

Read On As your students work with the *ALNTG*, encourage them to take risks and integrate their own experiences and knowledge into their reading. This workbook provides a guided format for them to impose their identity on their reading. Whatever their background, what students know matters, and each student has the ability to grow through focused exposure to note taking and active reading of high-quality texts. As they work at it, students will be able to apply new strategies and build a deeper reservoir of knowledge to connect with their reading.

Works Cited

Biancarosa, G., and Snow, C. E. 2004. Reading next—A vision for action and research in middle and high school literacy: A report to the Carnegie Corporation of New York. Washington, DC: Alliance for Excellent Education.

Fisher, D. 2001. "We're moving on up": Creating a schoolwide literacy effort in an urban high school. *Journal of Adolescent & Adult Literacy* 45:92–101.

Harvey, S., and Goudvis, A. 2000. *Strategies That Work: Teaching comprehension to enhance understanding.* York, MB: Stenhouse.

Hillocks, G., Jr. 1999. *Ways of Thinking, Ways of Teaching.* New York: Teacher's College Press.

Pauk, W. 1974. *How to Study in College.* Boston: Houghton Mifflin.

Wilhelm, J. D. 2006. *Inquiring Minds Learn to Read and Write: Inquiry, questioning and discussion strategies to improve reading and writing.* New York: Scholastic.

Introductory Text: The Anglo-Saxon Period and the Middle Ages 449–1485

Looking Ahead (p. 5)

Preview

- How did outside invasions affect Anglo-Saxon culture?

- How did the Church influence medieval culture?

- What was the medieval romance?

This introduction prepares you for the literature you will read in Unit 1 of your textbook. It explains the historical, social, and cultural forces at work during the earliest period of British literature.

As you read the introduction, use the Cornell Note Taking System to record important points and to remember what you have read.

Reduce

TO THE POINT *Note key words and phrases.* **Key** *words and phrases are the most important ones. They will help you remember what you read. For example:*

<u>Germanic tribe</u>

<u> invasions</u>

<u>evolution of English</u>

<u>European mainland</u>

<u>English literature</u>

ANY QUESTIONS? *Write them now; answer them as you reread your notes. For example: "What other foreign invasions?"*

<u> </u>

<u> </u>

Record

Looking Ahead

➡ *What historical and cultural forces shaped the earliest British literature? One has been listed for you.*

<u>Germanic tribes from Northern Europe invaded Britain.</u>

<u>The dialects these tribes spoke evolved into English.</u>

<u>Writers created literature in that English.</u>

<u> </u>

<u> </u>

Keep the following questions in mind as you read.

➡ *Each question is asking about one historical or cultural element. Which element is being asked about in each question? The first has been listed for you.*

<u>foreign invasions</u>

<u>the Roman Catholic Church</u>

<u>medieval romance</u>

<u> </u>

<u> </u>

<u> </u>

Introductory Text: The Anglo-Saxon Period and the Middle Ages 449–1485

Timeline *(pp. 6–7)*

Reduce

TO THE POINT *Note types of writing. For example:*

poetry
history
lyrics
ballad
autobiography

TO THE POINT *Note the general categories of British events. These categories will help you remember what you read. For example:*

Invasions
christianity
government
war
revolt
disease

Record

British Literature

➡ *Many kinds of literature were being created during this period. Identify some of the different categories, and list some examples. Two categories have been listed for you.*

poetry—"Beowulf", "Piers Plowman"
history—The Ecclesiastical History of the English People, History of the Kings of Britain
lyrics—Exeter Book
ballads—earliest ballads, c. 1300
autobiography—Margery Kempe

British Events

➡ *Below are some general categories—kinds or types—of British events that happened during this period? Under each category, list one or more events in each category. Two categories have been started for you.*

<u>Invasions</u>
449—Germanic tribes invade Britain.
787—Danish invasions begin.
1066 William the Conqueror invades England.

<u>Christianity</u>
597—St. Augustine established monastery.
664—Synod of Whitby
1170—murder of Archbishop of Canterbury

<u>Government</u>
<u>Disease</u>
<u>War</u>

Introductory Text: The Anglo-Saxon Period and the Middle Ages 449–1485

Timeline (pp. 6–7)

Reduce

TO THE POINT *Note general categories of world events.*

Roman Empire

Islam

Crusader

China

exploration

Japan

Aztecs

war

printing

Record

World Events

➡ *What are the general categories of world events? List the general catagories, or kinds of events. Then list one or two events in each category. Two categories have been started for you.*

Islam

c. 570—Muhammad, founder of Islam, born in Mecca

786—Harun al-Rashid becomes ruler of Muslim Empire

Roman Empire

476—fall of western Roman empire

Other possible categories might include the Crusades,

China, Japan, Aztecs, exploration, war, and printing.

Recap

➡ *Review your notes on the timeline. Then recap. Use a classification chart to organize the most important types of events. First list the important categories. Then list three events in that category. The chart has been started for you.*

Students might create such categories as literature, invasions, wars, the Church, government, and printing.

The Church	Invasions	Literature		
• 597, Canterbury monastery	•	•	•	•
• 664, Synod of Whitby	•	•	•	•
• 1170, Thomas à Becket	•	•	•	•

Introductory Text: The Anglo-Saxon Period and the Middle Ages 449–1485

By the Numbers *(p. 8)*

Reduce

ANY QUESTIONS? *Use them to organize your notes. For example: "What kinds of things would a rich person have in medieval England?"*

_____

_____

TO THE POINT *For the remaining heads, note key words and phrases. For example:*

harvest

sowing

wheat, hemp, rye

shearing

"man-price"

Record

Medieval Wealth

➡ *What does this information show?*
It shows what kinds of possessions a wealthy person (a butcher) had in medieval England.

_____

_____

Peasant's Wheel of Life

➡ *Complete this sentence in your own words: The life of English peasants in the Middle Ages . . .*
was a year-round cycle of endless work, depending on the season.

_____

➡ *What are the remaining headings on this page? What are they about? Underneath each, note what the information and statistics (numbers) tell you about this period. The first has been listed for you.*

Wergild
The Anglo-Saxons had a "man-price," which was a sum of money equal to a person's life. Since feuds were common, the price could be paid to the slain person's family to avoid an act of revenge.
Domesday Book
English rulers kept exact records of property for tax purposes.
The Black Death
The Black Death was a massive epidemic.
Percentage of Land Owned in England in the 11th Century
The king, nobles, and church leaders owned most of the land.

Introductory Text: The Anglo-Saxon Period and the Middle Ages 449–1485

Being There (p. 9)

Reduce

TO THE POINT *Note key words and phrases. For example:*

jousting

southern lowlands

kingdoms

highlands

Record

➡ *Pictures are part of the information in this introduction. What do these pictures show about life in Britain in the middle ages? One example has been done for you.*

Farmers worked by hand using simple tools.

Farmers had a harvest in July.

Cities had large, many-storied buildings made of stone.

People played a game with hobbyhorses, and knights participated in jousting.

➡ *The map shows towns and cities in medieval Britain. Where were most of the towns located?*

Most towns were located in the southeastern part of England.

Recap

➡ *Review your notes on By the Numbers and Being There. Then recap. Use the information to make several conclusions about medieval England. Two conclusions have been written for you.*

1. People in medieval England were unable to control the spread of epidemics such as the Black Death.

2. During this time the Church developed in England.

3. There were many foreign invasions, and society was unstable.

4. Kings, nobles, and high-ranking officials of the Church owned most of the land.

5. Life for peasants was a constant cycle of work.

Introductory Text: The Anglo-Saxon Period and the Middle Ages 449–1485

Historical, Social, and Cultural Forces *(pp. 10–11)*

Reduce

TO THE POINT *Note key words and phrases.*

Celtic tribes

Angles

Saxons

Jutes

Britons

Angle-land

Record

The Anglo-Saxons

➡ *What different peoples are discussed under this heading? Use a classification chart to organize your notes. The chart has been started for you.*

Romans	Celtic Britons	Anglo-Saxons
conquered the Celtic tribes of Britain introduced a better standard of living to Celtic tribes left Britain to defend Rome when their empire began to fall	according to legend, won victories under leader named Arthur driven into mountains by Anglo-Saxons took over mountain land as their territory	Angles, Saxons, and Jutes invaded Britain in 449 took over "Angle-Land" formed small tribal kingdoms later converted to Christianity

TO THE POINT *Note key words and phrases about the Vikings and Normans. For example:*

Danes and Norsemen

Saxon king Alfred

William, Duke of

Normandy

Battle of Hastings

Vikings and Normans

➡ *Use this chart to organize important information on the Vikings and Normans. The chart has been started for you.*

Vikings	Normans
other Germanic tribes Danes and Norsemen conquered most of England by mid-9th century defeated by Saxon king Alfred, 878 lost England to Alfred's son and grandson	from northwest France William, Duke of Normandy, claimed English throne, 1066 defeated Anglo-Saxon king at Battle of Hastings, ending Anglo-Saxon era

Introductory Text: The Anglo-Saxon Period and the Middle Ages 449–1485

Historical, Social, and Cultural Forces *(p. 11)*

ANY QUESTIONS? *Ask questions about headings. For example: "What does feudal mean?"*

_____

_____

_____

_____

_____

TO THE POINT *Note key words and phrases. For example:*

Hundred Years' War

Black Death

landed aristocracy

_____

_____

Feudal England

➡ *In your own words, define the important keywords, or terms, from this section. Ask yourself questions to organize the information, then define the terms. One term has been summarized for you.*

What is feudalism? Feudalism was a system in which lesser lords pledged loyalty and service to overlords in exchange for land.

Who are serfs? Serfs are the peasants at the lowest level of the social scale.

What was the Magna Carta? The Magna Carta was an agreement between King John and his barons that limited the king's power.

_____

War and Plague

➡ *Summarize the information in this section. Underneath each heading, list information. One heading has been done for you.*

Hundred Years' War

series of wars beginning in 1337 between England and France for control of lands in France.

Black Death

epidemic that swept through Europe starting in 1348. Outbreaks happened over next decades and nearly a third of all people in England died. Huge loss of life helped to destroy feudalism.

_____

_____

_____

_____

Introductory Text: The Anglo-Saxon Period and the Middle Ages 449–1485

Historical, Social, and Cultural Forces (pp. 10–11)

Reduce

TO THE POINT *Note key words and phrases.*

Epic warrior

undying fame

christian church

legendary heroes

popular ballad

Record

Preview Big Ideas of the Anglo-Saxon Period and the Middle Ages

➡ *Restate each of the Big Ideas to make them easier to remember. The first has been written for you.*

Epic Warrior

Anglo-Saxon culture believed in a world overwhelmed by dark forces. This inspired the idea of the epic warrior who wanted undying fame.

Power of Faith

Christianity influenced all of people's lives in medieval England.

World of Romance

Upper classes liked stories about legendary heroes. For common people ballads were their literature.

Recap

➡ *Review your notes on the Historical, Social, and Cultural Forces. Then recap. Use your summary notes to help you remember the main points. Some have been listed for you.*

Topic: The Anglo-Saxon Period and Medieval England 449–1485

Main Points:

Anglo-Saxons invaded Britain and defeated the Celtic Britons.

Anglo Saxons established small tribal kingdoms.

Vikings invaded England and conquered most of the country.

After King Alfred the Anglo-Saxons retook control of England.

Normans invaded England and defeated the Anglo Saxons.

Normans established feudalism, a system of loyalty and service.

King John forced by his barons to sign the Magna Carta.

English fought the French in the Hundred Years' War.

Black Death helped destroy feudalism.

Introductory Text: The Anglo-Saxon Period and the Middle Ages 449–1485

Big Idea 1: The Epic Warrior *(p. 12)*

Reduce

ANY QUESTIONS? *Use them to organize your notes. For example: "Who were the warlords?"*

_____

_____

_____

_____

TO THE POINT *For the remaining headings, note key words and phrases. They will help you remember what you read.*

scops

mead-halls

heroic-songs

wyrd

destiny

Record

A Warrior Society

➡ *What was the relationship between an Anglo-Saxon warlord and his followers? Summarize the main points under this heading. Two points have been summarized for you.*

Warfare—part of early Anglo-Saxon life

Tribes—made up of warrior families.

Warlords rewarded their bravest followers with treasure.

The followers of a warlord showed absolute loyalty.

Oral Literature

➡ *Who were the Anglo-Saxon storytellers? Why were they important? List major points. One has been listed for you.*

Storytellers created heroic songs about warriors.

Songs celebrated strength, courage, and loyalty.

Songs were performed at mead-halls of Anglo-Saxon rulers.

Germanic and Christian Traditions

➡ *Use a chart to organize the main characteristics of Germanic and Christian tradition. The chart has been started for you.*

Germanic traditions	Christian traditions

• tragic world: even gods die
• no promise of afterlife
• warriors' primary duty to
• achieve fame in lifetime
  Grendel: troll
	• omnipotent God
	• promise of eternal life
	• Grendel descended from
	  Cain, first murderer in
	  Bible

Importance of *Wyrd*

➡ *Complete this sentence: The Anglo-Saxons believed that wyrd, or fate . . .*

controlled human destiny and a person's unavoidable

death.

_____

Introductory Text: The Anglo-Saxon Period and the Middle Ages 449–1485

Big Idea 1: The Epic Warrior *(pp. 12–13)*

Reduce

TO THE POINT *Note key words and phrases. For example:*

Battle of Maldon

Oswald

Ealdwald

_____

_____

Record

from *The Battle of Maldon*

➥ *Paraphrase the following lines. To* **paraphrase** *is to restate the selection in your own words.* "*Heart must be braver, courage the bolder, / Mood the stouter as our strength grows less!*"

We must be braver and more courageous even as we

grow weaker.

_____

_____

_____

_____

Recap

➥ *Review your notes on Big Idea 1: The Epic Warrior. Then recap. Use a web to organize the key points about the Anglo-Saxon epic warrior. The web has been started for you.*

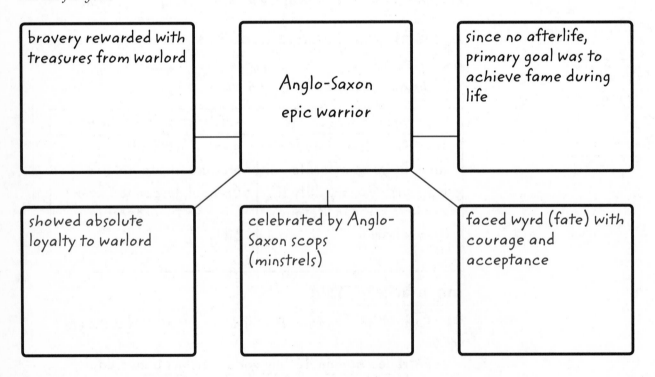

bravery rewarded with treasures from warlord	Anglo-Saxon epic warrior	since no afterlife, primary goal was to achieve fame during life
showed absolute loyalty to warlord	celebrated by Anglo-Saxon scops (minstrels)	faced wyrd (fate) with courage and acceptance

Introductory Text: The Anglo-Saxon Period and the Middle Ages 449–1485

Big Idea 2: The Power of Faith *(pp. 14–15)*

Reduce

ANY QUESTIONS? *Use them to organize your notes. For example: "Where was England's first monastery?" "What were decorated books called?" "What are some examples of decorated books?"*

_____

_____

_____

_____

_____

TO THE POINT *For the remaining heads, note key words and phrases. For example:*

scribes

Venerable Bede

Alfred the Great

The Anglo-Saxon

  Chronicle

pilgrimages

mystery plays

_____

_____

_____

_____

Record

Christianizing England

➡ *What events are described here? Order them in a timeline. The first two have been listed for you.*

596—Pope Gregory I sent missionaries to England.

650—England Christian in name, but many Anglo-Saxons still pagan in some practices and traditions.

Same time—Celtic monks from Ireland brought Christianity to other parts of England.

Eighth century—Anglo-Saxon culture reached its peak in Northumbrian monasteries.

Monasteries

➡ *What are the main ideas under this heading? One example has been listed for you.*

With spread of Christianity, some men and women chose to dedicate lives to prayer.

Monks copied manuscripts to preserve literature.

Venerable Bede wrote <u>The Ecclesiastical History of the English People</u>, in Latin.

Alfred the Great encouraged the use of Old English.

Pilgrimages

➡ *Complete this sentence: A medieval pilgrimage was . . .*

a journey to a sacred site to express religious devotion.

Religious Drama

➡ *What are the main ideas under this heading?*

Religious drama developed from enactments of biblical stories on feast days.

Mystery plays presented stories from the Bible.

Morality plays featured allegorical figures.

Introductory Text: The Anglo-Saxon Period and the Middle Ages 449–1485

Big Idea 2: The Power of Faith *(pp. 14–15)*

Reduce

TO THE POINT *Note key words and phrases.*

mystery plays

morality plays

guilds

_____

_____

Record

from *The Creation of Adam and Eve*

➡ *Ask yourself questions about this section. Then answer them in order to understand the main ideas. Two questions are listed.*

What was a mystery play?

A play performed by the guilds—mystery then meant

trade or craft

Who are the characters in this mystery play?

God, Adam, and Eve

What is happening in this scene?

God tells Adam and Eve about living in paradise.

_____

_____

_____

Recap

➡ *Review your notes on Big Idea 2: The Power of Faith. Then recap. Make several generalizations based on the information in this section. One has been listed for you.*

Christians of the Middle Ages often chose extreme ways of showing religious devotion,

such as joining religious orders or going on pilgrimages.

Students' generalizations may deal with Christianizing England,

monasteries, pilgrimages, and religious drama.

_____

_____

_____

_____

Introductory Text: The Anglo-Saxon Period and the Middle Ages 449–1485

Big Idea 3: The World of Romance *(pp. 16–17)*

Reduce

TO THE POINT *Note key words and phrases. For example:*

supremacy

feudal aristocracy

lords and vassals

jousting

Record

The Knight

➡ *Use a web to organize the main ideas under this heading. The web has been started for you.*

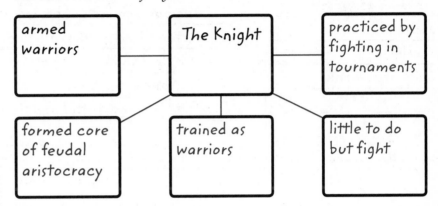

Chivalry and Courtly Love

➡ *Ask yourself questions to identify the information in this section. Then, answer the questions to understand the information. One question has been asked and answered for you.*

What was chivalry?

Chivalry was a code of ethics for knights that influenced much of the literature of the period. It helped improve the behavior of knights and raise the status of women.

What was courtly love?

Courtly love described the relationship between a knight and his lady and celebrated passionate love and total devotion.

The Rise of Romance

➡ *List two important examples of medieval romances.*

verse romance—"Sir Gawain and the Green Knight"

prose romance—Sir Thomas Malory's "Le Morte d'Arthur"

Introductory Text: The Anglo-Saxon Period and the Middle Ages 449–1485

Big Idea 3: The World of Romance *(pp. 16–17)*

Reduce

TO THE POINT *Note key words and phrases. For example:*

damsel

Sir Thomas Malory

Arthur

Merlin

Lady of the Lake

Record

from "Le Morte d'Arthur" by Sir Thomas Malory

➡ *How does this passage show the elements of chivalry? List a few examples. One has been listed for you.*

The passage includes two knights, Arthur and Merlin.

Arthur wants to have a sword, for he has none.

The Lady of the Lake offers him the sword if he does what she asks.

Arthur is respectful and agrees to do what she asks.

Recap

➡ *Review your notes on Big Idea 3: The World of Romance. Then recap. Use a classification chart to organize the main points. The chart has been started for you.*

Knights	Chivalry	Courtly Love	Romances
• heavily armed warriors • trained as warriors • practiced fighting in tournaments	• code of ethics for knights • stressed honor, courage, and respect for women • civilized knights' conduct and raised status of women	• relationship of knight and lady • popularized in songs and poems of troubadours • celebrated passionate love and devotion	• originated in France in 1100s • adventures of knights • celebrated chivalry and courtly love

Introductory Text: The Anglo-Saxon Period and the Middle Ages 449–1485

Wrap-Up *(p. 18)*

Reduce

TO THE POINT *Note key words and phrases. For example:*

watershed events

Germanic language

Norman Conquest

Magna Carta

Romantic movement

legends of King

Arthur

Record

Why It Matters

➡ *What is the main idea of each paragraph? The first has been listed for you*

paragraph 1—Germanic language of Anglo-Saxon invaders was the basis for English.

paragraph 2—Magna Carta established basic political rights and was the foundation of British law and government.

paragraph 3—Medieval Romances inspired the Romantic movement of the late 1800s and early 1900s that is still popular today.

Cultural Links

➡ *What cultural link is described in each paragragh? The first has been done for you.*

paragraph 1—"Beowulf" / John Gardner's <u>Grendel</u>

paragraph 2—<u>Canterbury Tales</u> / tales in a frame stories

paragraph 3—Malory's <u>Le Morte d'Arthur</u> /Tennyson's <u>Idylls of the King</u> and T. H. White's <u>The Once and Future King</u>

Recap

➡ *Review your notes on the Wrap-Up. Then recap. Use an evidence organizer to sum up your viewpoint on medieval England. Put details that support your viewpoint in the columns below. Take your details from the information in this section.*

Viewpoint		
The medieval romance was an influential form of literature.		
Supporting Detail	Supporting Detail	Supporting Detail
The Romantic movement found inspiration in medieval romances.	Tennyson's <u>Idylls of the King</u> was inspired by Malory's <u>Le Morte d'Arthur</u>.	T. H. White's <u>The One and Future King</u> was inspired by Malory's <u>Le Morte d'Arthur</u>.

Introductory Text: The Anglo-Saxon Period and the Middle Ages 449–1485

Summarize

➡ *Review your notes on this Introduction. Then recap. Create an outline using the Big Ideas. The outline has been started for you.*

Topic: The Anglo-Saxon Period and the Middle Ages, 449–1485

I. The Epic Warrior

   A. Anglo-Saxon society was organized around warfare.

   B. Anglo-Saxon scops celebrated the qualities of epic warriors.

   C. Anglo-Saxon oral tradition mixed Germanic and Christian elements.

   D. Wyrd was an idea of fate that controlled human destiny and person's
      unavoidable death.

II. The Power of Faith

   A. Christianity brought education and culture to England.

   B. Medieval monks copied manuscripts to preserve literature.

   C. People went on pilgrimages to express religious devotion.

   D. Drama developed from acting out biblical stories during church services.

III. The World of Romance

   A. Knights were the center of feudal aristocracy.

   B. Knights' behavior was governed by the codes of chivalry and courtly love.

   C. Medieval romances of knights' adventures celebrated chivalry and courtly
      love.

   D. Medieval romances had an influence on modern literature.

Introductory Text: The Anglo-Saxon Period and the Middle Ages 449–1485

Apply

Multiple Choice

Circle the letter of the best choice(s) for the following questions.

1. What were qualities of the Anglo-Saxon epic warrior? A, C, D
   A. showed absolute loyalty to warlord

   B. respectful to women

   C. faced *wyrd* with courage

   D. sought to achieve fame in lifetime

2. Which of the following is true of chivalry? D
   A. belief in wyrd

   B. promoted mock battles

   C. dishonored women

   D. stressed honor and courage

3. What was the origin of English drama in the Middle Ages? A
   A. enactments of stories from the Bible during church services

   B. epic poems

   C. morality plays that were popular at the time

   D. English courtly writers expressing their love for a lady

Matching

Write the letter of the choice in the second column that best matches each item in the first column.

4. Who fought the Hundred Years' War? _____ A

5. Who won victories under King Arthur? _____ C

6. Who formed small tribal kingdoms? _____ B

7. Whom did King Alfred defeat? _____ D
   A. English and French

   B. Anglo-Saxons

   C. Celtic Britons

   D. Vikings

How can you better remember and understand the material in this introduction? *Recite* your notes, *Reflect* on them, and *Review* them. **You can also use your notes for a quick review of the historical period or the Big Ideas of this unit. As you learn more about the ideas in the unit, add to your notes.**

Literary History: **The Epic and the Epic Hero**

(pp. 20–21)

Preview

- What is an epic?
- What is an epic hero?
- What is an epic form?

This article describes the epic and the epic hero. Both are part of our literary history. The epic is one of the earliest and most widespread forms of literature. This article will help you better understand the Anglo-Saxon epic *Beowulf* and other epic literature you will read in your textbook.

As you read the article, use the Cornell Note Taking System to record important points and to remember what you have read.

Reduce

ANY QUESTIONS? *Use them to organize your notes. For example: "What is discussed in the opening paragraphs?"*

_____

_____

_____

_____

_____

Record

➡ *Many opening paragraphs don't have headings. Based on the main ideas from the first paragraph listed below, what heading might you give to the paragraph?*

The First Epics

The epic is a long narrative poem that uses formal language.

Epics are found throughout the world.

Epics tell a familiar story about a superhero.

The earliest epics date to a time when people could not read.

The earliest epics were recited to music.

The earliest epic is the Sumerian Epic of Gilgamesh.

Epic Form

➡ *What are the important points in this section? List them under the headline. The list has been started for you.*

Standard Features of the Epic Form

regular meter and rhythm; formal, lofty language

heroic or superhuman main characters

gods or godlike beings who intervene

action on huge scale; fates of entire peoples

stories that begin in medias res ("in the middle of things")

kenning—standardized comparison in Beowulf

TO THE POINT *Note key words and phrases. For example:*

regular meter and
   rhythm

formal, lofty language

in medias res

epithet

kenning

_____

Literary History: The Epic and the Epic Hero

(p. 21)

Reduce

TO THE POINT *Note key words and phrases. For example:*

<u>Epic hero</u>: man of high
social status
destiny of his people
embodies values
warrior
noble
skilled

Record

The Epic Hero

➡ *What are the main ideas? Use a web to record them. This web has been started for you*

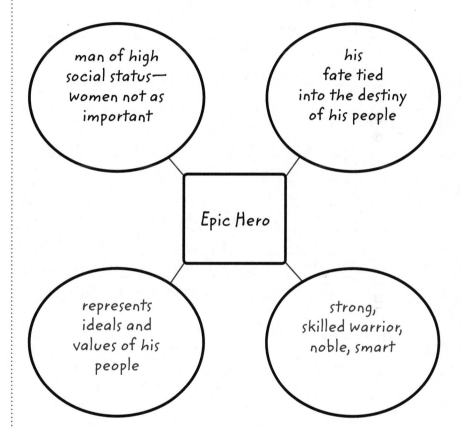

Literary History: The Epic and the Epic Hero

Summarize

➥   *Review your notes on this article. Then sum up the main points by using an outline. The outline has been started for you.*

The Epic and the Epic Hero

   I. The Epic

      A. long narrative poem recounts in formal language the adventures of a larger-than-life hero

      B. earliest epics were recited

      C. epic is found around the world

      D. legends transmitted from one generation to another

      E. earliest epic is Sumerian <u>Epic of Gilgamesh</u>

   II. Features of the Epic Form

      A. regular meter and rhythm; lofty language

      B. heroic or superhuman characters

      C. gods or godlike beings

      D. action on huge scale; fate of entire peoples

      E. stories that begin <u>in medias res</u> ("in the middle of things")

      F. epithet—word or brief phrase used to characterize person, place, or thing

      G. kenning—standardized comparison in <u>Beowulf</u> \

   III. Epic Hero

      A. man of high social status—women take subordinate role

      B. his fate affects the destiny of his people

      C. represents ideals and values of his people

      D. strong, skilled warrior, noble, quick-witted

Literary History: The Epic and the Epic Hero

Apply

Multiple Choice

Circle the letter of the best choice for the following questions.

1. Which are characteristics of the epic form? A, B, D
   A. lofty language
   B. heroic or superhuman characters
   C. written down
   D. action on a huge scale

2. Which is *not* a characteristic of the epic hero? D
   A. high social status
   B. skilled warrior
   C. embodies values of his people
   D. male or female

3. What does it mean when a story begins *in medias res*? C
   A. it begins at the beginning of the action
   B. it begins at the end of the action
   C. it begins in the middle of the action
   D. it begins as a form of media

Matching

Choose the best multiple-choice option for each question.

4. What is an epic? _____ D

5. What is a kenning? _____ C

6. What is the earliest known epic? _____ B

7. What means "in the middle of things"? _____ A
   A. *in medias res*
   B. *Epic of Gilgamesh*
   C. standardized comparison
   D. long narrative poem

How can you better remember and understand the material in this Literary History? *Recite* **your notes,** *Reflect* **on them, and** *Review* **them. You can also use your notes to help you read the literature in this unit—including Beowulf.**

Literary History: The Development of English

(pp. 90–91)

Preview

- What was Old English?
- How did Middle English develop?
- How is Middle English related to Modern English?

This article describes the early stages of the development of English, Old English, and Middle English. It will help you better understand the literature you will read in Unit 1 of your textbook.

As you read the article, use the Cornell Note Taking System to record important points and to remember what you have read.

Reduce

ANY QUESTIONS? *Use them to organize your notes. For example: "What is* **Old English?***"*

_____

_____

_____

TO THE POINT *Note key words and phrases. For example:*

<u>Middle English sources:</u>

Latin

Danish

Old Norse

Norman French

_____

Record

Old English: 450–1150

➡ *What was Old English? What does it have to do with modern English? List the important information in this section. One example has been written for you.*

Old English comes from mixture of Anglo-Saxon dialects.

was a form of English language used from mid-400s to early 1100s

had a significant effect on Modern English

most basic and functional words are from Old English

Middle English: 1150–1500

➡ *How did Middle English develop? List the important information in this section. One example has been written for you.*

Latin, Danish, Old Norse, and Norman French added words to English.

After Norman Conquest, aristocracy spoke French.

In Norman England, educated people had to speak three languages: French, Latin, and English.

Literary History: The Development of English

(pp. 90–91)

Reduce

TO THE POINT *Note key words and phrases. For example:*

linguistic diversity

dialect

Geoffrey Chaucer

Record

➡ *How did French contribute to Middle English? Make a list of the important points. The list has been started for you.*

French added 10,000 words to English vocabulary.

7500 of those words from French are still used.

French influence led to simplification of English

grammar and spelling.

➡ *What was the biggest problem with language diversity in the Middle English period? Look at the information and answer in your own words.*

People who lived in one part of England could not

understand people who lived in another part.

➡ *How was the problem of language diversity in the Middle English period solved? Look at the information and answer in your own words.*

The London dialect became the standard form of

English.

➡ *How is Chaucer's Middle English different from Beowulf's Old English? Look at the information and answer in your own words.*

Chaucer's Middle English is recognizable as English; Old

English looks like a foreign language.

Literary History: The Development of English

Summarize

➡ *Review your notes on this article. Then recap. Use a classification chart to organize the main points about Old and Middle English. The chart has been started for you.*

Old English	Middle English
• A mixture of Anglo-Saxon dialects is the basis of Old English. • Old English was the form of English language used from mid-400s to early 1100s. • Old English had a significant effect on Modern English. • The most basic and functional words are from Old English.	• Latin, Danish, Old Norse, and Norman French fed English. • After Norman Conquest, the aristocracy spoke French. • In Norman England, educated people spoke French, Latin, and English. • French increased English vocabulary by 10,000 words, 7500 of which are still in use. • French influence simplified English grammar and spelling.

Literary History: The Development of English

Apply

Multiple Choice

Circle the letter of the best choice for the following questions.

1. What is *not* an example of an Anglo-Saxon word? D
   A. Friday
   B. and
   C. for
   D. biology

2. What languages did well-educated people in Norman England need to know? A, C, D
   A. French, for dealing with nobility
   B. German, for dealing with clergy
   C. Latin, for scholarship
   D. English, for communication with the common people

3. What became the standard dialect in England? B
   A. the dialect spoken in France
   B. the dialect spoken in London
   C. the dialect spoken in Germany
   D. the dialect spoken by clergy

Matching

Choose the best multiple-choice option for each statement.

4. formed of Anglo-Saxon dialects
   _____ A

5. Old English poem shows the gap between Old and Middle English
   _____ B

6. when French language influenced English _____ F

7. dialect spoken in this city became standard _____ C

8. poem by Geoffrey Chaucer _____ D

9. language spoken by English aristocracy after Norman Conquest _____ E

   A. Old English
   B. *Beowulf*
   C. London
   D. *The Canterbury Tales*
   E. French
   F. Middle English

How can you better remember and understand the material in this Literary History? *Recite* your notes, *Reflect* on them, and *Review* them. You can also use your notes to help you read the literature in this unit.

Literary History: Miracle and Morality Plays

(pp. 152–153)

Preview

- How did medieval theater begin?
- What kinds of plays were performed?
- What was the purpose of these plays?

This article discusses the beginnings of theater in medieval Britain, which is part of our literary history. It describes the development of miracle and mystery plays performed in church, and then morality plays performed by professional actors.

As you read the article, use the Cornell Note Taking System to record important points and to remember what you have read.

Reduce

ANY QUESTIONS? *Use them to help you organize your notes. For example: "How did medieval theater begin?"*

_____

_____

_____

_____

TO THE POINT *Note key words and phrases. For example:*

miracle plays

mystery plays

pageants

_____

_____

Record

Rise of Medieval Drama

➡ *How did medieval drama develop? Identify the development discussed in this paragraph. Then, restate it in your own words. The list has been started for you.*

The church had condemned plays as being immoral in 692.

It later revived theater to use for religious purposes.

In the early 900s, medieval theater developed: priests performed events about the life of Christ.

Later, clerical plays were presented.

Miracle and Mystery Plays

➡ *What are the important points in this section? Summarize them in your own words. One example has been written for you.*

Priests performed <u>miracle plays</u> about Bible stories and the lives of saints.

Later, the plays were called <u>mysteries,</u> performed by trade guilds outside the church at fairs and marketplaces.

Guild members who staged the plays went on tour, traveling in wagons called "pageants." They performed everywhere from crossroads to castles.

There was music, dancing, comedy, and special effects during performances.

Audience members loudly cheered and booed.

Plays were performed in day-long cycles.

Literary History: Miracle and Morality Plays

(p. 153)

Reduce

ANY QUESTIONS? *Use them to organize your notes. For example: "What do I need to know about morality plays?"*

_____

_____

_____

_____

_____

Record

The Morality Play

➥ *What are the features of morality plays? One feature has been provided for you.*

Morality plays are about the moral struggles of everyday people.

Characters had names like Patience, Greed, and Good Works.

The plays taught lessons about virtue and vice.

They started a tradition leading to such playwrights as Shakespeare and Shaw.

Literary History: Miracle and Morality Plays

Summarize

➡️ *Review your notes on this article. Then use the classification chart on this page to sort information and identify key elements of miracle, mystery, and morality plays. The chart has been started for you.*

Miracle Plays	Mystery Plays	Morality Plays
• performed by priests • performed in church • about Bible stories and lives of saints • became elaborate and moved outside	• performed by trade guilds • performed outside church at fairs and markets • included sets and costumes, carried on wagons • included music, dancing, and comedy • audiences cheered heroes and booed villains	• performed by professional actors • about moral struggles of everyday people • included characters with names like Patience, Greed, and Good Works • started a tradition leading to Shakespeare and Shaw

Literary History: Miracle and Morality Plays

Apply

Multiple Choice

Circle the letter of the best choice for the following questions.

1. Which of the following is not true of mystery plays? C
   A. performed at fairs
   B. included costumes
   C. performed by professional actors
   D. included music and dancing

2. Which of the following are true of morality plays? B, C, D
   A. written by Shakespeare
   B. staging
   C. professional actors
   D. characters named Patience, Greed, and Good Works

3. What were "pageants"? C
   A. parades of medieval fashions
   B. a kind of mystery play
   C. wagons on which the scenery props and costumes were loaded
   D. a kind of room for performing plays

Matching

Choose the best options for each question.

4. What began in the early 900s? _____ B

5. What is true about a miracle play? _____ B, C

6. What is true about a mystery play? _____ B, D

7. What is true about a morality play? _____ A, B
   A. taught lessons about virtue and vice
   B. medieval drama
   C. performed by priests
   D. performed by guilds

How can you better remember and understand the material in this introduction? *Recite* your notes, *Reflect* on them, and *Review* them. You can also use your notes as you read *Everyman*.

BEFORE YOU READ

A DISTANT MIRROR

Building Background

Barbara Tuchman (1912–1989) was one of the most famous historians of the twentieth century. She received not one, but two Pulitzer Prizes. In 1963 she was awarded the honor for her book *The Guns of August,* an in-depth look at the first month of fighting during World War I. In 1972, she was honored for her book *Stilwell and the American Experience in China, 1911–1945,* about relations between China and the United States in the World War II era. Tuchman's book *A Distant Mirror* is a brilliant look at the life and society in fourteenth-century Europe. Tuchman discusses the plagues and wars that marked the period, how chivalry and knighthood changed medieval European society, and how dangerous life was for a knight.

Setting Purposes for Reading

What do honor and status mean to you? Have you ever done something well and became known for the good job you did, or admired for what you have? The knights of the Middle Ages valued honor and status a great deal.

With a classmate discuss the following questions:

- Think of a time you had to exert great physical effort to achieve a goal. What was the result?
- What would you risk in order to win someone's admiration?

Read to learn about how the historical realities of chivalry and knighthood are different from how they are described in medieval romances.

Reading Strategy | Analyzing Historical Context

Analyzing historical context means:

- collecting background information
- looking at the social forces that influence a work of literature

Active Reading Focus | Monitoring Comprehension

To **monitor comprehension,** you take pauses while reading to:

- ask yourself: Do I understand what I am reading?

- summarize or paraphrase a passage—write the main ideas in your own words.
- spend extra time to monitor comprehension with difficult passages.

Literary Element | Imagery

Imagery is the series of "word pictures" that writers create. Imagery causes readers to have an emotional response. To create effective images, writers use sensory details—descriptions that appeal to one or more of the five senses. Imagery helps the reader "see" or visualize what the writer is describing.

Big Idea | The World of Romance

Picture a "knight in shining armor." That is probably the strongest image we have of the Middle Ages. This is partly due to the medieval romance, a long-popular form of literature. The world of the medieval romance is full of knights and ladies, castles and tournaments. But real life for medieval knights was often far less glamorous than what was depicted in medieval romances.

Vocabulary

Read the definitions of these words from *A Distant Mirror.* The origin of each word, or its *etymology,* can be found in a dictionary. A word's origin reflects its history and development. Knowing the background of a word can help you unlock its meaning.

martial (mär′ shəl) *adj.* of or having to do with war, combat, or military life; p. 31 *Duane began his study of the martial arts with a class in karate.*

moral (môr′ əl) *adj.* what is known to be right and fair in terms of society; p. 31 *Roger believed in moral behavior, and always tried to do the right and fair thing.*

chronically (kron′ i kəl lē) *adv.* continuing for a long time; on a regular basis; p. 31 *Esther is chronically late for class.*

stamina (stam′ ə nə) *n.* strength and endurance; p. 31 *Michelle built up a lot of stamina for the long-distance race.*

peril (per′ əl) *n.* exposure to the chance of injury; danger; p. 31 *Phil put us in peril when he drove too fast.*

A Distant Mirror
By Barbara Tuchman

Chivalry was a moral system, governing the whole of noble life. It developed at the same time as the great crusades of the 12th century as a code intended to fuse the religious and **martial** spirits and somehow bring the fighting man into accord with Christian theory. A **moral** gloss was needed that would allow the Church to tolerate the warriors in good conscience and the warriors to pursue their own values in spiritual comfort. With the help of Benedictine thinkers,[1] a code evolved that put the knight's sword arm in the service, theoretically, of justice, right, piety, the Church, the widow, the orphan, and the oppressed.

Chivalry could not be contained by the Church, and bursting through the pious veils, it developed its own principles. Prowess, that combination of courage, strength, and skill that made a chevalier *preux*,[2] was the prime essential. Honor and loyalty, together with courtesy—meaning the kind of behavior that has since come to be called "chivalrous"—were the ideals, and so-called courtly love the presiding genius.[3] Designed to make the knight more polite and to lift the tone of society, courtly love required its disciple to be in a **chronically** amorous[4] condition, on the theory that he would thus be rendered[5] more courteous, gay, and gallant, and society in consequence more joyous.

Prowess was not mere talk, for the function of physical violence required real **stamina**. To fight on horseback or foot wearing 55 pounds of plate armor, to crash in collision with an opponent at full gallop while holding horizontal an eighteen-foot lance half the length of an average telephone pole, to give and receive blows with sword or battle-ax that could cleave[6] a skull or slice off a limb at a stroke, to spend half of life in the saddle through all weathers and for days at a time, was not a weakling's work. Hardship and fear were part of it. "Knights who are at the wars . . . are forever swallowing their fear," wrote the companion and biographer of Don Pero Niño, the "Unconquered Knight" of the late 14th century. "They expose themselves to every **peril**; they give up their bodies

---

1. *Benedictine thinkers* refers to monks of the Order of Saint Benedict.
2. *Chevalier* is French for "knight." *Preux* means "valiant" in French.
3. Here, *genius* means "guiding principle."
4. *Amorous* means "to be in love."
5. Here, *rendered* means "made."
6. *Cleave* means "to cut" or "to slash."

Reading Strategy

Analyzing Historical Context To analyze **historical context** is to look at the cultural background and social forces behind a work. Ask questions of this passage to analyze the article's historical context:

- When did it take place?

  12th century

- What is the main idea?

  To make fighting and religion

  related

Big Idea

The World of Romance Why do you think it was necessary to develop such a code of honor for knights?

Without such a code, the knights,

trained to be wariors, might be a

dangerous element in courtly life.

Vocabulary

martial (mär′ shəl) *adj.* of or having to do with war, combat, or military life

moral (môr′ əl) *adj.* what is known to be right and fair in terms of society

chronically (kron′ i kəl lē) *adv.* continuing for a long time; on a regular basis

stamina (stam′ ə nə) *n.* strength and endurance

peril (per′ əl) *n.* exposure to the chance of injury; danger

Imagery Recall that **imagery** is language that appeals to one or more of the five senses.

Which of the senses do the images in this passage appeal to?
These images appeal to the senses
of sight, smell, taste, and touch.

Monitoring Comprehension One way to **monitor comprehension** is to paraphrase or restate a passage in your own words.

How would you paraphrase this passage?
Possible response: "When both
sides were too tired to keep
fighting, Pero Niño's shield and
sword were badly damaged, and
his sword was covered with
blood."

✔ Reading Check

What ideals distinguished chivalrous behavior?
Chivalrous behavior was
distinguished by the ideals of
honor, loyalty, and courtesy.

to the adventure of life in death. Moldy bread or biscuit, meat cooked or uncooked; today enough to eat and tomorrow nothing, little or no wine, water from a pond or a butt,[7] bad quarters, the shelter of a tent or branches, a bad bed, poor sleep with their armor still on their backs, burdened with iron, the enemy an arrow-shot off. 'Ware! Who goes there? To arms! To arms!' With the first drowsiness, an alarm; at dawn, the trumpet. 'To horse! To horse! Muster! Muster!' As lookouts, as sentinels,[8] keeping watch by day and by night, fighting without cover, as foragers,[9] as scouts, guard after guard, duty after duty. 'Here they come! Here! They are so many—No, not as many as that—This way—that—Come this side—Press them there—News! News! They come back hurt, they have prisoners—no, they bring none back. Let us go! Let us go! Give no ground! On!' Such is their calling."

Horrid wounds were part of the calling. In one combat Don Pero Niño was struck by an arrow that "knit together his gorget[10] and his neck," but he fought on against the enemy on the bridge. "Several lance stumps were still in his shield and it was that which hindered him most." A bolt[11] from a crossbow "pierced his nostrils most painfully whereat he was dazed, but his daze lasted but a little time." He pressed forward, receiving many sword blows on head and shoulders which "sometimes hit the bolt embedded in his nose making him suffer great pain." When weariness on both sides brought the battle to an end, Pero Niño's shield "was tattered and all in pieces; his sword blade was toothed like a saw and dyed with blood . . . his armor was broken in several places by lance-heads of which some had entered the flesh and drawn blood, although the coat was of great strength." Prowess was not easily bought.

In the performance of his function, the knight must be prepared, as John of Salisbury[12] wrote, "to shed your blood for your brethren"—he meant brethren in the universal sense—"and, if needs must, to lay down your life." Many were thus prepared, though perhaps more from sheer love of battle than concern for a cause. Blind King John of Bohemia[13] met death in that way. He loved fighting for its own sake, not caring whether the conflict was important.

7. Here, *butt* means "ditch."
8. *Sentinels* are guards.
9. *Foragers* are scavengers.
10. A *gorget* is a piece of armor worn around the neck.
11. Here, *bolt* refers to a type of small arrow.
12. *John of Salisbury* (1115–1180) was a writer, historian, secretary to two archbishops of Canterbury, and the Bishop of Chartres.
13. *King John of Bohemia* (1296–1346) was a popular heroic figure who ruled from 1311 until his death at the Battle of Crécy in France.

As an ally of Philip VI,[14] at the head of 500 knights, the sightless King fought the English through Picardy,[15] always rash and in the avant-garde. At Crécy he asked his knights to lead him deeper into the battle so that he might strike further blows with his sword. Twelve of them tied their horses' reins together and, with the King at their head, advanced into the thick of the fight, "so far as never to return." His body was found next day among his knights, all slain with their horses still tied together.

Fighting filled the noble's need of something to do, a way to exert himself. It was his substitute for work. His leisure time was spent chiefly in hunting, otherwise in games of chess, backgammon, and dice, in songs, dances, pageants, and other entertainments. Long winter evenings were occupied listening to the recital of interminable[16] verse epics. The sword offered the workless noble an activity with a purpose, one that could bring him honor, status, and, if he was lucky, gain. ↄ

Reading Strategy

Analyzing Historical Context What is a difference between how kings or rulers of today, and how kings of the Middle Ages, are involved with their troops?

Today, kings and rulers do not go into battle with the troops. They are far more removed from the results of the orders they give. They are safer from harm than the soldiers they order to fight.

Vocabulary

Using Word Origins Look up the words *interminable* and *terminate* in the dictionary.

How are they related?
Students may understand that both originate from the word *term*, meaning period of time. They may relate *interminable* (endless) to *terminate* (to stop).

✔ Reading Check

What was the daily life of a knight like, when he was not at court?
When he was not at court, the daily life of a knight was very difficult, requiring great strength, stamina, and endurance of uncomfortable and perilous conditions.

---

14. *Philip VI* (1293–1350) was king of France from 1328 until his death.
15. *Picardy* is a region of northern France.
16. *Interminable* means "never-ending."

AFTER YOU READ

Graphic Organizer

A **K-W-L chart** can help you track what you are learning.

- The *K* stands for what you *know* already.
- The *W* stands for what you *want* to know.
- The *L* stands for what you *learned* from your reading.

Complete the organizer by reading the information in the first box and filling in the information in the remaining boxes. If you prefer, construct a Foldable™ to display the information.

Active Reading Focus

Monitoring Comprehension In the space below, paraphrase (restate in your own words) the first paragraph of this excerpt from *A Distant Mirror.* As you write, check to make sure you understand what the author is saying. Use words that make sense to you.

Responses will vary. Possible response: "Chivalry was a code, or system, or behavior that affected all areas of the lives of the nobility. In the twelfth-century crusades, the Church needed a way to relate the warriors to Christian beliefs. Benedictine monks came up with the code that put the knights on the side of good, as helpers of the weak and in the service of the Church."

What I Know

Knights were the warriors of medieval Europe. They wore armor and fought battles on horseback or by hand. When they weren't battling, they participated in jousts as exhibitions, entertainment, and practice.

What I Want to Know

Responses will vary. Possible response: "What hardships did the knights face when they were away from court? What was the daily life of the knight like, away from court? Did the knight's armor really protect him in battle?"

What I Learned

Responses will vary. Possible response: "Knights faced hunger, thirst, poor sleeping conditions, and terrible danger from surprise attacks. Their daily life was spent mostly in the saddle, wearing heavy armor and fighting horrible battles. The knight's armor could be penetrated by lances, swords, and battle-axes."

Reading Strategy

Analyzing Historical Context Reread the last paragraph of the selection. How does knowing this historical context help explain why anyone would want to live the dangerous life of a knight?

Responses will vary. Possible response: Most nobles

had nothing meaningful to do, since they did not work.

By knowing that nobles' leisure time was mostly taken

up with entertainment, the reader is better able to

understand why a noble who wanted a fuller life might

turn to knighthood and the seeking of honor, status,

and financial gain.

Literary Element

Imagery With a classmate, look back over the selection.

- Note passages in which the language appeals to your senses and helps you imagine, or picture the scene.
- Find a passage you find the easiest to "see."
- How does the imagery help you understand the scene?

Student responses will vary, but they should be able to

pinpoint a passage with rich imagery. They should be

able to explain how the imagery from the passage

helped them better understand what was going on.

For example, images of battle made them understand

how dangerous the life of a knight was.

Vocabulary Practice

Using Word Origins Word origins, or *etymology*, reflect the history and development of words. Use the clue to each word's origin to determine the correct word from the choices.

1. This word comes from the Greek word *stemon*, which means "standing."
    - (a) peril
    - (b) stamina
    - (c) martial

2. This word comes from a Latin word that refers to Mars, the god of war.
    - (a) piety
    - (b) peril
    - (c) martial

3. This word comes from the Latin word *periculum*, meaning "danger."
    - (a) peril
    - (b) moral
    - (c) chronically

4. This word has origins in the Greek word for time, *chronos*.
    - (a) martial
    - (b) chronically
    - (c) peril

1. (b) stamina

2. (c) martial

3. (a) peril

4. (b) chronically

Literary History: The Ballad Tradition

(p. 208)

Preview

- What is a folk ballad?
- What are the subjects of ballads?
- What are the characteristics of ballads?

This article discusses the nature and history of the English folk ballad, which is a part of our literary history. It discusses the subjects and forms of ballads, and the influence of ballads on later literary works. Reading this article will help you understand the ballads in Unit 1 that follow this article.

As you read the article, use the Cornell Note Taking System to record important points and remember what you have read.

Reduce

TO THE POINT *Note key words and phrases. For example:*

minstrels

balladeers

tropes

Lord Randall

ANY QUESTIONS? *Write them now; answer them as you reread your notes. For example: "What was the influence of folk ballads?"*

Record

➡ *Sometimes opening paragraphs do not have headings. What heading would you give to the opening paragraph of this article? Some of the main ideas have been listed below. Write your idea of the heading above them.*

Origin and Nature of Folk Ballads

Folk ballads originated about six centuries ago.

They were created by traveling minstrels.

They are rhymed poems that are recited or sung.

They were often based on local stories and tall tales.

usual topics included murders, revenge, tragic

accidents and disasters.

The Ballad's Influence

➡ *What are the key ideas in this paragraph? One has been listed for you.*

The authors of these early ballads are unknown.

Many versions of the same ballad may exist.

Ballads were first collected and published in the late

18th and early 19th centuries.

Romantic poets wrote literary ballads.

Robin Hood—Ballad Hero

➡ *Complete the following sentence: Robin Hood, who robbed from the rich and gave to the poor, is an example . . .*

of a popular folk ballad theme: the noble outlaw.

Literary History: The Ballad Tradition

(p. 209)

TO THE POINT *Note key words that explain the italicized items. For example:*

reflection

dialogue

rhyme scheme

refrain

burden

Characteristics of the Folk Ballad

➡ *List the characteristics of the folk ballad. After each, briefly explain the characteristic in your own words. Two examples have been written for you.*

about a single incident—little characterization, description or background

little reflection—focuses on story, not emotions or thoughts

includes dialogue—story told through characters

simple beat and rhyme—differs from literary ballad

refrain— lines repeated throughout ballad

burden—use of a complete repeated stanza repeated after a narrative stanza

suggests, not states—folk wisdom implied, not told directly

actual events—some ballads based on real incidents, such as shipwrecks, accidental deaths, like today's headlines.

MY VIEW *Write your comments here.*

➡ *What were some of the influences of the folk ballads on popular music? One example has been written for you.*

still popular among Irish folk singers today

influenced such musicians as Bob Dylan and B. B. King

themes, rhythms and rhymes still an influence

Literary History: The Ballad Tradition

Summarize

➡ *Review your notes on this article. Then summarize the important points of the article. List each point under the appropriate heading below. The summary has been started for you.*

<u>Origin of Ballad Tradition</u>

dates to 15th century

minstrels and storytellers entertained with songs that told stories

portray real events

<u>Typical Ballad Topics</u>

murder

revenge

accidents

disasters

heroic deeds

love

<u>The Influence of Folk Ballads</u>

Late 18th century writers collected and published ballads.

Romantic poets wrote literary ballads imitating them.

Contemporary folk and pop artists imitate them.

<u>Folk Ballad Characteristics</u>

recounts a single incident with little commentary

uses dialogue

a simple beat

repeated lines or stanzas

often about real incidents

can contain implied folk wisdom

Literary History: The Ballad Tradition

Apply

Multiple Choice

Circle the letters of the best choice for the following questions.

1. Which of the following are true of folk ballads? B, C
   A. They first appeared in the eighteenth century.

   B. Some recount real events.

   C. Minstrels entertained with them.

   D. Keats wrote folk ballads.

2. Which of the following are folk ballad topics? A, C, D
   A. revenge

   B. epic battles

   C. love

   D. disasters

3. When did the folk ballad tradition begin? C
   A. The eighteenth century

   B. The sixth century

   C. the fifteenth century

   D. 600 A.D.

4. What were stories in folk ballads often based on? C
   A. religious texts

   B. old myths and legends

   C. actual events

   D. earlier forms of poetry and song

Matching

Choose the best option to complete each of the following items.

5. Romantic poets _____ A

6. Robin Hood _____ C

7. Scottish ballads _____ B

8. Bob Dylan _____ A, D
   A. imitated the folk ballad form.

   B. are typical folk ballads.

   C. is a popular folk ballad hero.

   D. wrote modern variations of folk ballads.

How can you better remember and understand the material in this Literary History? *Recite* **your notes,** *Reflect* **on them, and** *Review* **them. You can also use your notes as you read the ballads in this unit.**

Introductory Text: The English Renaissance 1485–1650

Looking Ahead *(p. 237)*

Preview

- What was the Renaissance?
- Who was William Shakespeare?
- What was the King James version of the Bible?

This introduction prepares you for the literature you will read in a unit of your textbook. It explains the historical, social, and cultural forces of the English Renaissance. This era produced the plays of William Shakespeare and the King James version of the Bible.

As you read the introduction, use the Cornell Note Taking System to record important points and to remember what you have read.

Reduce

TO THE POINT *Note key words and phrases. For example:*

Renaissance
William Shakespeare
King James Bible

ANY QUESTIONS? *Ask questions about terms in each section. For example: "What is humanism?"*

Record

Looking Ahead

➡ *What events in history and culture are mentioned here? The first item has been listed for you.*

cultural movement known as Renaissance reaches
England, end of 1400s
next 150 years includes conflicts at home, military
threats from abroad
same time also produces great literary works, such as
Shakespeare's plays and the King James Bible

Keep the following questions in mind as you read

➡ *What cultural terms are mentioned here? One has been listed for you.*

Renaissance humanism
Shakespeare's works
metaphysical poets
Cavalier poets

Introductory Text: The English Renaissance 1485–1650

Timeline *(pp. 238–239)*

Reduce

TO THE POINT *Note types of writing. For example:*

morality play

religious text

poem collection

essay

sonnet

TO THE POINT *Note general categories of events. For example:*

exploration and settlement

Record

British Literature

➡ *Based on the timeline, what types of literature were being created during this period? List types. Next to it, list one or two examples of each type. Two types and examples have been listed for you.*

morality play—Everyman

religious texts—Book of Common Prayer, King James Bible

collections of poems—Tottel's Miscellany

essays—Sir Francis Bacon

sonnets—Shakespeare and John Donne

British Events

➡ *What types of events take place in this section of the timeline? List one or two examples of each type of event. Use words that make the event clear to you. One type of event has been listed for you.*

Exploration and Settlement

1580—Sir Francis Drake circles globe

Other possible categories might include rulers, Christianity, and war.

Introductory Text: The English Renaissance 1485–1650

Timeline *(pp. 238–239)*

Reduce

TO THE POINT *Note general categories of events. For example:*

Native Americans

_____

_____

_____

_____

Record

World Events

➡ *What types, or categories, of events take place in this section of the timeline? List one or two events in each category. Use words that make the event clear to you. One category has been started for you.*

Native Americans

1521—Hernán Cortés conquers the Aztec empire

Other possible categories might include religion, rulers, science and technology, literature, Japan, art, slavery.

Recap

➡ *Review your notes on the Timeline. Then recap: Use classification notes to organize events by the most important types. One type has been started for you.*

Students might create such categories as exploration, English theater, rulers, war, Christianity, or science. They should list appropriate entries in each category.

English Theater				
c. 1500— *Everyman,* morality play, performed 1576—First professional playhouse in London				

Introductory Text: The English Renaissance 1485–1650

By the Numbers *(p. 240)*

Reduce

TO THE POINT *For the headings on this page, note key words and phrases. For example:*

Philip II

Spanish Armada

Protestant monarch

Whitsun

Mary I

Elizabeth I

plague

Globe

shilling

Record

Spanish Armada; Spanish and English Losses

➡ *Summarize the main points in this section. The first two points have been listed for you.*

In 1588 England became a great sea power.

That year, King Philip II of Spain tried to invade and overthrow Protestant England.

The fleet was called the Spanish Armada.

The English navy defeated the Spanish Armada.

Spain lost over a third of their ships; England lost none.

Introductory Text: The English Renaissance 1485–1650

By the Numbers *(p. 240)*

Reduce

TO THE POINT *Write the remaining heads on this page.*

holidays
executions
London's population
earning power
theater prices

➡ *List the remaining headings on this page. What is each about? Under each heading, note what the statistics tell you. The first has been listed for you.*

<u>Holidays</u>
Renaissance England had many religious holidays.

<u>Executions</u>
Many people were executed for treason (including having the wrong religion) in Renaissance England, including royalty.

<u>London's Population</u>
London's population grew steadily despite many epidemics.

<u>Theater Prices</u>
Theater prices in London's playhouses were different depending on where you sat or stood.

<u>Earning Power</u>
There was a huge gap between rich and poor in Renaissance England.

Introductory Text: The English Renaissance 1485–1650

Being There *(p. 241)*

Reduce

ANY QUESTIONS? *Ask questions about the pictures. For example: "What is the subject of the picture, Musicians at Wadley House?"*

_____

_____

_____

TO THE POINT *Note key words and phrases. For example:*

Glasgow

_____

_____

_____

_____

Record

➡ *Pictures are part of the information in this introduction. What do these pictures tell you about life in Renaissance England? One fact has been done for you.*

groups of musicians performed

wealthy people built giant estates

townspeople gathered for celebrations

_____

_____

➡ *What cities and towns were becoming important during this period? Look at this map and list some examples. One has been listed for you.*

Glasgow

Plymouth

Southampton

Birmingham

Stratford-upon-Oxford

Recap

➡ *Review your notes on By the Numbers and Being There. Then recap: Use the information to draw several conclusions about Renaissance England. One example has been written for you.*

People in Renaissance England enjoyed theater and music.

Students' conclusions might relate to the Spanish Armada, holidays,

executions, London's population, theater prices, and earning power.

_____

_____

_____

Introductory Text: The English Renaissance 1485–1650

Historical, Social, and Cultural Forces *(p. 242)*

Reduce

TO THE POINT *Note key words and phrases. For example:*

Henry VII

War of the Roses

golden age

_____

_____

_____

TO THE POINT *Note key words and phrases. For example:*

Renaissance

Francesco Petrarch

_____

_____

_____

_____

ANY QUESTIONS? *Ask questions about headings. For example:*

"What was important about humanism?"

"Who was Geoffrey Chaucer?"

Record

Tudor England

➡ *What events happened in England under the Tudor rulers? Two have been listed for you.*

Henry VII started a new royal line when he became king in 1485.

The 30-year civil war (Wars of the Roses) ended

the monarchs brought many changes to England

the country was divided by religious and political conflicts

England enjoyed a creative golden age

The Renaissance

➡ *What are the main ideas in this section? List them in your own words. Two ideas have been written for you.*

The Renaissance was a cultural movement that began in Italy and spread to Western Europe.

Renaissance means "rebirth."

This was a time of transition from the Middle Ages to the modern world.

There was a renewed interest in science, art, and Greek and Roman learning.

Scholars of this era rediscovered classical works.

Humanism

➡ *What was humanism? Why was it important? How did it reach England? Summarize the main ideas to answer these questions. The first has been answered for you.*

Humanism was a new movement that believed humans could do great things.

Humanism was important because it helped cause great achievements in the arts and sciences.

Humanism also helped cause the Protestant Reformation.

Introductory Text: The English Renaissance 1485–1650

Historical, Social, and Cultural Forces *(p. 243)*

Reduce

TO THE POINT *Note key words and phrases. For example:*

Martin Luther

Catherine of Aragon

Anglican Church

_____

_____

Record

The Protestant Reformation

➡ *What happened during the Protestant Reformation? Use a flow chart to organize events. The chart has been started for you.*

> Martin Luther protested abuses in the Roman Catholic Church.

↓

> Luther's protests caused a widespread rejection of the pope's authority.

↓

> Henry VIII proclaimed himself head of the Protestant Church of England.

↓

> A split led to religious conflict in England that lasted until the end of the 1600s.

Introductory Text: The English Renaissance 1485–1650

Historical, Social, and Cultural Forces *(p. 243)*

Reduce

TO THE POINT *Note key words and phrases.*

wordly subjects

Shakespeare

_____

_____

Record

Preview Big Ideas of the English Renaissance

➥ *Restate each of the Big Ideas to make them easier to remember. Use words that make the ideas clear to you. The first has been written for you.*

Influenced by the humanists' idea that human activity was worthwhile by itself, English writers moved from religious subjects to worldly ones.

The greatest product of the English Renaissance was William Shakespeare, whose plays present individual heroes and villains struggling with difficult choices.

The English Renaissance produced works dealing with subjects as different as religious meditations and erotic love.

Introductory Text: The English Renaissance 1485–1650

Historical, Social, and Cultural Forces *(pp. 242–243)*

Recap

 *Review your notes on the Historical, Social, and Cultural Forces. Then recap: Use your summary notes to help you remember the main points. Two main points have been listed for you.*

<u>Topic: The English Renaissance 1485–1650</u>

<u>Main Points:</u>

Tudor kings—ended the Wars of the Roses, a 30-year civil war.

Renaissance—cultural movement that began in Italy and spread to Western Europe.

Renaissance—characterized by interest in science, art, and Greek and Roman learning

humanism—proclaimed unlimited human potential

humanism—fostered achievements in art and science

The Protestant Reformation—protest against the Roman Catholic Church

Martin Luther—began Reformation by protesting perceived Church abuses.

Henry VIII—declared himself head of Protestant Church of England

religious conflict—continued in England until the end of the 1600s

Introductory Text: The English Renaissance 1485–1650

Big Idea 1: Humanists and Courtiers *(p. 244)*

Reduce

ANY QUESTIONS? *Use them to organize your notes. For example:*

Sir Thomas More
Desiderius Erasmus
The Praise of Folly
"a man for all seasons"
Utopia

TO THE POINT *Note key words and phrases. For example:*

Elizabeth I
Sir Walter Raleigh
History of the World
James I

TO THE POINT *Note key words and phrases. For example:*

Stuart family
Britain
King James Bible
Lord Chamberlain's Men

Record

Humanism in England

➡ *What were some characteristics of humanism and humanists? Two examples have been listed for you.*

personal contact and friendships
friendships inspired important works
humanists had sharp intellect
humanists were witty
humanists valued deep learning
Thomas More was considered an ideal humanist

Elizabeth I and Her Court

➡ *Who was Queen Elizabeth I? What were some of her characteristics? Two examples have been listed for you.*

Henry VII's second daughter
famous for her wit and eloquence
knew Greek, Latin, and several modern languages
loved music, dancing, and theater
admired displays of wit
poet, scientist, and adventurer Sir Walter Raleigh was
a favorite member of her court

The Court of James I

➡ *How was King James I like Queen Elizabeth I? How was he unlike Elizabeth I?*

Like

They both loved theater.

Unlike

Elizabeth I was worldly and practical; James I was
interested in arguments about theology.

Introductory Text: The English Renaissance 1485–1650

Big Idea 1: Humanists and Courtiers *(p. 245)*

Reduce

TO THE POINT *Note key words and phrases. For example:*

Puritan attacks

immoral

Sir Philip Sidney

Record

from *A Defence of Poesie* by Sir Philip Sidney

➡ *Complete the sentence to paraphrase the following lines from the passage: "So is it in men (most of which are childish in the best things, till they be cradled in their graves): glad they will be to hear the tales of Hercules, Achilles, Cyrus, and Aeneas; . . . "* Actually, most men (who are like children in the best ways), would love to hear stories of Hercules, Achilles, Cyrus and Aeneas.

Recap

➡ *Review your notes on Big Idea 1: Humanists and Courtiers. Then recap: Use a classification chart to summarize key points about Sir Thomas More and Elizabeth I.*

Sir Thomas More	Elizabeth I
ideal humanist	famous for her wit and eloquence
friendship with Erasmus typical of humanists	knew Greek, Latin, and several modern languages
cultivated intellect	loved music, dancing, and theater
sparkling wit	admired daring displays of wit
deep learning	her favorites, such as poet, scientist, and adventurer Sir Walter Raleigh, showed qualities she admired most
broad culture	worldly and practical

Introductory Text: The English Renaissance 1485–1650

Big Idea 2: A Bard for the Ages (p. 246)

Reduce

ANY QUESTIONS? *Use them to organize your notes. For example:*

Stratford-upon-Avon

Lord Chamberlain's Men

Globe Theater

Thames

As You Like It

Blackfriars

TO THE POINT *For the remaining headings on this page, note keywords and phrases. For example:*

Ovid

Plautus

Seneca

Montaigne

Record

Shakespeare's Theaters

➡ *What information is given in each paragraph in this section? Create a heading for each paragraph. Then organize the main ideas under it. The first has been done for you.*

<u>Shakespeare's career</u>

profitable career—retired in 1610

good businessman—part owner of popular acting

company, Lord Chamberlain's Men

built Globe Theatre in 1599

<u>The Globe</u>

located on south bank of Thames River

held 3,000 people

open-air playhouse built in shape of an O

<u>Blackfriars Theatre</u>

more intimate and expensive

for more sophisticated audience

Shakespeare's Learning

➡ *What are the main ideas in this section? One has been written for you.*

Shakespeare probably did not learn any Greek

Read latin works by poet Ovid and playwrights Plautus

and Seneca that were big influence

incorporated what he read into his plays

Shakespeare's Humanism

➡ *Complete this sentence in your own words: Shakespeare's plays show his humanism by . . .*

focusing on characters who seek to fulfill their potential

and by writing about the many sides of human nature.

Introductory Text: **The English Renaissance 1485–1650**

Big Idea 2: A Bard for the Ages *(p. 247)*

Reduce

TO THE POINT *Note key words and phrases. For example:*

Richard III

villain

deformity

Record

from *Richard III*, Act 1, Scene 1

➡️ *To paraphrase means to restate writing using your own words. Paraphrase these lines: "And therefore, since I cannot prove a lover, / To entertain these fair well-spoken days, / I am determined to prove a villain."*

Possible response:

Since I can't have love and enjoy this pleasant time, I have decided to become evil.

Recap

➡️ *Review your notes on Big Idea 2: A Bard for the Ages. Then recap. Use a web to organize key points about Shakespeare. The web has been started for you.*

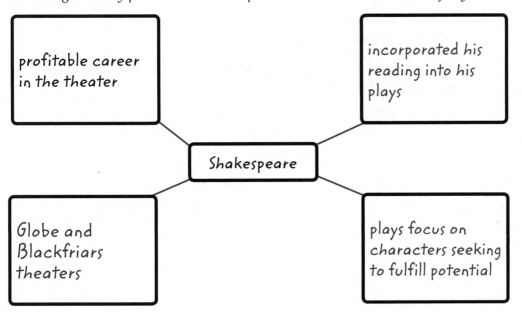

profitable career in the theater

incorporated his reading into his plays

Shakespeare

Globe and Blackfriars theaters

plays focus on characters seeking to fulfill potential

Introductory Text: The English Renaissance 1485–1650

Big Idea 3: The Sacred and the Secular *(p. 248)*

Reduce

TO THE POINT *Note key words and phrases. For example:*

Roman Catholic

sacred

secular

Record

Humanism and Religion

➡ *Complete this sentence in your own words: Sir Thomas More's opposition to Henry VIII's divorce, and his practice of private prayer, show that More's humanism . . .*

was based on his religious beliefs.

The Bible in English

➡ *When did the Bible get translated into English? Organize the events in a timeline. The first event has been written for you.*

1522—Luther translates New Testament into German

1520s and 1530s—William Tyndale translates Bible into English

1536—Tyndale burned at stake as punishment for his unauthorized translation

Later—King James Bible writers borrowed heavily from Tyndale's work

ANY QUESTIONS? *Use them to organize your notes. For example: "What was Metaphysical poetry?"*

Metaphysical and Cavalier Poets

➡ *What are the main features of Metaphysical and Cavalier poetry? The list has been started for you.*

Metaphysical poetry

removed from complex religious issues of day

strong sense of contradictions in life, such as between beauty of sensual world and ravages of time

poets included John Donne and Andrew Marvell

Cavalier poetry

Italian word for knight

celebrated earthly pleasures, especially quick-blooming love, and lamented its fading

poets included Robert Herrick, Sir John Suckling, Richard Lovelace

Introductory Text: The English Renaissance 1485–1650

Big Idea 3: The Sacred and the Secular *(p. 249)*

Reduce

TO THE POINT *Note key words and phrases. For example:*

usurped

viceroy

betrothed

Record

Batter my heart, three-personed God **by John Donne**

➥ *Consider the lines from the poem: "Yet dearly I love you, and would be loved fain/But am betrothed unto your enemy." How do these lines, and this poem, express the idea of contradiction in Metaphysical poetry?*

Possible response:

The poet writes about his own awareness of the

contradiction between his own sinful nature and his

desire for God.

Recap

➥ *Review your notes on Big Idea 3: The Sacred and the Secular. Then recap: Use summary notes to help you remember the main points. The recap has been started for you.*

Topic: The Sacred and the Secular

Main Points:

Many humanists, such as Sir Thomas More, combined humanism
with religious belief.

Protestant leader William Tyndale translated the Bible into
English.

Tyndale was burned at the stake as punishment for his
unauthorized translation.

But later, scholars writing the King James Bible borrowed heavily
from Tyndale's work.

Metaphysical poetry expressed a strong sense of contradictions in
life, such as between beauty of sensual world and ravages of time.

Cavalier poetry celebrated earthly pleasures, especially quick-
blooming love, and lamented its fading.

Introductory Text: **The English Renaissance 1485–1650**

Wrap-Up *(p. 250)*

TO THE POINT *Note key words and phrases. For example:*

Sir Francis Bacon

English Renaissance

William Shakespeare

British Empire

Protestant Reformation

King James Bible

Record

Why It Matters

➡ *What is the main idea of each paragraph in this section? The main idea of the first paragraph has been written for you.*

paragraph 1—The value humanism placed on human experience led to modern scientific methods.

paragraph 2—The plays of Shakespeare are masterpieces of world literature.

paragraph 3—The King James Bible and Book of Common Prayer have enriched faith and language.

Cultural Links

➡ *What cultural link to the present is described in each paragragh?*

paragraph 1—Shakespeare is still performed in modern adaptations

paragraph 2—King James Bible had a profound influence on development of English language.

Recap

➡ *Review your notes on the Wrap-Up. Then recap: Use an evidence organizer to sum up a viewpoint on Renaissance England based on information drawn from this section. The organizer has been started for you.*

	Viewpoint	
Shakespeare has become an essential part of world culture.		
Supporting Detail	Supporting Detail	Supporting Detail
English culture was spread around the world by the British Empire.	Modern adaptations of Shakespeare's works are performed in many different styles and forms.	Biographies and novels about Shakespeare continue to appear.

Introductory Text: The English Renaissance 1485–1650

Summarize

➡ *Review your notes on this introduction. Then recap: Create an outline using the big ideas. The outline has been started for you.*

The English Renaissance, 1485–1650

   I. Humanists and Courtiers

     A. Humanists valued intellect, wit, learning, and culture.

     B. Sir Thomas More was an ideal humanist.

     C. Smart, learned, and cultured, Elizabeth I encouraged culture at her court.

     D. Though different from Elizabeth as a ruler, James I was like her in his love of theater.

   II. A Bard for the Ages

     A. Shakespeare had a very successful career in the theater.

     B. He established the Globe Theatre as a playhouse for inexpensive entertainment.

     C. He wrote plays for the Blackfriars Theatre for a more sophisticated audience.

     D. His characters express humanism's goal of fulfilling potential.

   III. The Sacred and the Secular

     A. Many humanists, such as Sir Thomas More, combined humanism and religion.

     B. Humanists and Protestants translated the Bible as a challenge to Church authority.

     C. Metaphysical poetry expressed a strong sense of contradictions in life.

     D. Cavalier poetry celebrated earthly pleasures.

Introductory Text: The English Renaissance 1485–1650

Apply

Multiple Choice

Circle the letter of the best choice for the following questions.

1. What was *not* true of the Renaissance? D
   A. rediscovered classical works

   B. renewed interest in science and art

   C. spread to Western Europe

   D. led to religious conflict in England

2. Which of the following describe(s) humanism? A, B, C
   A. valued this world

   B. proclaimed unlimited human potential

   C. helped cause Protestant Reformation

   D. ended Wars of the Roses

3. Which literature was a product of the Protestant Reformation? C, D
   A. William Shakespeare's sonnets

   B. William Shakespeare's plays

   C. The King James Bible

   D. The Book of Common Prayer

4. Which is a quality of Cavalier poetry? D
   A. sense of contradictions in life

   B. sense of unlimited human potential

   C. sense of importance of culture

   D. sense of quick-blooming love

Matching

Write the letter of the choice that best matches each numbered item.

5. Who wrote *Utopia*?_____ A
6. Who was a worldly and practical ruler? _____ B
7. Who translated the Bible into English? _____ C
8. Who was one of the Cavalier poets? _____ D

   A. Sir Thomas More

   B. Elizabeth I

   C. William Tyndale

   D. Robert Herrick

How can you better remember and understand the material in this introduction? *Recite* your notes, *Reflect* on them, and *Review* them. **You can also use your notes for a quick review of the historical period or the Big Ideas of this unit. As you learn more about the ideas in the unit, add to your notes.**

Literary History: **The Development of the Sonnet** (p. 252)

Preview

- What is a sonnet?
- What are the different types of sonnet?
- Why were sonnets a popular form?

This article describes the history of the sonnet. Many popular poems in English and world literature took this form. The article describes sonnets' major types, traditional themes, and essential terms. The information will help you read the sonnets in Unit 2 of your textbook.

As you read the article, use the Cornell Note Taking System to record important points and to remember what you have read.

Reduce

TO THE POINT *Note key words and phrases. For example:*

<u>iambic pentameter</u>
<u>stressed</u>
<u>unstressed</u>
<u>rhyme scheme</u>

ANY QUESTIONS? *Ask questions as you read the headings. Then, answer them as you read the information under the headings. Review the questions when you reread your notes. For example: "What are the sonnet forms? How are they different?"*

Record

Meter and Rhyme Patterns

➡ *Group information according to characteristics and symbols. First, list the key characteristics of a sonnet. Then, list the symbols used for marking stresses and rhyme in poetry. The information has been started for you.*

<u>Characteristics:</u>
14 lines
iambic pentameter: each line has 5 metric units/feet
each foot has an unstressed syllable followed by a
stressed syllable
sonnets have a rhyme scheme

<u>Symbols:</u>
symbol for unstressed syllables: ˘
symbol for stressed syllables: ′
rhyme scheme: letters in alphabetical order
(a, b, c, etc.) mark the sound of a line's last word—the
lines that rhyme share the same letter

Sonnet Forms

➡ *What different forms do sonnets have? List them to help you remember them. One has been listed for you.*

There are three types of sonnets:
Italian/Petrarchan
English/Shakespearean, and Spenserian

Literary History: The Development of the Sonnet (p. 253)

TO THE POINT *Note key words and phrases. For example:*

Petrarchan sonnet

Francesco Petrarch

octave

sestet

turn

The Italian Sonnet

➡️ *Divide this information on the Italian sonnet into these categories: history, themes, and form. Then list information under each category. Some information has been listed for you.*

History: often called Petrarchan sonnet: named for Francesco Petrarch

Theme: unrequited love

Form:

first eight lines (octave)—problem or situation

last six lines (sestet)—answer or resolution

rhyme scheme in octave: <u>abbaabba</u>

rhyme scheme in sestet: <u>cdecde</u> or <u>cdcdcd</u>

The English Sonnet

➡️ *Summarize the main ideas. One idea has been written for you.*

Shakespeare was a master of this type of sonnet, which is also known as the Shakespearean sonnet.

It has three quatrains—each quatrain is four lines, each with its own rhyme scheme.

Rhyme scheme is usually <u>abab cdcd efef gg</u>.

A couplet ends the sonnet—a couplet is two lines.

TO THE POINT *Note key words and phrases. For example:*

Shakespearean sonnet

quatrains

couplet

Spenserian sonnet

The Spenserian Sonnet

➡️ *Use this chart to organize the main ideas in this section. Two main ideas have been written for you.*

History and Development	Characteristics
named for its creator, Edmund Spenser	similar to Shakespearean sonnet: three quatrains and a couplet different rhyme scheme: abab bcbc cdcd ee

Literary History: The Development of the Sonnet

Summarize

➡ *Review your notes on this article. Then summarize: Use this classification chart to sort information and identify key characteristics associated with the sonnets of three major writers. The writers are Petrarch, Shakespeare, and Spenser. The chart has been started for you.*

Francesco Petrarch	William Shakespeare	Edmund Spenser	Shared by All
created Italian sonnet, also called the Petrarchan sonnet	master of English sonnet, also called the Shakespearean sonnet	Spenserian sonnet similar to Shakespearean sonnet—three quatrains and a couplet	14 lines
themes of unrequited love	three quatrains— a quatrain is a group of four lines, each with its own rhyme scheme	rhyme scheme: <u>abab bcbc cdcd ee</u>	themes of unrequited love and mortality
octave and sestet		interlocking rhyme pushes toward final couplet	iambic pentameter: 5 metric units/feet per line—each foot contains an unstressed syllable followed by a stressed syllable
octave is first 8 lines—presents a problem or situation	ends with a couplet—a couplet is two lines		two parts: first part establishes problem, situation or question— second part provides resolution, summary, or answer
sestet is final 6 lines—resolves the problem or situation	rhyme scheme: <u>abab cdcd efef gg</u>		transition between two parts—called "turn"
rhyme scheme in octave: <u>abbaabba</u>			some variation of rhyme scheme
rhyme scheme in sestet: <u>cdecde</u> or <u>cdcdcd</u>			

Literary History: **The Development of the Sonnet**

Apply

Multiple Choice

Circle the letters of the best choice or choices for the following questions.

1. What is characteristic of a sonnet? B, D
   A. dialogue

   B. iambic pentameter

   C. free verse

   D. 14 lines

2. What symbols are used to mark stressed and unstressed syllables in poetry? C, D
   A. *

   B. !

   C. ˘

   D. ´

3. What are the three main kinds of sonnets? D
   A. English, Italian, and Shakespearean

   B. English, Italian, and Petrarchan

   C. English, Italian, and French

   D. English, Italian, and Spenserian

4. How many lines does it take an English sonnet to answer its own question? A
   A. two

   B. six

   C. eight

   D. twelve

Matching

Write the letter of the choice that best matches each numbered item.

5. originated the Italian Sonnet _____ C

6. created the Spenserian Sonnet _____ B

7. master of the English Sonnet _____ A

8. group of four lines _____ D
   A. William Shakespeare

   B. Edmund Spenser

   C. Francesco Petrarch

   D. quatrain

How can you better remember and understand the material in this Literary History? *Recite* **your notes,** *Reflect* **on them, and** *Review* **them. You can also use your notes as you read the sonnets in this unit.**

Literary History: Shakespeare's Theater *(p. 314)*

- When and why was the Globe Theatre built?

- What was the Globe like?

- What was a performance there like?

This article describes the Globe Theatre and the productions that were presented there. Reading this article will provide you with information to help imagine how Shakespeare's *Macbeth* was first performed on stage.

As you read the article, use the Cornell Note Taking System to record important points and to remember what you have read.

Reduce

TO THE POINT *Note key words and phrases. For example:*

William Burbage

Globe

_____

_____

ANY QUESTIONS? *Ask questions about the headlines. Answer them as you read the information under the headings. Review the information in your notes. For example: "What are groundlings?"*

_____

_____

Record

➥ *Why was the first theater in England built? Answer in words that make sense to you.* Possible response:

The London city council would not allow players to work in the city of London in 1574. So William Burbage built a playhouse outside the city in 1576.

The Globe

➥ *Complete this sentence in your own words: Burbage had trouble renewing the lease on his theater . . .*
so he built the Globe in another spot, using wood from the old theater.

This Wooden O

➥ *List words and phrases that describe the Globe's structure and appearance. The description has been started for you.*

Building: circular; three-tiered galleries; open courtyard

Stage: raised platform; two-tiered gallery above; rear inner stage

Literary History: Shakespeare's Theater *(pp. 314–315)*

Reduce

TO THE POINT *Note key words and phrases. For example:*

blank verse

Elizabethan dress

_____

_____

_____

Record

Lords and Groundlings

➡ *Describe the audience at the Globe in your own words. The description has been started for you.*

Well-to-do patrons sat in the galleries.

Common people were called "groundlings," and stood in the courtyard.

The audience shouted comments to actors onstage.

Theatrical Conventions

➡ *Summarize the theatrical conventions that were typical of a production at the Globe Theatre. Two have been listed for you.*

Actors spoke in blank verse that mimics the rhythm of spoken English.

Female roles were played by boys.

Colorful costumes matched Elizabethan dress, regardless of the play's time and setting.

There was little or no scenery.

Trumpets announced the beginning; characters' entrances signaled new scenes.

Plays lasted about two hours.

The Globe's Comeback

➡ *What happened to the Globe Theatre? List three events in its history. One has been written for you.*

The original Globe was destroyed by a fire in 1613.

A replacement was torn down in 1644 to make room for housing.

A replica of the Globe funded by actor Sam Wanamaker now stands on the south bank of the Thames in London.

_____

Literary History: Shakespeare's Theater

Summarize

➡ *Review your notes on this article. Then summarize: Use a classification chart to list details about the history, physical features and audience, and theatrical conventions of the Globe Theater. The chart has been started for you.*

History	Physical Features / Audience	Theatrical Conventions
Originally built by Burbage in 1599 with wood from previous theater. The Globe was destroyed by fire in 1613. A replacement torn down in 1644. A replica opened in 1997.	A circular building surrounded an open courtyard. Three-tiered galleries provided audience seating. A platform stage jutted into courtyard. A two-tiered performance gallery was above stage. A small, curtained inner stage was in the back. Well-to-do patrons sat in the galleries. Common people— "groundlings"—stood in the courtyard. The audience shouted comments to actors onstage.	Actors spoke in blank verse. Boys played female roles. Costumes matched Elizabethan dress. There was little or no scenery. Trumpets signaled the beginning of a play; characters' entrances signaled new scenes. Plays lasted about 2 hours.

Literary History: Shakespeare's Theater

Apply

Multiple Choice

Circle the letter of the best choice for the following questions.

1. Which of the following is true of the Globe Theater? B
   A. was first theater in England
   B. had open courtyard
   C. did not allow common people
   D. produced 3–4 hour plays

2. Which of the following does *not* describe the Globe? D
   A. tiered galleries for seating
   B. performance galleries above stage
   C. curtained inner stage
   D. circular main stage

3. Why did Burbage build a theater outside the city? C
   A. it was easier to build due to unlimited timber supplies
   B. traveling actors generally preferred to work outside London
   C. the city council banned traveling actors from performing in the city
   D. the city council wanted to tax Burbage for his ticket receipts

4. What were groundlings? A
   A. common people who stood in the courtyard to watch the performance
   B. common people who had to sit up in the galleries to watch the performance
   C. the city council's name for traveling actors
   D. the crew that moved and set up the theatrical scenery and props

Matching

Write the letter of the choice in the second column that best matches each item in the first column.

5. Costumes . . . _____ C
6. Scenery and props . . . _____ D
7. Actors . . . _____ A
8. The stage . . . _____ B
   A. spoke in blank verse.
   B. had no front curtain.
   C. were similar to Elizabethan styles.
   D. were sparse.

How can you better remember and understand the material in this Literary History? *Recite* your notes, *Reflect* on them, and *Review* them. You can also use your notes to help you read *Macbeth.*

THRONE OF BLOOD

Building Background

Shakespeare's great drama *Macbeth* has inspired many works in other art forms. One well-known treatment of *Macbeth* is the 1957 Japanese film *Throne of Blood*. The movie was created by one of Japan's finest directors, Akira Kurosawa. Kurosawa's film is greatly influenced by Noh (nō). Noh is a centuries-old Japanese theatrical form. It uses brightly painted, white face masks. Its costumes symbolize a character type or position in society. Its vocal lines are chanted, not spoken, in an unrealistic style.

In the following selection from his book *Shakespeare on Screen*, Daniel Rosenthal describes how Kurosawa adapted *Macbeth* into *Throne of Blood*.

Setting Purposes for Reading

How do you make a play into a movie? Translating a work of art from one medium to another is not easy. With a classmate, discuss these questions:

- What is the difference between a movie and a stage play?
- What can you do in a movie but not in a play?

Read to find out how Kurosawa adapted *Macbeth* into *Throne of Blood*.

Reading Strategy | Comparing and Contrasting Genres

- To **compare** is to show how things are similar.
- To **contrast** is to show how they are different.

When you **compare and contrast genres**, you identify the similarities and differences between two or more types (or genres) of art.

Active Reading Focus | Identifying Sequence

Identifying sequence means finding the logical order of ideas or events. In his essay, Rosenthal discusses the chronological sequence of events in Kurosawa's film. A chronology is an arrangement of events in terms of time: which came first, which came next, etc. As you read, ask yourself:

- in what ways does Kurosawa's movie follow the same sequence of events as Shakespeare's play *Macbeth*?
- how does Kurosawa change the sequence?

Literary Element | Imagery

Imagery refers to the "word pictures" an author creates by using sensory details, or descriptions that appeal to the five senses. In his essay, Rosenthal uses strong verbs and clear adjectives to help readers understand what viewers of the film saw.

Big Idea | A Bard for the Ages

In his work, William Shakespeare captured the drama and excitement of Renaissance England. His plays often focus both on practical concerns, such as war and governing, and on personal matters, such as vengeance and concern for family. Their themes are relevant to human behavior today.

Vocabulary

Read the definitions of these words from *Throne of Blood*. As you read, think about **synonyms**—words with the same or similar meanings. Knowing the synonyms of an unfamiliar word can help you understand the word's meaning.

sparse (spärs) *adj.* thinly spread; not dense or crowded; p. 68 *Vegetation in that desert region is sparse and stunted.*

shrouded (shrou´ dəd) *adj.* covered; hidden from view; p. 68 *All the furniture in our vacation cabin was shrouded in old bed sheets.*

exploits (eks´ ploits) *n.* bold deeds; remarkable actions; p. 68 *Zeke couldn't get enough of hearing about his older brother's exploits in the navy.*

treacherous (trech´ ər əs) *adj.* traitorous; disloyal; p. 68 *The spy's treacherous actions may have resulted in her country's defeat.*

raze (rāz) *v.* to tear down completely; level to the ground; p. 70 *The houses were so damaged by the flood that the city engineers decided to raze them.*

Comparing and Contrasting Genres To compare and contrast is to show how things are alike and different.

- What is being compared and contrasted in this passage?
  Kurosawa's film and Shakespeare's

  play

- In what ways are these two works the same?
  in powerful atmosphere and

  imagery

Literary Element

Imagery Descriptions that appeal to the senses are known as **imagery**.

- How does the description of the evil spirit add to the supernatural setting in this passage?
  The imagery of white makeup

  adds a pale and ghostly look to

  the character, and adds to the

  mysterious, supernatural setting.

Vocabulary

sparse (spärs) *adj.* thinly spread; not dense or crowded

shrouded (shrou′ dəd) *adj.* covered; hidden from view

exploits (eks′ ploits) *n.* bold deeds; remarkable actions

treacherous (trech′ ər əs) *adj.* traitorous; disloyal

Throne of Blood
from *Shakespeare on Screen*
By Daniel Rosenthal

Washizu, the Macbeth figure in *Throne of Blood* has all of his Shakespearean counterpart's courage, but none of his eloquence.[1] This wild-eyed samurai[2] (Toshiro Mifune at his fiercest) rarely says more than a dozen words at a time, and his language is as plain as the floorboards of his castle. There is no poetry in *Throne of Blood*'s **sparse** dialogue, and little subtlety in its characterization, but its pace, atmosphere and imagery have a power that is absolutely Shakespearean.

The Bard's evocation of 11th-century Scotland and Kurosawa's depiction of late 15th-century Japan are both marked by bestial omens and foul weather. In *Throne of Blood* a horse's wild behavior presages[3] its master's murder; galloping warriors are buffeted by howling wind and driving rain, or **shrouded** in fog or mist. The music of Shakespeare's verse is replaced by the woodwind and percussion of Masaru Sato's distinctively Japanese score.

Washizu's story is told in flashback, beginning with a shot of the monument that marks the site of Cobweb Castle, as a male chorus sings of its destruction. Next, we see the impregnable[4] castle in its former glory, as Tsuzuki (the Duncan figure) learns of heroic **exploits** by Washizu and his best friend, Miki (Minoru Chiaki as a jovial, trusting Banquo), against Inui (the King of Norway) and the **treacherous** Fujimaki (the thane of Cawdor).

Meanwhile, in a marvelously dynamic and eerie sequence, Washizu and Miki become lost in the maze-like Cobweb Forest, and meet an aged "evil spirit" (Chieko Naniwa). Her white make-up resembles the ghost-masks of Noh theater[5] (the ancient Japanese form that Kurosawa adored), and she prophecies in the husky, expressionless tones of Noh actors: Washizu, commander of Fort One, will rule North Mansion and then Cobweb Castle. Miki will take over Fort One, and his son will eventually rule the castle.

Tsuzuki installs Washizu and his wife, Asaji, in North Mansion, and Kurosawa immediately uses Noh to associate Asaji (the mesmerizing Isuzu Yamada) so closely with the forest spirit that the suspicion arises they are in league together. Yamada's long, oval face is like a Noh mask, she walks heel to toe, like Noh actors,

---

1. *Eloquence* means "powerful speech."
2. A *samurai* is a noble warrior of medieval and early modern Japan.
3. *Presages* means "foreshadows."
4. *Impregnable* means "unconquerable."
5. *Noh theater* is a highly stylized form of Japanese drama that developed in the fourteenth and fifteenth centuries. Noh plays are performed by actors wearing symbolic masks.

The ambitious general Washizu (Toshiro Mifune) and his ruthless wife Asaji (Isuzu Yamada) ponder their next move.

and adopts an expressionless voice to suit Asaji's pitiless ambition. She convinces the unambitious Washizu that Tsuzuki and Miki are plotting his death and that he must strike while Tsuzuki is their guest.

Here, Kurosawa devises a night-time sequence of such stealth that it perfectly distills the dreadful tension of Duncan's murder in *Macbeth*. For seven minutes, in the build-up to and bloody aftermath of the crime, no words are spoken—nor are they necessary: the horror of the deed is writ large on Mifune and Yamada's faces.

The "guilty" flight of Kunimaru, Tsuzuki's son, and Noriyasu (Macduff) makes Washizu lord of the castle, and from now on the script begins to work devastating variations on *Macbeth*. With no children of his own, Washizu has agreed to let Miki's son, Yoshiteru, inherit the castle, but then Asaji suddenly announces that she is pregnant: Washizu will have an heir, so Miki and Yoshiteru must die.

Kurosawa now pulls off a unique feat: improving on Shakespeare by *not* showing a murder that is invariably depicted on stage. Miki's horse refuses to be saddled, but he ignores this omen and sets off for Washizu's feast. The horse gallops, riderless, back into Fort One, showing that Miki is dead; his dazed ghost's appearance during the feast provides confirmation.

Vocabulary

Understanding Synonyms
Synonyms are words with the same or similar meanings. Consider this passage from the excerpt: "the suspicion arises that they are in league together."

Based on your understanding of the meaning of the passage, find a synonym for the phrase "in league."

Students should be able to recognize that the passage is about someone suspecting two people of something, and be able to find a synonym such as *working*, *in partnership*, or *planning*.

Big Idea

A Bard for the Ages Shakespeare's plays often focus both on practical concerns, such as war, and personal matters, such as vengeance.

- What Shakespearean theme does Kurosawa focus on in the part of the plot described here?
  The focus here is on the desire for vengeance, which shapes the behavior of the characters in both the play and the movie.

Literary Element

Imagery Picture this image of a riderless horse. How do you think this image suggests the death of Miki?

A riderless horse always suggests that something terrible has happened to its rider. The galloping horse acts as if it has been frightened.

After having his comrade Miki killed, Washizu imagines he sees his ghost at a banquet.

Reading Strategy

Comparing and Contrasting Genres A *soliloquy* is a long monologue spoken by a character in a play. Shakespeare wrote masterful soliloquies.

• What does the writer mean here by "the closest Mifune gets to a soliloquy"?

Here, instead of a long

monologue, Mifune says only two

words in this scene.

Vocabulary

Synonyms are words with the same or similar meanings.

➡ Circle the words in this sentence that work as a synonym for the word "soliloquy":

The character stood at the center of the stage to deliver his long speech on his misfortunes and fate.

Students should circle the words "long speech."

Vocabulary

raze (rāz) *v.* to tear down completely; level to the ground

A final reckoning

Months pass, Asaji has a stillborn child, and the realization that Yoshiteru (who escaped his father's assassin) will still inherit prompts a self-mocking shout from Washizu: "Fool! Fool!"—the closest Mifune gets to a **soliloquy**.

With Asaji madly washing Tsuzuki's invisible blood from her hands, and his enemies preparing to attack, Washizu rides back to the spirit, who guarantees him invincibility[6] "until Cobweb Forest comes to Cobweb Castle."

He reassures his soldiers with this promise, but when they see an army of pines approaching through the mist, we get the last, greatest twist on *Macbeth*: Washizu is killed by his own men. Dozens of arrows whistle into his armor, until one last arrow transfixes his neck a nd he collapses. Beyond the gates, Noriyasu's men prepare to **raze** the castle and the screen fades back to its opening image of the monument.

Astonishingly, on its first release, Kurosawa's film was dismissed by *The New York Times* for an "odd amalgamation[7] of cultural contrasts [that] hits the occidental[8] funnybone." However, by 1965, Britain's *Sight and Sound* magazine was making a bold and not unreasonable claim for *Throne of Blood* as the only work that "completely succeeded in transforming a play of Shakespeare's into a film."

---

6. *Invincibility* means the characteristic of being impossible to defeat.
7. *Amalgamation* means "blending."
8. *Occidental* means "relating to Europe and the Western Hemisphere."

AFTER YOU READ

Graphic Organizer

A **Venn diagram** can help you understand the similarities and differences between two things. In the left box of the diagram, list details that describe only Shakespeare's play *Macbeth;* in the right box, list details that describe only Kurosawa's film *Throne of Blood.* Where the boxes overlap, list details that describe both the play and the film. If you prefer, construct a Foldable™ to display the information.

Macbeth
spoken in poetry and verse, eloquent
11th century Scotland
music contained in the sounds of the verse

Both
supernatural forces
desire for vengeance
concern for family

Throne of Blood
spoken in dialogue, spare, not as many words
15th century Japan
musical score by Japanese composer
Noh theater tradition

Active Reading Focus

Identifying Sequence ➥ In the passage below, certain words and phrases convey the sequence of events.

Months pass, Asaji has a stillborn child, and the realization that Yoshiteru (who escaped his father's assassin) will still inherit prompts a self-mocking shout from Washizu.

- Underline the words and phrases that convey an order of events.

  Students should underline "months pass," "Asaji has," "who escaped," "will still," and "prompts a"

- What happened first? What happened last?

  Students should identify first event: Yoshiteru escaped his father's assassin. Last event: Realization of that makes Washizu shout out loud.

Reading Strategy

Comparing and Contrasting Genres Compare Shakespeare's play and Kurosawa's movie: list two ways that the play and the movie are similar. Then, contrast them: list two ways that they are different. Students should be able to list possible similarities such as same themes and same basic story, and possible differences such as setting and the medium in which the story is told.

Literary Element

Imagery With a partner, look back over the selection. What words and phrases, strong verbs, or clear, precise adjectives did the author use that helped you imagine the scene? List at least three sensory details and explain how they made a scene "come alive" for you. Possible responses: "warriors buffeted by howling wind and driving rain or shrouded in fog or mist"; "maze-like Cobweb Forest"; "build-up to and bloody aftermath of the crime"; "horse galloping riderless into fort"; "ghost's appearance at banquet"; "Asaji madly washing invisible blood from her hands"; "army of pines approaches through the mist"; "one last arrow in Washizu's neck."

Vocabulary Practice

Understanding Synonyms Recall that synonyms are words that have the same or nearly the same meaning. Determine each word's synonym from the choices given.

1. Trees are **sparse** on the plain, as thinly spread as signs of human habitation.

    (a) few

    (b) tall

    (c) flowering

    (d) natural

2. **Shrouded** in the mist, the landscape looked hazy, indistinct.

    (a) vivid

    (b) invisible

    (c) dampened

    (d) screened

3. A superhero is judged by his or her **exploits**, or heroic actions.

    (a) costume

    (b) identity

    (c) deeds

    (d) admirers

4. The city council voted to **raze** the old firehouse and to rebuild it from the ground up.

    (a) destroy

    (b) repair

    (c) repaint

    (d) dedicate

1. (a) few

2. (d) screened

3. (c) deeds

4. (a) destroy

Literary History: The Metaphysical Poets *(p. 428)*

- Who were the metaphysical poets?
- What is metaphysical poetry?
- How is it different from Elizabethan poetry?

This article presents information about metaphysical poetry, including who wrote it, its characteristics, and how it differs from Elizabethan poetry. Information in this article will help you read the selections in this unit by John Donne.

As you read the article, use the Cornell Note Taking System to record important points and to remember what you have read.

Reduce

TO THE POINT *Note key people and definitions. For example:*

John Donne

George Herbert

Richard Crashaw

Andrew Marvell

complex metaphors

irregular meter

unconventional

imagery

Record

➡ *Summarize the main points in the opening section. Use the headings to guide your notes. The list has been started for you.*

   <u>Metaphysical Poets</u>

     wrote in the 17th century

     John Donne, George Herbert, Richard Crashaw,

     Andrew Marvell

     complex metaphors; irregular meter; unconventional

     imagery from philosophy, science, religion, arts

   <u>Origin of the Term "Metaphysical Poetry"</u>

     Samuel Johnson created term in 1700s.

     Johnson himself disliked this poetry—thought it

     "unnatural."

     Johnson used term to categorize poetry with

     philosophical, abstract, and theoretical topics.

The Metaphysical Style

➡ *Describe the key characteristics of John Donne's poetry. The list has been started for you.*

     less formal than Elizabethan poetry

     irregular rhythm, startling figurative language

     intellectually challenging—complex metaphors, witty

     arguments, and philosophical speculation

TO THE POINT *Note key words and phrases. For example:*

elaborate metaphor

witty argument

use of conceits

Literary History: The Metaphysical Poets (p. 428–429)

ANY QUESTIONS? *Ask them about headings and information. Answer them as you reread your notes. For example:*

What did

metaphysical poets

write about?

The Characteristics of Metaphysical Poetry

➡ *What subjects did metaphysical poets write about? The list has been started for you.*

physical love, death, brevity of human life, an individual's relationship to God

➡ *How is Metaphysical Poetry different from Elizabethan poetry? Both are discussed on pages 428 and 429. Summarize the differences using the information on those pages. The list has been started for you.*

Both often take the form of an argument.

Metaphysical arguments appeal to intellect, while Elizabethan arguments appeal solely to emotion.

Both include conceits—elaborate metaphors.

Metaphysical metaphors are more complex than Elizabethan metaphors.

Metaphysical imagery refers to objects and ideas, while Elizabethan imagery refers to nature.

Metaphysical poets used casual language, everyday speech—"plain style," while Elizabethan poets used elegant, formal language—"high style."

Metaphysical poets violated conventional forms, while Elizabethan poets followed conventional poetic forms.

TO THE POINT *Note key writers and literary periods. For example:*

Yeats

Eliot

Auden

Modernist poets

The Legacy of the Metaphysical Poets

➡ *How did metaphysical poetry influence literature to come? An example has been written for you.*

Writers in the 18th and 19th centuries undervalued metaphysical poetry.

Yeats, Eliot, and Auden praised the metaphysical poets.

Modernist poets compared the metaphysical poets' response to Elizabethan poetry to their own response to Romanticism.

Literary History: The Metaphysical Poets

Summary

➡ *Review your notes on this article. Then summarize: Use this classification chart to list what you've learned about metaphysical poetry. The chart has been started for you.*

Metaphysical Poets	John Donne George Herbert Richard Crashaw Andrew Marvell Ben Jonson
Origin of term "Metaphysical Poetry"	Neoclassicist Samuel Johnson created the term in the 1700s. He created it to categorize abstract and philosophical poems, which he disliked. These works were written by a group of poets in the 1600s.
Differences from Elizabethan Poetry	more intellectual did not observe traditional forms more complex metaphors plainer language irregular meter scandalous topics
Effects	undervalued by Neoclassicists, Romantics, and Victorians influenced Yeats, Eliot, Auden, and Modernist writers of the early 20th century

Literary History: The Metaphysical Poets

Apply

Multiple Choice

Circle the letter(s) of the best choice for the following questions.

1. Which of the following is *not* true of metaphysical poetry? B
   A. extended, complex metaphors

   B. formal, elegant language

   C. images drawn from philosphy

   D. everyday subjects such as physical love, death, and faith

2. How did metaphysical poetry differ from Elizabethan poetry? B, D
   A. included elaborate metaphors

   B. more challenging to interpret

   C. often takes form of an argument

   D. written in "plain style"

3. Which of the following were typical subjects of metaphysical poems? A, B, C
   A. physical love

   B. death

   C. the shortness of life

   D. elaborate conceits

4. Which of the following defines conceits? A
   A. elaborate, extended metaphors

   B. characters who were self-involved

   C. unnatural, complex images

   D. witty arguments

Matching

Write the letter(s) of the choice in the second column that best matches each item in the first column.

5. Samuel Johnson _____ B

6. John Donne _____ A

7. W. H. Auden _____ C

   A. wrote metaphysical poems.

   B. created the term "metaphysical poetry."

   C. praised the metaphysical poets for their appeal to the mind.

How can you better remember and understand the material in this Literary History? *Recite* your notes, *Reflect* on them, and *Review* them. You can also use your notes as you read the following selections in this unit.

Literary History: The Cavalier Poets (pp. 452–453)

Preview

- Who were the Cavalier poets?

- What defines the work of the Cavalier poets?

- What political forces affected these writers?

This article describes the literary style and social flair expressed by the Cavalier poets. The article discusses the social and cultural scene surrounding these writers. It also discusses their rise and fall. The information in this article will help you read their poetry in Unit 2.

As you read the article, use the Cornell Note Taking System to record important points and to remember what you have read.

Reduce

TO THE POINT *Note key words and phrases. For example:*

Cavalier poets
aristocrats
King Charles I
Ben Jonson
Sir John Suckling
Robert Herrick
Richard Lovelace
roundheads

Record

➡ *Summarize the main points in this opening section. Two main points have been written for you.*

Cavalier poets: aristocrats
King Charles I's court:
educated, talented, sociable
some were king's soldiers
Sir John Suckling, Robert Herrick, Richard Lovelace
supported monarchy and had a bold personal style
"Roundheads" supported the more strict Puritans

Features of Cavalier Poetry

➡ *You may find that many sections of informational text are divided with run-in headings—boldfaced headings set on the same line as the following text. For each run-in heading on this page, note a key idea about Cavalier poetry. The list has been started for you.*

<u>Conversational Style</u>—Rhythm of everyday speech
<u>Elaborate Conceits</u>— Cavalier poems are accessible
<u>Meditative Tone</u>—Cavalier poets often self-mocking.
<u>Classicism</u>— Cavalier poems refer to Greek and Roman mythology.

ANY QUESTIONS? *As you read, ask yourself questions about headings and information. Then, answer them as you reread your notes. For example: "What is conversational style?"*

Literary History: The Cavalier Poets (pp. 452–453)

Reduce

TO THE POINT *Note boldfaced and italicized words:*

eclogues

heroic couplet

carpe diem

MY VIEW *Write your thoughts and comments here. What interests you about the Cavalier poets?*

Record

➡ *Continue to track the run-in headings in this section. Under each, summarize the effects of classical poetry and ideas on the Cavaliers. The list has been continued for you.*

Regular Poetic Form Classical poets influenced Cavaliers to use regular poetic forms. Lovelace: 4- or 8-line stanzas with abab or aabb rhyme

Many: heroic couplet—two unrhymed iambic pentameter lines. Poetry is easily set to music.

Carpe Diem Two main subjects of Cavalier poetry influenced by classical poetry: love and carpe diem.

Carpe diem is Latin for "seize the day."

Cavalier love poems written to women with classical names, such as Julia, Althea, and Lucasta.

Cavaliers felt life was fragile during the English Civil War.

Political and Poetical Fortunes

➡ *Take sequence notes on the effects of the English Civil War on the Cavalier Poets. The diagram has been started for you.*

1. Intense civil wars occur between Royalists (the Cavaliers' side) and Parliamentarians.

⬇

2. Charles I is sentenced to death in 1649.

⬇

3. Puritan Oliver Cromwell new head of Commonwealth, Cavalier poets fall into disgrace. Some arrested, imprisoned, others escape to London.

⬇

4. In 1660 Charles II becomes King and the monarchy is restored; of the Cavaliers, only Herrick is still alive.

Literary History: **The Cavalier Poets**

Summarize

➡ *Review your notes on this introduction. Then summarize: Use this concept map to organize what you've learned about the Cavalier poets and their world. Part of the concept map has been started for you.*

Possible response:

Details

Cavaliers associated with King Charles I.

Cavalier poets had a bold, fashionable appearance—including long hair and elaborate clothing.

Details

Cavaliers were disliked by Roundheads, who were strict Puritans.

Cavaliers lost prestige when Puritans came to power after the English Civil War.

Definition

The Cavalier poets led a literary movement fueled by the good times of court society under Charles I. They based their poetry on classical forms and ideas as well as an awareness of social life and a desire to "seize the day."

Cavalier Poets

Examples

Cavalier poets were inspired by classical poets—including Horace's <u>carpe diem</u> poems.

There are many references to Greek and Roman mythology in Cavalier poetry.

Examples

Inspired by Ben Jonson, Cavaliers were called "Sons of Ben."

Cavaliers responded to the fragility of life in the Civil War era with poems about love and living in the moment.

Literary History: The Cavalier Poets

Apply

Multiple Choice

Circle the letter(s) of the best choice for the following questions.

1. Which ruler helped Cavalier poets flourish? B
   A. Oliver Cromwell
   B. King Charles I
   C. King Charles II
   D. Queen Elizabeth

2. Who were the "sons of Ben"? B, C, D
   A. Andrew Marvell
   B. Sir John Suckling
   C. Robert Herrick
   D. Richard Lovelace

3. When did the Cavalier poets fall into disgrace? D
   A. during the reign of Charles I
   B. during the reign of Charles II
   C. when Queen Elizabeth took power
   D. when the Puritans took power

4. How did the Cavalier poets dress? C
   A. elegantly but with restraint
   B. in modern clothes for their day
   C. with bold style and flamboyance
   D. with short hair and plain dress

Matching

Write the letter(s) of the choice that best matches each numbered item.

5. strict Puritans who opposed the Cavaliers _____D
6. an elaborate metaphor _____B
7. "seize the day"_____ A
8. two lines of unrhymed iambic pentameter _____C
   A. *carpe diem*
   B. conceit
   C. heroic couplet
   D. Roundheads

How can you better remember and understand the material in this Literary History? *Recite* your notes, *Reflect* on them, and *Review* them. You can also use your notes as you read the literature in this part.

Introductory Text: From Puritanism to the Enlightenment 1640–1780

Looking Ahead (p. 501)

Preview

- What was Puritanism?
- What was the Restoration?
- What was the English Enlightenment
- What was Neoclassicism?

This introduction prepares you for the literature you will read in a unit of your textbook. It explains English Puritanism, the English civil war, Restoration, Enlightenment, and Neoclassicism. It also provides information about literature in England during that time.

As you read the introduction, use the Cornell Note Taking System to record important points and to remember what you have read.

Reduce

TO THE POINT *Note key words and phrases. **Key** words and phrases are the most important ones. They will help you remember what you have read. For example:*

conflict between king
and Parliament
Restoration culture
the Enlightenment

ANY QUESTIONS? *Write questions as you read. Then, answer them as you reread your notes. For example: "What is Puritanism?"*

Record

Looking Ahead

➡ *What history and culture are previewed here? The first item has been listed for you.*
conflict between King Charles I and Puritan supporters
of Parliament
Restoration culture
the Enlightenment

Keep the following questions in mind as you read.

➡ *What cultural terms are mentioned in this section? One term has been listed for you.*
Puritanism
English civil war
English Enlightenment

Introductory Text: From Puritanism to the Enlightenment 1640–1780

Timeline *(pp. 502–503)*

Reduce

TO THE POINT *Note types of writing. For example:*

| diary |
| translation |
| dictionary |
| encyclopedia |
| history |

Record

British Literature

➡ *Based on the timeline, what types of writing were being created during this period? List types and examples. Two have been listed for you.*

diary—Samuel Pepys

translation—Alexander Pope's translation of <u>Iliad</u>

dictionary—Samuel Johnson's <u>A Dictionary of the English Language</u>

encyclopedia—<u>Encyclopaedia Britannica</u>

history—Edward Gibbon's <u>The Decline and Fall of the Roman Empire</u>

TO THE POINT *Note general categories of British events. For example:*

| religion |
| disasters |
| science |
| revolution |
| art, theater, music |

British Events

➡ *Based on the timeline, what are some general categories of British events? List one or more events in each category. Use words that make the event clear to you. Two categories have been started for you.*

<u>Religion</u>

1647—George Fox founds Quakers

<u>Disasters</u>

1665—Plague ravages London

Other possible categories might include institutions, rulers, science, revolution, art, theater, and music.

Introductory Text: From Puritanism to the Enlightenment 1640–1780

Timeline *(pp. 502–503)*

Reduce

TO THE POINT *Note general categories of world events. For example:*

religion

disasters

colonies

empires

revolution

Record

World Events

➡ *Based on the timeline, what are the general categories of world events? List one or two events in each category. Use wording that makes the event clear to you. Two categories have been started for you.*

Architecture

1650—Taj Mahal completed in India

Disasters

1650—Japanese capital Edo is nearly destroyed by fire

Other possible categories might include rulers, theater, colonies, empires, wars, music, technology, literature, and revolution.

Recap

➡ *Review your notes on the Timeline. Then recap. Create a specific timeline of entries relating to one of the major categories of the period, such as science and technology, disaster, or architecture.*

Science and Technology

1668—Anton van Leeuwenhoek develops simple microscope

1687—Newton publishes theory of gravitation

1721—Smallpox inoculation introduced by Lady Mary Wortley Montagu

1752—Ben Franklin invents the lightning rod

Introductory Text: From Puritanism to the Enlightenment 1640–1780

By the Numbers *(p. 504)*

Reduce

TO THE POINT *For the headings on this page, note key words and phrases. They will help you remember what you have read. For example:*

four-day long fire
Puritan
Commonwealth
first coffeehouses
express coaches
Royal African Company
West African slave trade

Record

The Great Fire of London

➡ *Summarize the main points of this section. The first two main points have been listed for you.*

In September 1666, a four-day fire destroyed much of London.
Only five people were killed because the fire spread slowly.
Damage to buildings and property was great.
100,000 people were left homeless.
Rebuilding London cost millions of pounds.

London's Population, 1600–1800

➡ *How much did London's population increase in 200 years? Summarize the information on this graph.*

From 1600 to 1800, London's population increased from 200,000 to 800,000.

➡ *List the remaining headings on this page. For each, note what the statistics tell you about the period. The first has been listed for you.*

<u>Punishment for Swearing</u>
The Puritan government punished swearing with fines, which depended on the person's social rank.
<u>Tea and Coffee</u>
Tea and coffee were expensive but became very popular during this period.
<u>Travel Rates</u>
Stagecoach travel became faster, but was still very slow.
<u>The Slave Trade</u>
The British became involved in the slave trade beginning in 1672.

Introductory Text: From Puritanism to the Enlightenment 1640–1780

By the Numbers *(p. 504)*

ANY QUESTIONS? *Ask any questions about the statistics on this page.*

_____

_____

_____

_____

_____

Tea and Coffee

➡ *Cite the evidence that supports the conclusion that drinking tea and coffee was popular during the Restoration.*

The number of coffeehouses in London increased from 82 in 1663 to somewhere between 500–2000 by 1700.

_____

_____

_____

_____

Travel Rates

➡ *What was the gain of distance traveled by stage coach between 1719 and 1765?*

Stage coaches gained a distance of 24 miles a day between 1719 and 1765.

_____

_____

_____

The Slave Trade

➡ *What was the increase in the number of Africans transported to slavery after the Royal African Company lost its monopoly?*

The number increased from five thousand to between forty and fifty thousand.

_____

_____

_____

Introductory Text: From Puritanism to the Enlightenment 1640–1780

Being There *(pp. 505)*

Reduce

ANY QUESTIONS? *Ask questions about pictures. For example: "What kind of clothing are people wearing here?"*

_____

_____

_____

_____

TO THE POINT *Note key words and phrases. For example:*

Act of Union

Great Fire of London

London Europe's

largest city

_____

_____

Record

➡ *Pictures are part of the information in this introduction. What do these pictures show about life in Britain in the seventeenth and eighteenth centuries? An example has been written for you.*

Many people went to London coffeehouses.

People wore formal dress and fancy clothing.

People kept animals as pets.

Wealthy people lived on large country estates.

_____

➡ *Compare this map to the map of Renaissance England on page 241. What cities and towns have become more important in this era? One example has been written for you.*

Newcastle, Leeds, Hull, Manchester, Derby, Liverpool

_____

_____

_____

Recap

➡ *Review your notes on By the Numbers and Being There. Then recap. Use the information to draw several conclusions about Britain in the seventeenth and eighteenth centuries. Two conclusions have been written for you.*

1. The slave trade was very profitable.
2. London's population increased tremendously and it became Europe's largest city.

Students' conclusions might relate to the Great Fire of London, Puritan government, tea and coffee, stagecoach travel, or the slave trade.

_____

_____

Introductory Text: From Puritanism to the Enlightenment 1640–1780

Historical, Social, and Cultural Forces *(pp. 506–507)*

Reduce

ANY QUESTIONS? *Ask questions about headings as you read. Then answer them as you reread your notes on this section. For example: "What is the 'divine right of kings'?"*

_____

_____

_____

_____

_____

TO THE POINT *Note key words and phrases. For example:*

Charles I

Parliament

Anglican rituals

eleven years' tyranny

Cavaliers

Roundheads

Record

The Divine Right of Kings

➡ *What was the principle of the divine right of kings? How did it affect Britain under the rule of James I? List the main points of this section. One point has been written for you.*

divine right of kings—belief that the regent derives power directly from God

James I—forced subjects to observe rules of Church of England.

Catholics and Puritans—emigrated to the European continent to be able to practice their religions.

Growing Conflict

➡ *Organize the information in this section in a timeline. The timeline has been started for you.*

1625—Charles I succeeds James I

1629—Parliament and king unable to agree; Charles dissolves Parliament and rules alone

1640—Charles recalls Parliament, but compromise fails

1642—Civil war begins between king and Parliament

Civil War

➡ *Who were the two sides in the civil war? Who won and why? What was the final outcome? Summarize the main points of this section to answer these questions. One answer has been written for you.*

1. War was fought between Royalist Cavaliers—supporters of king, and Puritan Roundheads—supporters of Parliament

2. Parliament won mainly because of Oliver Cromwell's New Model Army.

3. At the end, Charles I was put on trial for tyranny and publicly executed. The Parliament abolished the monarchy.

Introductory Text: From Puritanism to the Enlightenment 1640–1780

Historical, Social, and Cultural Forces (p. 507)

Reduce

TO THE POINT *Note key words and phrases. For example:*

Oliver Cromwell, Lord

Protector

Puritanical rules

"graven images"

ANY QUESTIONS? *Ask questions about headings as you read. Then answer them as you reread your notes on this section.*

Record

The Commonwealth

➡ *Complete this sentence in words that make sense to you: As Lord Protector of Britain, Oliver Cromwell . . .*

closed theaters, banned dancing and music, destroyed

religious icons, and forbade people from celebrating

Christmas.

The Restoration

➡ *What happened during the Restoration? How did the Restoration differ from the Commonwealth? List the main points of this section to answer these questions. One answer has been written for you.*

1. In 1660, during the Restoration, Charles II reclaimed the British throne in 1660.

2. Unlike during the Commonwealth, intellectual and cultural life began to thrive during the Restoration. Theaters were reopened, public festivals were celebrated, and new European fashions in clothes, food, and ideas flooded Britain.

The Enlightenment and Neoclassicism

➡ *What was the Enlightenment? What was Neoclassicism? Define these terms in your own words.*

Enlightenment or "Age of Reason" —

European philosophical and literary movement

characterized by a profound faith in power of human

reason and a devotion to clarity of thought

Neoclassicism —

literary movement related to the Enlightenment; held

that rules and norms of classical authors of ancient

Greece and Rome should govern literature

Introductory Text: From Puritanism to the Enlightenment 1640–1780

Historical, Social, and Cultural Forces (pp. 506–507)

Reduce

TO THE POINT *Note key words and phrases.*

Puritanism

Civil War

Restoration

Enlightenment

Neoclassicism

Record

Preview Big Ideas of Puritanism to the Enlightenment

➡ *Restate each of the Big Ideas to make them easier to remember. The first has been written for you. Possible response:*

The English civil war was caused by conflict between the Anglican supporters of the king and the Puritan supporters of Parliament. Many English writers took sides in the civil war.

The Puritans ruled harshly for ten years and then a new king, Charles II, took power. Restoration writing was witty, scornful, and worldly.

The Enlightenment, which saw reason as the highest authority, was a reaction to religious extremism. Neoclassicists wanted to revive classical literary principles.

Recap

➡ *Review your notes on the Historical, Social, and Cultural Forces. Then recap. Define the key terms using words that make sense to you. One key term has been defined for you.*

divine right of kings—belief that the regent gets power directly from God

civil war—war between royalist Cavaliers who supported the king and Puritan Roundheads who supported the Parliament

Commonwealth—government under Oliver Cromwell as Lord Protector, when public behavior and religious worship was strictly controlled

Restoration—period after Charles II reclaimed throne

Enlightenment or "Age of Reason"—European philosophical and literary movement characterized by a deep faith in power of human reason and a belief in clarity of thought

Neoclassicism—literary movement related to the Enlightenment; held that rules and norms of classical authors of ancient Greece and Rome should govern literature

Introductory Text: From Puritanism to the Enlightenment 1640–1780

Big Idea 1: Puritanism and the Civil War *(p. 508)*

Reduce	Record

Reduce

ANY QUESTIONS? *Ask questions about headings as you read. For example: "What kind of religion was Puritanism?"*

_____

_____

_____

_____

_____

TO THE POINT *Note key words and phrases. For example:*

Royalist forces

Oliver Cromwell

Battle of Naseby

treason

Record

What Was Puritanism?

➡ *What are the main ideas of this section? One has been listed for you.*

Puritanism was a radical form of Calvinistic Protestantism. Puritans believed in the "pure" word of God.

Its goal was purifying the Church of England of Catholic rites and doctrines.

Liberal Puritans such as John Milton balanced religious views with civil liberties.

Religious Conflict

➡ *Complete the following sentence in your own words: The English civil war began over . . .*

questions of who had authority and how it should be divided.

The Civil War

➡ *List the main ideas in this section. One has been listed for you.*
The Royalists won battles at the beginning of the war.

Cromwell's leadership gave Parliament victory.

The king made a bad mistake in the Battle of Naseby.

In 1649, King Charles was tried and executed, but people had mixed feelings about the execution.

Puritan Rule

➡ *What were the positive and negative effects of Puritan rule?*
positive effects—religious tolerance (except for Catholics); stable government; economic prosperity
negative effects—destruction of religious images; ban on music and theater

Introductory Text: From Puritanism to the Enlightenment 1640–1780

Big Idea 1: Puritanism and the Civil War *(p. 509)*

Reduce

TO THE POINT *Note key words and phrases. For example:*

John Milton

Areopagitica

freedom of the press

censorship

Commonwealth

Record

from *Areopagitica* by John Milton

➡ *John Milton wrote this selection in 1644, defending freedom of the press, in response to the government's imposing censorship on its people. Write down two phrases that show Milton's support for civil liberties.*

"who destroys a good book, kills reason itself"

"a good book is the precious life-blood of a master spirit"

Recap

➡ *Review your notes on Big Idea 1: Puritanism and the Civil War. Then recap. Use summary notes to help you remember the main points. The summary has been started for you.*

Topic: Puritanism and the Civil War

Main Points:

Puritanism was a radical form of Calvinistic Protestantism.

Its goal was purifying the Church of England of Catholic rites and doctrines.

Liberal Puritans such as John Milton balanced religious views with civil liberties.

The English civil war began over questions of who had authority and how it should be divided.

Royalists won early battles, but Cromwell's leadership gave Parliament victory.

King Charles was tried and executed, though people had mixed feelings about his death.

The positive effects of Puritan rule included religious tolerance (except for Catholics), stable government, and economic prosperity.

The negative effects included destruction of religious images, and a ban on music and theater.

Introductory Text: From Puritanism to the Enlightenment 1640–1780

Big Idea 2: The Restoration *(pp. 510–511)*

Reduce

TO THE POINT *Note key words and phrases. For example:*

Restoration Court

John Dryden, poet

laureate

Tower of London

Record

The Restoration Court

➡ *What was the character of Charles II? Based on the information in this section, describe it in your own words. One example has been written for you.*

known as the merry monarch

enjoyed pleasures of all kinds

forgave his father's old enemies

did not forgive the judges who condemned his father

to death, or Oliver Cromwell, who he had reburied in

a common grave

Public Pleasures

➡ *What words and phrases are used to describe the comedies of the Restoration? One example has been written for you.*

witty, bawdy, and amoral

treated love and money with silliness and cynicism

pleasure-loving attitude and carpe diem spirit

vivacious

Plague and Fire

➡ *Use a chart to organize information about the outbreak of plague and the Great Fire of London. The chart has been started for you.*

Outbreak of Plague	Great Fire of London
started in 1665	affected both rich and poor
affected mostly the poor	
dead buried in communal pits	destroyed most of old London
official death toll of 68,000	king rebuilt city in stone
actual death toll may have been 100,000	rebuilding plan under Sir Christopher Wren

Introductory Text: From Puritanism to the Enlightenment 1640–1780

Big Idea 2: The Restoration *(pp. 510–511)*

Reduce	**Record**
TO THE POINT *Note key words and phrases. For example:* satire John Wilmot, Earl of Rochester	**from *A Satire Against Mankind* by John Wilmot** ➡ *In this passage by John Wilmot, what phrases reflect the cynicism of the Restoration?* "Were I (who to my cost already am One of those strange, prodigious creatures, man)" I'd be a dog, a monkey, or a bear, Or anything but that vain animal Who is so proud of being rational"

Recap

➡ *Review your notes on Big Idea 2: The Restoration. Then recap. Use a web to organize key points about the period. The web has been started for you.*

- The merry monarch, Charles II, loved pleasures of all kinds.
- Outbreak of plague in 1665 may have killed 100,000; mostly poor.
- Comedy of the day was witty, bawdy, amoral, cynical, pleasure-loving, *carpe diem* spirit
- Great Fire of London destroyed most of old city; it was rebuilt by Sir Christopher Wren.

(Restoration Period)

Introductory Text: From Puritanism to the Enlightenment 1640–1780

Big Idea 3: English Enlightenment and Neoclassicism *(p. 512)*

Reduce

TO THE POINT *Note key words and phrases. For example:*

"natural philosophers"

Royal Society of
London for the
Promotion of Natural
Knowledge
Christopher Wren
Robert Boyle
Edmund Halley
Isaac Newton

ANY QUESTIONS? *Ask questions as you read the headings and information within them. Then use those questions to organize your notes. For example: "What was the Rule of the Ancients?"*

_____
_____
_____
_____
_____

Record

A Scientific Revolution

➡ *Complete this sentence in your own words: Because of Sir Isaac Newton's work, eighteenth-century scientists believed that . . .*

the mechanical workings of the universe were no longer mysterious, but could be understood by humans.

The Rule of Reason

➡ *What are the main ideas in this section? One idea has been listed for you.*

Royal Society members believed in the importance of experiment and observation.

Communicating to others in a clear and accurate manner was part of their methodology.

The Rule of the Ancients

➡ *What were the basic beliefs of eighteenth-century philosophers and poets? One belief has been stated for you.*

Nature is rational and orderly, and these underlying patterns are harmonious and beautiful.

Poetry is governed by natural, not man-made, laws.

Ancient texts explained the natural laws that governed literature.

Satire can cause improvements in moral and social behavior.

Introductory Text: From Puritanism to the Enlightenment 1640–1780

Big Idea 3: English Enlightenment and Neoclassicism (pp. 511–512)

Reduce

TO THE POINT *Note key words and phrases.*

vengeance, Aegis,

vulture of the chair,

wounded, unmanly,

shrieks, red deluge

Record

from *The Odyssey*, Book 22, translated by Alexander Pope

➡ *How does Pope's translation of the Greek writer Homer's work,* The Odyssey, *express the values of Neoclassicism?*

Translating a Greek writer showed the admiration for

classical culture, which was a large part of

Neoclassicism.

Recap

➡ *Review your notes on Big Idea 3: English Enlightenment and Neoclassicism. Then recap. Use a chart to help you remember key beliefs and goals of the Enlightenment and Neoclassicism. The chart has been started for you.*

Enlightenment	Neoclassicism
The mechanical workings of the universe can be understood by humans.	Nature is rational and orderly.
	Poetry is governed by natural, not man-made, laws.
Experimentation and observation are important.	Ancient texts explain natural laws that governed literature.
Communicating to others in a clear and accurate manner is crucial.	Satire can improve moral and social behavior.

Introductory Text: From Puritanism to the Enlightenment 1640–1780

Wrap-Up (p. 514)

TO THE POINT *Note key words and phrases. For example:*

John Locke

Declaration of Independence

the Federalist Papers

U.S. Constitution

scientific method

MY VIEW *Write your own thoughts on this section. For example, which of these cultural links do you find the most interesting?*

_____

_____

_____

_____

Why It Matters

➥ *What is the main idea of each paragraph? The list has been started for you.*

paragraph 1—The Enlightenment encouraged British freedom of thought and expression.

paragraph 2—Enlightenment thinkers shaped the ideals of the American Revolution and U.S. government.

paragraph 3—The scientific revolution and the Enlightenment helped establish the modern rational, secular worldview.

Cultural Links

➥ *What link is described in each paragragh?*

paragraph 1—English Puritanism—American colonial literature

paragraph 2—Milton's Satan in <u>Paradise Lost</u>—Mary Shelley's monster in <u>Frankenstein</u> and Melville's Captain Ahab in <u>Moby-Dick</u>

paragraph 3—Jonathan Swift's <u>Gulliver's Travels</u>—words <u>Lilliputian</u>, <u>Brobdignagian</u>, and <u>Yahoo</u>

➥ *Review your notes on the Wrap-Up. Then sum up a viewpoint on this period. The organizer has been started for you.*

Viewpoint		
Puritanism and the Enlightenment had a major effect on American history and culture		
Supporting Detail	Supporting Detail	Supporting Detail
Enlightenment thinkers helped shape the ideals of the American Revolution and U.S. government.	English Puritanism was a basic element in American colonial literature.	Milton's rebel hero Satan in <u>Paradise Lost</u> influenced Herman Melville's character Captain Ahab in <u>Moby-Dick</u>.

Introductory Text: From Puritanism to the Enlightenment 1640–1780

Summarize

➡ *Review your notes on this introduction. Then recap. Make several generalizations about the events of this period.*

Students' generalizations may relate to the positive and negative aspects of Puritanism,

the English civil war, the Restoration, the Enlightenment, or Neoclassicism.

Sample generalization:

Both Puritanism and the Enlightenment encouraged people to write more clearly

and plainly.

Introductory Text: From Puritanism to the Enlightenment 1640–1780

Apply

Multiple Choice

Circle the letter(s) of the best choice for the following questions.

1. What describes Puritans? B, C
   A. emphasized importance of experimentation
   B. wanted to purify the Church of England
   C. radical Calvinistic Protestants
   D. faith in power of reason

2. Which of the following does *not* describe Restoration comedy? B
   A. bawdy
   B. orderly
   C. amoral
   D. cynical

3. Which of the following describes the Enlightenment? D
   A. an American religious movement
   B. a European religious movement
   C. an American philosophical and literary movement
   D. a European philosophical and literary movement

4. Which of the following describes the Commonwealth? B
   A. a celebration of all common people and everyday life
   B. a clampdown on public behavior and religious worship
   C. a group of nobles and statesmen
   D. a European philosophical and literary movement

Matching

Write the letter of the choice in the second column that best matches each item in the first column.

5. Who defended civil liberties? B

6. Who was executed by Parliament? C

7. Who was a leader of the scientific revolution? D

8. Who led the New Model Army? A
   A. Oliver Cromwell
   B. John Milton
   C. Charles I
   D. Sir Isaac Newton

How can you better remember and understand the material in this introduction? *Recite* your notes, *Reflect* on them, and *Review* them. You can also use your notes for a quick review of the historical period or the Big Ideas of this unit. As you learn more about the ideas in the unit, add to your notes.

Literary History: The Essay

(pp. 612–613)

Preview

- What is an essay?
- How did the essay develop?
- What are formal and informal essays?

This article describes the development of the essay, which is a part of our literary history. It discusses characteristics of formal and informal essays and will help you better understand the essays you will read in your textbook.

As you read the article, use the Cornell Note Taking System to record important points and to remember what you have read.

Reduce

ANY QUESTIONS? *Use them to organize your notes. For example, "What are some characteristics of Montaigne's essays?"*

_____

_____

_____

_____

TO THE POINT *Note the boldfaced terms in the section. For example:*

formal essay

thesis

_____

_____

_____

Record

Michel de Montaigne

➡ *Create a list to describe the essays of Michel de Montaigne. The list has been started for you.*

short and personal

titles that were not pretentious, such as "Of Smells and Odors"

called his works <u>essais</u>, or "attempts"

Sir Francis Bacon

➡ *What was the subject matter of Sir Francis Bacon's essays? Use information from this section to answer this question. The answer has been started for you.*

Bacon wrote systematic examinations of scholarly subjects. He wrote in a formal style. His subjects were in such areas as philosophy, religion, and science. He often quoted ancient writers or made aphorisms, which are short concise observations about human experience.

The Formal Essay

➡ *What is a formal essay? What is a thesis?*

A formal essay is written with impersonal, objective authority on a particular subject to instruct or persuade readers.

A thesis is the main idea of a formal essay.

Literary History: The Essay

(p. 612)

Reduce

TO THE POINT *Note key words and phrases. For example:*

Addison and Steele

The Tatler

The Spectator

Robert Louis Stevenson

Max Beerbohm

G.K. Chesterton

Virginia Woolf

George Orwell

blogs

Internet

Record

The Informal Essay

➥ *Create an outline to describe key characteristics of the informal essay. The outline has been started for you.*

I. The Informal, or Personal Essay

    A. lighter tone

    B. personal details

    C. humor

    D. uses fictional techniques

    E. Joseph Addison and Richard Steele

    F. The Tatler and The Spectator

    G. Robert Louis Stevenson, Max Beerbohm,
       G. K. Chesterton, Virginia Woolf, George Orwell

    H. Blogs and the Internet have helped increase the
       amount and popularity of informal essays.

Literary History: The Essay

Summarize

➡ *Review your notes on this article. Then summarize. Use the two-column chart to organize information on the formal and informal essay. The chart has been started for you.*

The Formal Essay	The Informal Essay
• impersonal, objective • develops a thesis • intended to instruct or persuade • authoritative • Bacon	• lighter tone • less structured • personal details • humor • uses, or incorporates fictional techniques • blogs • Montaigne

Literary History: The Essay

Apply

Multiple Choice

Circle the letter(s) of the best choice for the following questions.

1. What is an *aphorism*? D
   A. a French word for "attempts"

   B. the main idea of an essay

   C. systematic explanations of subjects in such areas as religion and science

   D. short observation about human experience

2. Why is an informal essay often referred to as a "personal" essay? C, D
   A. it is about one person

   B. it instructs a person how to do something

   C. it includes personal details

   D. it uses a conversational style

3. Which of the following is characteristic of a formal essay? A
   A. its author writes with an impersonal authority

   B. its author writes in a very casual tone

   C. its author uses humor rather than seriousness

   D. its author writes in the first person

4. Which of the following is another characteristic of a formal essay? C
   A. its purpose is to entertain

   B. its purpose is to pose questions

   C. its purpose is to instruct and persuade

   D. its purpose is to be friendly rather than logical

Matching

Write the letter of the choice that best matches each item.

5. This man is considered the father of the informal essay. _____ A

6. This literary form is characterized by a lighter tone and humor. _____ B

7. This essayist wrote objectively, used aphorisms in his writing. _____ C

8. Newspaper editorials and opinion pieces are an example of this. _____ D
   A. Michel de Montaigne

   B. the informal essay

   C. Sir Francis Bacon

   D. the formal essay

How can you better remember and understand the material in this Literary History? *Recite* your notes, *Reflect* on them, and *Review* them. You can also use your notes to help you read the essays in this unit.

SAMUEL JOHNSON

Building Background

Walter Jackson Bate (1918–1999) was a biographer with a long and successful career. He won two Pulitzer Prizes. The first, in 1964, was for his biography *John Keats*, about the famous English Romantic poet who died of tuberculosis at only 25 years old. The second, in 1978, was for his vivid biography of Samuel Johnson, another English literary giant.

The following excerpt is from Bate's biography. It describes a key figure in Johnson's life, James Boswell. Here, Bate discusses Boswell's family background, his relationship with Johnson, his biography of Johnson, and the importance of his biographical masterpiece.

Setting Purposes for Reading

The influence of other people can have a tremendous impact on our lives. With a classmate discuss the following questions:

- Have you known a person that you admire for a long time? Why do you admire that person?
- Have you ever wanted to be like another person? How did this make you feel?

Read to learn more about James Boswell's life and his famous biography of Samuel Johnson.

Reading Strategy | Determining Main Idea and Supporting Details

Determining main idea and supporting details involves reading:

- carefully to identify the most important idea in a work of literature. This idea may be stated, or it may be suggested (or implied).
- closely to identify the details that support that main idea.

Active Reading Focus | Questioning

Questioning involves:

- asking if information in a selection is important.
- pausing as you read to ask yourself if you have understood what you have read.
- asking yourself questions to check your comprehension throughout the selection.

Literary Element | Motivation

Motivation is the stated or implied reason or cause for a character's statements and actions.

Big Idea | The English Enlightenment and Neoclassicism

The Enlightenment was a European philosophical and literary movement. Its principles included:

- faith in the power of human reason
- devotion to clarity of thought
- skeptical attitude toward traditional organized religion.

As you read the selection, ask yourself how Boswell's role models did or did not reflect these principles.

Vocabulary

Read the definitions of these words from *Samuel Johnson*. As you read, use context clues to help unlock the meaning of these and other words you do not know.

acquaintance (ə kwānt′ əns) *n.* a knowledge of someone or something; p. 104 *He first made the writer's acquaintance at a bookstore reading.*

moralistic (môr′ ə lis′ tik) *adj.* characterized by or expressive of a concern with morality; p. 104 *The judge was fair, although many considered her to be a bit moralistic.*

gregarious (gri gār′ ē əs) *adj.* very friendly and sociable; p. 105 *Charles thought that Boswell's gregarious nature was the sign of a very lonely man.*

eminent (em′ ə nənt) *adj.* prominent; famous; p. 106 *The eminent historian was much in demand as a public speaker.*

empathy (em′ pə thē) *n.* the ability to identify with and understand another person's feelings or troubles; p. 106 *He was good at writing about other people because his empathy enabled him to understand them.*

Samuel Johnson
By W. Jackson Bate

On Monday, May 16, when he[1] dropped into the small bookshop kept by his friend Tom Davies, there occurred one of the famous meetings in literary history, which began an **acquaintance** that was ultimately to result in one of the masterpieces of world literature—James Boswell's *Life of Johnson* (1791). The admiring young Scot was the son of Alexander Boswell, Laird of Auchinleck, a man about Johnson's age, who had studied law at Leyden and was now a judge on the Scottish bench. Though Boswell's name, because of his great work, was to become a household word not long after his death, he himself was drastically underrated until our own generation. He has proved, at the very least, to be a far more complicated person than was ever imagined. The most celebrated literary discovery of this century was the vast journal—or series of journals—he kept through most of his life, **chronicling** with complete frankness his own personal experiences and, more important, recording conversations and interviews with noted people he met. When published, the writings—*The Private Papers of James Boswell from Malahide Castle* (1928–34)—filled eighteen volumes, and they were later to be supplemented by other material. The conversations in the *Life of Johnson*, together with those in Boswell's earlier *Journal of a Tour to the Hebrides with Samuel Johnson* (1785), are carved from this enormous collection of diaries.

We should remind ourselves (it is often forgotten) how extremely young Boswell was when he met Johnson—he was only twenty-two; Johnson was fifty-three—just as we should remind ourselves that he had many interests, and spent most of his adult life as an able and busy lawyer in Edinburgh, visiting London only on vacations. In some ways, he was even younger than twenty-two at this time, and was generally to remain younger than his years. The identity for which the young Boswell was searching—and continued to search—was one that could define itself against the example of his father, Lord Auchinleck, who was firm and **moralistic**, a Whig[2] and a Presbyterian, and who proudly spoke

---

1. *He* refers to James Boswell.
2. The *Whig* party was the dominant political faction in England at the time.

broad Scots. In reaction, the son was all the father was not: romantically imaginative, promiscuous, impulsively idealistic and open-natured, pliable,[3] and with an impressionable genius for mimicry.

In his search for identity, a shadow in the background was always there to make him uneasy if he allowed himself to think of it. There was a strain of mental instability in his family; and Boswell's own younger brother John, after the age of nineteen, was to suffer from marked insanity for most of his remaining life. The stability for which Boswell was always to crave was something that his **gregarious**[4] nature could acquire only through others. And his profoundest enjoyment, if not at the start, certainly as the years passed, was the company, example, and if possible the approval, of older men whom he admired—men of acknowledged standing who were also interesting in themselves, knew the world, and, like Johnson, symbolized the moral rectitude he wanted desperately to impose on his own wayward nature.

Hence his injunctions to himself in his journal to identify with admired models, and acquire a stronger mind and character ("*be Johnson*"). At first the ideals suggest conventional notions of sophistication and elegance. After arriving in London, for example, he writes, "I felt strong dispositions to *be a Mr. Addison*."[5] Months later—he has by now met and talked a good deal with Johnson—the rather frightened youth is to set off for Harwich to get the boat to Holland, where he is to study law. And the models now, basically so different from each other (the father from whom he is in part fleeing, Lord Chesterfield,[6] and Johnson), show what he really wants most to acquire—inner strength, reserve, calmness, and courage: "[Be] like Father, grave . . . composed. . . . Go abroad with a manly resolution. . . . Never despair. . . . Study [to be] like Lord Chesterfield, manly. . . . Resemble Johnson . . . your mind will strengthen" (August 1763); or, later in the year, "Be like the Duke of Sully." As he approaches and enters his thirties, there are moments of satisfaction (when he says "you," he is addressing himself—a common practice in his diaries, and typical of his attempt at detachment):

"You felt yourself . . . *like a Johnson* in comparison of former days" (1766). "Was *powerful* like Johnson, and very much satisfied with myself" (1767). "I was in such a frame as to *think myself an Edmund Burke*"[7] (1774). "Fancied myself like Burke, and drank moderately . . ." (1775).

---

3. *Pliable* means "changeable."
4. *Gregarious* means "outgoing" or "social."
5. Joseph *Addison* (1672–1719) was a famed essayist.
6. *Lord Chesterfield* (1694–1773) was a statesman and the patron of many writers.
7. *Edmund Burke* (1729–1797) was a conservative British political thinker and statesman.

Questioning As you read this section, ask yourself if you understand the idea of this passage. What is Bate saying about what makes Boswell unique among writers?

Responses will vary. Bate is saying

that even if writers had the chance

Boswell had to know their subject,

Boswell had the talent they did not

have.

Reading Strategy

Determining Main Idea and Supporting Details What is the main idea of the paragraph?

●● Underline two major supporting details.

Boswell possessed the ideal

combination of opportunity and talent

that enabled him to write a unique

biography of a fascinating man.

Students may underline "Nor has

anything comparable been written

since, because that special union of

talents, opportunities, and subject

matter has never been duplicated,"

and "his ability to draw people out

and get them to talk freely, his

astonishing memory for conversations,

his zest and gusto…".

Vocabulary

eminent (em′ ə nənt) *adj.* prominent; famous

empathy (em′ pə thē) *n.* the ability to identify with and understand another person's feelings or troubles

One of the touching entries is near the end, toward the close of his life. Much of his despair—he is now fifty—is that he felt he had no more inner strength to meet difficulties now, when he needed it badly, than he had as a youth—that he seemed to have gone through life "without any addition to my character from my having had the friendship of Dr. Johnson and many **eminent** men."

Many readers assume that he was constantly in Johnson's presence. But during the twenty-one years he knew Johnson, the total number of days he spent in Johnson's company amounted to 325, plus another 101 during their trip to Scotland and the Hebrides in 1773.[8]

Even so, by 1772—ten years after he met Johnson—he had accumulated what he justly called "a vast treasure of his conversation at different times," and decided that he would someday try to write a life of Johnson using these materials. It was to be a new kind of biography—a "life in Scenes," as though it were a kind of drama. And when the "life in Scenes" did appear, nothing comparable to it had existed. Nor has anything comparable been written since, because that special union of talents, opportunities, and subject matter has never been duplicated. If there were writers who had Boswell's opportunities of knowing their subject as well, they have not had his unusual combination of talents. If they had his talents, they have lacked his opportunities. The talents include his gift for **empathy** and dramatic imitation, his ability to draw people out and get them to talk freely, his astonishing memory for conversations, his zest and gusto, his generous capacity for admiration, and his sheer industry as a reporter—qualities that are by no means often found together. Bringing these qualities into focus and sustaining his industry was his prevailing sense of what he called "the *waste* of good if it be not preserved," of the rapid erosion and loss of human experience through life's enemy, time, and the need to rescue it as far as possible through the recorded word. But the final indispensable element in Boswell's great work is Johnson himself. Fascinating as they are, the interviews with others—David Hume, Voltaire, Rousseau, the elder Pitt[9]—rarely approach in range of topics and personal interest any section of equal length dealing with Johnson.

8. The *Hebrides* are islands off the western coast of Scotland.
9. *David Hume* (1711–1776) was a Scottish philosopher. *Voltaire* (1694–1778) and Jean-Jacques *Rousseau* (1712–1778) were famed French writers and philosophers. William *Pitt* (1708–1778) was a powerful British statesman and orator.

The picture of Johnson, which for better or worse remains permanently imprinted because of this classic work, is inevitably, given the circumstances, somewhat specialized. Most important, it is a picture of Johnson in his later years. The first half of Johnson's life occupies little more than a tenth of the work. Less than a quarter takes him up to fifty-three, when his life was more than two-thirds over; and a full half of the book is devoted to Johnson's last eight years, from sixty-seven to seventy-five. There are also personal sides of Johnson even after fifty-three of which Boswell could never know, but of which others—above all, Mrs. Thrale[10]—knew or suspected a great deal, though they did not always care to proclaim their knowledge. Moreover, it is a very masculine world in which Boswell presents him—the world of The Club and the taverns. In addition, he saw Johnson through the spectacles of his own romantic Toryism,[11] with the result that Johnson has been—and perhaps will unfortunately always be—viewed as an "arch-conservative." Even his minor dramatic touches have proved permanent: for example, his exaggerated insertion of "Sir" before so many of Johnson's remarks, as if to give them a kind of thunderous and formal authority; or his decision to change his references to him from "Mr. Johnson" to "Dr. Johnson," with the result that Johnson alone, of all great writers who have ever received a doctor's degree, is forever known to most people as "Dr. Johnson." (Ironically Johnson himself—according to Hawkins[12]—rather disliked being called Dr. Johnson. At least, as even Boswell once admitted, he hardly ever assumed it in formal notes or on cards—"but called himself *Mr.* Johnson"; and when Boswell once noticed a letter addressed to him with the title "Esquire," and said he thought it a title inferior to "Doctor," Johnson "checked me, and seemed pleased with it.") Yet whatever its limitations, large or small, the work remains unique among all writings by one human being about another—unique in the way Boswell himself foresaw when he decided as a mature man to undertake it: that is, in the drama, fidelity, and range of interests in the conversation of one of the most fascinating individuals in history.

---

10. Hester *Thrale* (1741–1821) and her husband Henry Thrale were Johnson's friends and traveling companions.
11. The principles of the English Tory party, which opposed those of the Whigs, are known as *Toryism*.
12. Sir John *Hawkins* (1719–1789) was a close friend and biographer of Johnson.

Literary Element

Motivation What might have been Boswell's motivation for referring to Johnson as "Dr. Johnson," despite Johnson's objections?

Boswell's use of "Dr. Johnson" to refer to his friend and mentor suggests a very high level of respect even though Johnson preferred to be called "Mr. Johnson."

✔**Reading Check**

What qualities separate Boswell apart from other biographers of his day?

He knew his subject, remembered each conversation, freely gave praise and admiration, and could make others comfortable. Other biographers may have had some of these talents or opportunities, but only Boswell had all of them.

Graphic Organizer

A **timeline** can help you organize and order information in a text. In the excerpt from *Samuel Johnson*, the author does not present the information chronologically. Look back through the excerpt. Then, fill in some of the events that happened in the years listed on the timeline. If you prefer, construct a foldable to display the information.

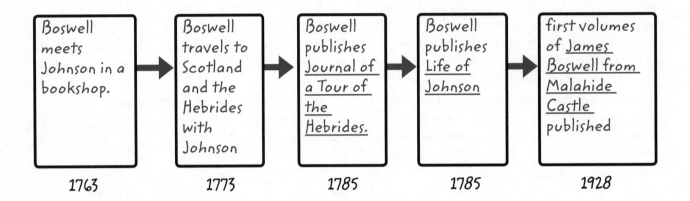

Boswell meets Johnson in a bookshop.	Boswell travels to Scotland and the Hebrides with Johnson	Boswell publishes <u>Journal of a Tour of the Hebrides.</u>	Boswell publishes <u>Life of Johnson</u>	first volumes of <u>James Boswell from Malahide Castle</u> published
1763	1773	1785	1785	1928

Active Reading Focus

Questioning In the space below write two questions you would suggest that readers ask themselves to make sure they understand the excerpt from *Samuel Johnson*.

What was James Boswell's relationship to

Samuel Johnson?

What distinguished Boswell as a biographer?

Reading Strategy

Determining Main Idea and Supporting Details
Reread the last paragraph of the excerpt. What is the main idea of that paragraph? Write a short statement summarizing its main idea.

Even in its imperfections, Boswell's biography is
unique and outstanding partly because his subject was
a fascinating man and partly because of his unique
opportunity and talents.

Literary Element

Motivation Consider Boswell's phrase: "the waste of good if it not be preserved." How do you think that may have motivated Boswell to write a biography of Johnson?

The "waste of good" means that it doesn't matter how
good something is if it doesn't live on. Boswell,
completely taken with Samuel Johnson and believing
him to be an amazing thinker and individual, wanted
to make sure he lived on. That was a motivation that
contributed to his writing a biography.

Vocabulary Practice

Using Context Clues Recall that when using difficult words, writers often provide clues to the meaning of those words. Some common context clues include:

- definitions or synonyms
- concrete examples
- contrast clues (opposite meanings)
- descriptions
- modifying words or phrases

For each passage from the text, study the underlined parts. How does that information give you a clue to the boldfaced word's meaning?

1. "The identity for which the young Boswell was searching—and continued to search—was one that could define itself against the example of his father, Lord Auchinleck, who was firm and **moralistic**, <u>a Whig and a Presbyterian…</u>"

   The passage gives concrete examples to reveal the
   meaning of **moralistic**.

2. "… he felt he had no more inner strength to meet difficulties now, when he needed it badly, than he had as a youth—that he seemed to have gone through life 'without any addition to my character from my having had the friendship of <u>Dr. Johnson</u> and many **eminent** men.'"

   The passage gives a concrete example of an
   eminent man.

3. "The most celebrated literary discovery of this century was the vast journal—or series of journals—he kept through most of his life, **chronicling** with complete frankness his own personal experiences and, more important, <u>recording</u> conversations and interviews with noted people he met."

   "Recording" is a synonym for chronicling.

Introductory Text: The Triumph of Romanticism 1750–1837
Looking Ahead (p. 693)

Preview

- What was English Romanticism?

- How did it influence English literature?

- How was it connected to political and social changes?

This introduction prepares you for the literature you will read in Unit 4 of your textbook. It explains Romanticism, a cultural movement of the 1800s. Romanticism was connected to political and social changes sweeping through Europe. Unlike the Enlightenment ideal, Romanticism valued feeling and imagination over reason.

As you read the introduction, use the Cornell Note Taking System to record important points and to remember what you have read.

Reduce

TO THE POINT *Note key words and phrases. For example:*

revolution

Romanticism

folk culture

conception of the

imagination

_____

_____

ANY QUESTIONS? *Ask questions as you read the headings and information. Answer them as you reread your notes. For example: "How was this period a 'Triumph'"?*

_____

_____

_____

_____

Record

Looking Ahead

➡ *Summarize the key characteristics of Romanticism. Two have been listed for you.*

happened at end of the 1700s

time of industrial and political revolution and change

challenged Enlightenment's belief in reason

believed in feeling and imagination

inspiration found in nature, folk culture, medieval past,

  passions

Keep the following questions in mind as you read

➡ *Use a KWL chart to preview this introduction. Return to this chart later to fill in the third colum. The chart has been started for you.*

	What I <u>K</u>now	What I <u>Want</u> to <u>K</u>now	What I <u>L</u>earned
Romanticism	"Romantic" often refers to love.	What else does "Romantic" refer to in literature?	
Nature in Romanticism			
Imagination in Romanticism			

Introductory Text: The Triumph of Romanticism 1750–1837

Timeline *(pp. 694–695)*

TO THE POINT *Note types of literature in the Timeline.*

gothic novel

historical novel

science fiction novel

_____

_____

British Literature

➡ *Based on the timeline, group entries into the categories provided for you below. The list has been started for you.*

<u>Firsts in Literature</u>

first gothic novel 1763—Horace Walpole's <u>The Castle of Otranto</u>

first historical novel 1814—Sir Walter Scott's <u>Waverly</u>

first science fiction novel 1818—Mary Shelley's <u>Frankenstein</u>

<u>Women Authors</u>

Ann Radcliffe

Jane Austen

Mary Shelley

<u>Writers Listed Twice</u>

William Wordsworth

Samuel Taylor Coleridge

Jane Austen

George Gordon, Lord Byron

TO THE POINT *Note key words and phrases. For example:*

technology

railway

American colonists

steam engine

British Events

➡ *What are the general categories of events in this part of the Timeline? List two categories, and list a few events in each category. The list has been started for you.*

<u>Technology</u>

1769—steam engine invented

1814—first steam locomotive designed

1830—first public railway line

<u>War</u>

1805—British defeat Napoleon's naval forces at Trafalgar

1812—War between U.S. and Great Britain

1819—Peterloo massacre

Introductory Text: The Triumph of Romanticism 1750–1837

Timeline (pp. 694–695)

Reduce

ANY QUESTIONS? *Use them to organize your notes. Answer them as you reread your notes. For example: "Why were there so many revolutions and revolts in this period?"*

_____

_____

_____

_____

Record

World Events

➡ *What type of event is most prominent in this section of the Timeline? List the events in this category. One example has been listed for you.*

<u>Revolution and revolt</u>

1789—French Revolution

1794—Toussaint L'Ouverture's Haitian revolt

1810—Father Hidalgo's Mexican revolt

1819—Simón Bolívar's revolt against Spain

1821—Greece revolts against Turkey

Recap

➡ *Review your notes on the Timeline. Then recap: Make a few generalizations about this period based on your notes.*

Possible generalization:

This was a time marked by many revolutions and revolts.

_____

_____

_____

_____

Introductory Text: The Triumph of Romanticism 1750–1837

By the Numbers *(p. 696)*

Reduce

ANY QUESTIONS? *Ask questions about heads. For example: "Why was it important to maintain 'Gentility'"?*

_____

_____

_____

_____

_____

TO THE POINT *For the remaining heads, note key words and phrases.* **Key** *words and phrases are the most important ones. They will help you remember what you have read. For example:*

Grand Tour
Waterloo
Metropolitan Police
Act
first public railway

Record

The Cost of Gentility

➡ *Use the statistics in this section to create a budget chart on the cost of maintaining economic and social status. How much could a family afford? The chart has been started for you.*

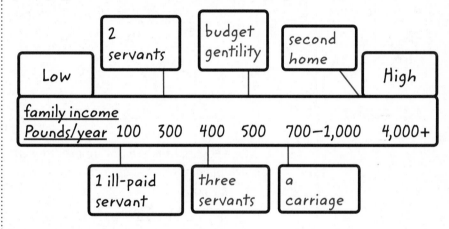

Travel Expenses

➡ *What are the main ideas in this section? One has been listed for you.*

A Grand Tour of Europe was part of a "genteel" education.

Young Englishmen would take a 3-4 year trip.

British people could live cheaper in other countries in Europe.

Introductory Text: The Triumph of Romanticism 1750–1837

By the Numbers *(p. 696)*

Reduce

TO THE POINT *Note key words and phrases.*

  Napoleon

  Cotton consumption

  Population increase

  London police

  Railroads

Record

Military Expansion

➡ *Use the Timeline on pages 694 and 695 to help increase your understanding of this section. What are examples of military expansion? One example has been listed for you.*

  many battles with Napoleon

  1812 war with the U.S.

➡ *List the remaining headings on this page. For each, note what increase or development each heading describes. One has been listed for you.*

  British Cotton Consumption

  increased from 0 tons to 790 tons in 1800-1900

  Population Boom

  increased dramatically during the 1800s

  Policing London

  first London police force established

  Growth of Railroads

  first public railway, 1830

Introductory Text: The Triumph of Romanticism 1750–1837

Being There *(p. 697)*

Reduce

TO THE POINT *For the map information, note key words and phrases. For example:*

growing blight of

factories, slums

Lake District

Great Britain and

Ireland united

Record

➡ *Compare this map with the maps on pages 9, 241, and 505. Note new labels that appear on the map in Unit 4. Note the information given under the heading, "Being There." What conclusion can you draw based on the way the maps change with time, and based on the information in that section? The new labels have been listed for you.*

New labels:

United Kingdom and Lake District are new labels on the map.

Conclusion:

The United Kingdom became united during this period. Many industrial towns were developed. Because of the growth of factories and slums, people began to go to remote areas, like the Lake District.

Recap

➡ *Review your notes on By The Numbers and Being There. Then recap: Use an evidence organizer to summarize the main idea and supporting details. Select details that support the main idea below. One idea has been listed for you.*

Main Idea
British society was becoming larger, more technological, and more developed. Britain also was involved in wars that required many resources.

Supporting Detail	Supporting Detail	Supporting Detail	Supporting Detail
British cotton consumption increased greatly.	The British military expanded and there were many conflicts.	The London police force was established.	The first railroads connected cities in England.

Introductory Text: The Triumph of Romanticism 1750–1837

Historical, Social, and Cultural Forces (pp. 698–699)

Reduce

MY VIEW *Indicate what you find most interesting or surprising about this information.*

_____

_____

_____

_____

_____

TO THE POINT *Note key dates, events, and people in the rest of these sections. For example:*

1776

French Revolution

Reign of Terror

Saint Domingue
  (Haiti)

Toussaint L'Ouverture

Napoleon Bonaparte

_____

Record

The Industrial Revolution

➡ *What changes did the Industrial Revolution cause in the English society and economy? Organize your notes into cause-and-effect statements. One example has been done for you.*

It caused the economy to shift from being based on farming to being based on manufacturing.

It caused people to move from the country to the city.

It caused factory owners to get rich while workers stayed poor and worked in dangerous conditions.

The American and French Revolutions

➡ *Identify the key, or major, characteristics of these revolutions.*

American Revolution ended, 1781

French Revolution began, 1789—started with good intentions but led to brutal Reign of Terror

Latin American Revolutions

➡ *What are the main idea and supporting details here?*

Main idea:

Revolutions led by American colonists and the French inspired people in Latin America to revolt.

Supporting details:

Toussaint L'Ouverture's 1804 revolt against France in Haiti

independent by 1824: Argentina, Chile, Mexico, Peru, Uruguay, Paraguay, Columbia, Venezuela, Bolivia

The Napoleonic Wars

➡ *Summarize the main ideas. One has been listed for you.*

Britain vs. France—fought between 1793 and 1815

Napoleon Bonaparte— French military commander

British naval commander Horatio Nelson—hero, beat Napoleon at battle of Trafalgar, 1805

Introductory Text: The Triumph of Romanticism 1750–1837

Historical, Social, and Cultural Forces *(p. 699)*

Reduce

TO THE POINT *Note key words and phrases.*

extreme

exotic

nature

imagination

feelings

Record

Romanticism

➥ *Use a concept web to organize the key ideas of English Romanticism. This web has been started for you.*

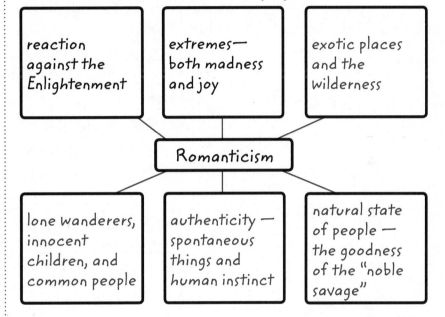

reaction against the Enlightenment

extremes— both madness and joy

exotic places and the wilderness

Romanticism

lone wanderers, innocent children, and common people

authenticity — spontaneous things and human instinct

natural state of people — the goodness of the "noble savage"

➥ *As you read, you will see display quotes, or quotes set in large letters apart from the rest of the text. They often provide important information. What conclusions can you draw from the display quote by Walter Pater? One example has been written for you.*

Pater is probably an expert on art and Romanticism.

This quote is probably a famous definition of Romanticism.

"Strangeness" and "beauty" are major themes in the literature of Romanticism.

Introductory Text: The Triumph of Romanticism 1750–1837

Historical, Social, and Cultural Forces (p. 699)

Reduce

MY VIEW *Write comments here. What interests you the most about this section?*

_____

_____

_____

_____

Record

Preview Big Ideas of The Triumph of Romanticism

➡ *Identify the main idea of each Big Idea. Then paraphrase the main idea. To paraphrase is to restate information in your own words. Use words that make sense to you. One main idea has been written for you.*

The Stirrings of Romanticism—In the late 1700s people began to challenge the established values of the Enlightenment.

Nature and Imagination—As factories and industry made society more complicated and change the nation, writers looked to nature, children, and common people for inspiration.

The Quest for Truth and Beauty—Lord Byron, Percy Shelley, and John Keats continued the Romantic quest.

Recap

➡ *Review your notes on the Historical, Social, and Cultural Forces. Then Recap: Sum up these forces using this thinking tree. Some of it has been filled in for you.*

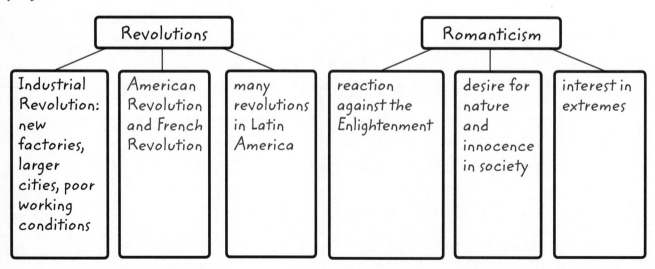

Revolutions			Romanticism		
Industrial Revolution: new factories, larger cities, poor working conditions	American Revolution and French Revolution	many revolutions in Latin America	reaction against the Enlightenment	desire for nature and innocence in society	interest in extremes

Introductory Text: The Triumph of Romanticism 1750–1837

Big Idea 1: The Stirrings of Romanticism *(pp. 700–701)*

Reduce

TO THE POINT *Note key writers and ideas. For example:*

Jean-Jacques
    Rousseau
noble savage
society corrupts

_____

_____

_____

ANY QUESTIONS? *Write them as you read the headings and information in these sections. Then answer them as you reread your notes.*

_____

_____

_____

Record

The "State of Nature"

➥ *List the key ideas of Jean-Jacques Rousseau. One has been listed.*
was Enlightenment thinker who lived in France
believed that people are naturally good, curious, and
    have only basic needs
believed that society corrupts people—making them
    want status symbols, money, and vacations.

Sensibility and the Emotions

➥ *What was the "cult of sensibility" among Romantic writers? List the main points of this section. One has been listed for you.*
young writers wanted to shift away from
    Enlightenment emphasis on reason
believed in "sensibility," or sympathetic feeling
heart represents origin of emotion

The Imagination

➥ *How did Romanticism differ from the Enlightenment? Organize your notes in this chart which has been started.*

Enlightenment	Romanticism
reason, logic	irrational thoughts, feelings
science and philosophy	imagination
truth	vision

The Pre-Romantics

➥ *Group information: writers and themes.*
Thomas Gray—elevated language
Robert Burns—common farmers, Scottish dialect
William Blake—supernatural topics and imaginative
    experimentation (broke with Neoclassical tradition)

Introductory Text: The Triumph of Romanticism 1750–1837

Big Idea 1: The Stirrings of Romanticism *(p. 701)*

MY VIEW *Write your responses to the text. Then use them to remember your notes.*

_____

_____

_____

_____

_____

Record

from *Proverbs of Hell* from *The Marriage of Heaven and Hell*

➡ *Paraphrase this idea from the excerpt: "No bird soars too high, if he soars with his own wings." To paraphrase is to rewrite a passage in your own words.*

Possible response:

If an individual uses his or her own mind and strength, his or her potential is unlimited.

_____

_____

Recap

➡ *Review your notes on Big Idea 1: The Stirrings of Romanticism. Then fill out this Venn diagram to identify similarities and differences that marked the transition from the Enlightenment to Romanticism. What ideas did Enlightenment and Romanticism have separately? What ideas did they share? The diagram has been started for you.*

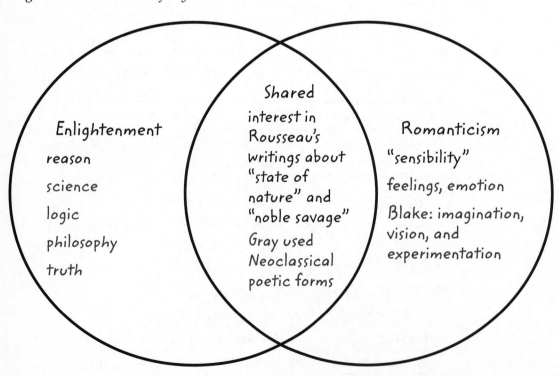

Enlightenment

reason

science

logic

philosophy

truth

Shared interest in Rousseau's writings about "state of nature" and "noble savage" Gray used Neoclassical poetic forms

Romanticism

"sensibility"

feelings, emotion

Blake: imagination, vision, and experimentation

Introductory Text: The Triumph of Romanticism 1750–1837

Big Idea 2: Nature and the Imagination *(p. 702)*

Reduce

TO THE POINT *Note descriptive phrases next to key words. For example:*

Enlightenment —
nature is laboratory
Romanticism — nature
is wild garden

ANY QUESTIONS? *Ask them as you read the headings and information in these sections. Then answer them as you reread your notes. For example: "How did Romantic writers feel about science?"*

Record

What is Nature?

➡ *How were Enlightenment and Romantic views of nature different? Organize the ideas in a chart to find the differences. The chart has been started for you.*

Nature to Enlightenment	Nature to Romanticism
needed to be tamed	best left wild and untamed
farms	tangled, winding gardens
laboratories	Swiss Alps
orderly gardens	feeling of awe

The Child and the Common Man

➡ *Use compare-and-contrast statements to organize the information about Romantic beliefs and writers compared to Enlightenment beliefs and writers. One has been written for you.*

Unlike the Enlightenment view that children were ignorant, deficient adults, Romantics believed children were innocent and imaginative.

Instead of using regular poetic form, ornate language and traditional subjects, in the 1798 Lyrical Ballads William Wordsworth and Samuel Taylor Coleridge used simple forms like folk ballads and hymns and used the lives of uneducated people as subjects.

Dreams and Nightmares

➡ *What did romantic writers believe? Group information according to each writer listed in this section. One has been listed for you.*

William Wordsworth: suspicious of science—"We murder to dissect"

Mary Shelley: science deforms natural life—Frankenstein

Coleridge: famous poem "Kubla Khan" appeared to him in a drug-induced dream-vision

Introductory Text: The Triumph of Romanticism 1750–1837

Big Idea 2: Nature and the Imagination (p. 703)

Reduce	**Record**
TO THE POINT *Note key words and phrases. For example:*	**from the Preface to *Lyrical Ballads***

Reduce

TO THE POINT *Note key words and phrases. For example:*

common life

low and rustic life

essential passions of

the heart

Record

from the Preface to *Lyrical Ballads*

➡ *List the key adjectives and phrases in this excerpt of Romantic writing by Wordsworth. Make a generalization about how each relates to Romanticism. One example has been written for you.*

"common life" — Romantics appreciated children and common people.

"language really used by men" — Romantics believed the ideas in poetry were more real and powerful if written in everyday language

"low and rustic life" — Romantics were interested in working and uneducated people.

"more durable" — Romantics believed people and things in their natural state were stronger than things and people that were polished.

Recap

➡ *Review your notes on Big Idea 2: Nature and the Imagination. Then recap: Use a web to organize the main ideas. Part of this web has been filled out for you.*

Nature and the Imagination (in Romanticism)

- interest in wildness and awe-inspiring power of untamed nature
- appreciation of innocence and imagination of children and common people
- a desire to explore magic of dreams, distrust of science

Introductory Text: The Triumph of Romanticism 1750–1837

Big Idea 3: The Quest for Truth and Beauty *(p. 704)*

Reduce

MY VIEW *Indicate what you find most interesting or surprising about this information.*

_____

_____

_____

_____

TO THE POINT *Note key words and phrases. For example:*

folk culture

Greek fight for

independence

George Gordon, Lord

Byron

Record

The Revolutionary Spirit

➡ *How did the French Revolution influence English Romanticism? One example has been listed for you.*

The success of the revolution inspired belief that

fighting for a cause was worthwhile.

The spirit of the French Revolution—"Liberty, Equality,

Fraternity"—inspired Wordsworth and Coleridge.

The Reign of Terror followed and made Wordsworth

and Coleridge rethink their idealism.

The Spirit of Nationalism

➡ *What information is contained under this heading? One point has been listed for you.*

political aspect to Romantic interest in folk culture

romantics inspired by Greek fight for independence

from Turkey

Exotic Places and Times

➡ *Summarize the key points about the exotic places, times, and settings described here. One point has been written for you.*

Travel writing from the Near East inspired the Romantics.

Mary Shelley's <u>Frankenstein</u> set in Scottish highlands

and Alps

The Poetic Quest

➡ *What are the main ideas here? One has been listed for you.*

This was an age of rebellion.

Wordsworth, Shelley wrote statements on poetry's

supremacy

Some Romantic poems are about poetry itself.

John Keats was famous poet with brief life, wrote

about power of books and the imagination.

Introductory Text: The Triumph of Romanticism 1750–1837

Big Idea 3: The Quest for Truth and Beauty *(p. 705)*

Reduce

MY VIEW *Write comments here.*

_____

_____

_____

_____

Record

from *A Defense of Poetry*

➡ *Paraphrase this idea from the excerpt by Percy Bysshe Shelley: "Poets are the unacknowledged legislators of the world." To paraphrase is to restate a passage or idea in your own words. Use words that make sense to you.*

Sample response:

Although people don't realize it, the ideas of poetry change the way they see the world.

_____

_____

Recap

➡ *Review your notes on Big Idea 3: The Quest for Truth and Beauty. Then recap: Sort your notes to preview the three English Romantic writers in unit 4, part 3: George Gordon, Lord Byron; Percy Bysshe Shelley; and John Keats. After you identify the characteristics of each writer, make a generalization about all three writers. Organize your ideas in this chart. The chart has been started for you.*

Possible response:

George Gordon, Lord Byron	Percy Bysshe Shelley	John Keats
joined Greek fight for independence from Turkey gave money, then died going to fight	felt betrayed that Wordsworth and Coleridge became conservative still believed in revolution	short life wrote about the power of books and the imagination
Generalization: These three poets believed poetry was . . . bigger than an academic pursuit. They believed poets affected the entire world, and believed their work was similar to the work of people who led revolutions and wars. They led idealistic lives similar to their writings.		

Introductory Text: The Triumph of Romanticism 1750–1837

Wrap-Up *(p. 706)*

Reduce

TO THE POINT *Note key words and phrases. For example:*

Rousseau

Blake

Wordsworth

unique experiences of
    childhood

"gothic"

Ralph Waldo Emerson

Henry David Thoreau

Record

Why It Matters

➡ *What was the legacy of English Romanticism? Summarize the main points. One example has been written for you.*

values: power of nature and imagination, dignity of
    artist

inspired today's environmental movements and art
    programs

improved how we think of and treat children

showed that the medieval period was interesting

inspired U.S. writers like Emerson, Thoreau, Poe

Cultural Links

➡ *What links are described here? The chart has been started for you.*

Romanticism		Link
William Blake	→	Yeats, Roethke, Ginsberg
gothic novel and historical novel	→	popular today
<u>Frankenstein</u>	→	"mad scientists" and androids

Recap

➡ *Review your notes on the Wrap-Up. Then recap: write a brief paragraph on why English Romanticism was important, and in what ways.*

Students' responses might mention the influence of English

Romanticism on art, literature, and social or political movements. They

might connect English Romanticism to their own experience,

discussing movies or music that relate to Romantic ideas.

Introductory Text: The Triumph of Romanticism 1750–1837

Summarize

➡ *Review your notes on this introduction. Then summarize: Fill in the concept map with what you've learned about English Romanticism. The map has been started for you.*

Key Writers & Works

Gray

Burns

Blake

Wordsworth & Coleridge — <u>Lyrical Ballads</u>

Mary Shelley — <u>Frankenstein</u>

Percy Bysshe Shelley

Keats

Types of Literature

poetry

manifestos (statements)

gothic novels

historical novels

science fiction

Definition

English Romanticism was a movement . . . led by writers who disliked the coldness of science and excitedly pushed the boundaries of the imagination.

English Romanticism

Themes & Subjects

children and common people

imagination

wild nature

  exotic places

  extremes

  sensibility

  beauty

  dreams and madness

  human instinct

Influences

dislike of the Enlightenment's belief in only reason

"state of nature" and the "noble savage"

reaction to Industrial Revolution

response to multiple revolutions

medieval culture

Introductory Text: The Triumph of Romanticism 1750–1837

Apply

Multiple Choice

Circle the letters of the best choice(s) for the following questions.

1. What historical events occurred during this period? B, C, D
    - **A.** English civil war
    - **B.** Industrial Revolution
    - **C.** American Revolution
    - **D.** French Revolution

2. What did the Romantic poets believe in? A, B, C, D
    - **A.** the wisdom of children
    - **B.** the value of folk traditions
    - **C.** the truths revealed in dreams
    - **D.** the use of everyday speech in poetry

3. What were the Napoleonic Wars? C
    - **A.** wars between England and Italy
    - **B.** wars between France and Italy
    - **C.** wars between England and France
    - **D.** wars between England and America

4. Who wrote the gothic novel *Frankenstein?* D
    - **A.** Kubla Khan
    - **B.** William Blake
    - **C.** Lord Byron
    - **D.** Mary Shelley

Matching

Write the letter of the choice in the second column that best matches each item in the first column.

5. led revolt in present-day Haiti _____ C

6. fought for Greece _____ D

7. wrote about the "noble savage" _____ B

8. wrote poems with Romantic themes and Neoclassical style _____ A
    - **A.** Thomas Gray
    - **B.** Jean-Jacques Rousseau
    - **C.** Toussaint L'Ouverture
    - **D.** George Gordon, Lord Byron

How can you better remember and understand the material in this introduction? *Recite* your notes, *Reflect* on them, and *Review* them. You can also use your notes for a quick review of the historical period or the Big Ideas of this unit. As you learn more about the ideas in the unit, add to your notes.

Literary History: **The Two Sides of Blake** (pp. 766–767)

Preview

- Who was William Blake?

- What were the "two sides" of Blake?

- What are some characteristics of Blake's artwork?

This article discusses the career of poet and artist William Blake, who is a part of our literary history. The article will help you better understand the poetry you will read in your textbook.

As you read the article, use the Cornell Note Taking System to record important points and to remember what you have read.

Reduce

ANY QUESTIONS? *Ask questions as you read. Answer them as you reread your notes. For example: "What kind of background did Blake have?"*

_____

_____

_____

_____

_____

TO THE POINT *Note key words and phrases. For example:*

Milton's <u>Paradise Lost</u>

Dante's <u>Divine</u>

   <u>Comedy</u>

"Nebuchadnezzar"

"Infant Joy"

_____

Record

Early Influences

➡ *What were Blake's family life and education like? Paraphrase the information in this section to answer the question. The answer has been started for you.*

Blake grew up in an unusual family. His parents encouraged his individuality and artistic interest. At age 10, he began studying Italian and German Renaissance artists. At age 15, he was an apprentice to an engraver. Then he enrolled in the Royal Academy of Art. In school, he preferred to create art based on his own imagination.

Visionary Art

➡ *List key details that describe Blake's artistic style. One detail has been listed for you.*

believed line was the most important element

did not like techniques like shadowing that made
   contours of a painting unclear

liked to paint from religious works—Milton's <u>Paradise</u>
   <u>Lost</u>, Dante's <u>Divine Comedy</u>

startling images: "Nebuchadnezzar"

often made engravings from his poetry—"Infant Joy"
   and "Songs of Innocence"

Literary History: The Two Sides of Blake (pp. 766–767)

Reduce

TO THE POINT *Note key words and phrases. For example:*

commision

mastery of engraving

overarching belief

credo: live by own

    rules

_____

_____

_____

Record

➡ *Use a classification chart to organize details about Blake's engravings. List the details of three important works. The chart has been started for you.*

"Nebuchadnezzar"	"Infant Joy"	"The Lord Answering Job Out of the Whirlwind"
illustrates episode from the biblical Book of Daniel stark, clear lines very scary	based on poem from "Songs of Innocence" energy and spontaneity mother, child, angel	engraving of episode from the Book of Job in Bible majestic, circular lines shows masterful skill

Literary History: **The Two Sides of Blake**

Summarize

➡ *Review your notes based on the information in this article. Then organize them: Complete the web diagram below. The web has been started for you.*

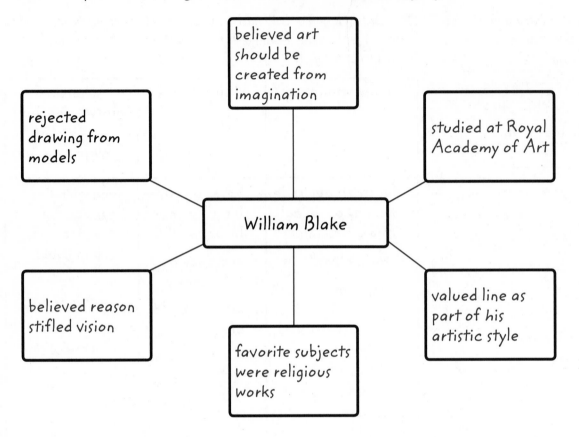

Literary History: **The Two Sides of Blake**

Apply

Multiple Choice

Circle the letter of the best choice for the following questions.

1. What tradition was part of conventional art in the eighteenth century? B
   A. art created by imagination
   B. Greek and Roman art
   C. the rejection of still-life
   D. Asian art

2. Which of the following is *not* a fundamental element of pictorial art? C
   A. line
   B. shape
   C. content
   D. tone

3. What materials did Blake use to create "Nebuchadnezzar"? B
   A. engraving
   B. ink and watercolor
   C. oil paint
   D. sculpture

4. What "artistic credo" did Blake believe in? C
   A. traditional art was the best model
   B. always follow the rules of conventional art
   C. live by your own rules, not someone else's
   D. Greek and Roman art should be your subject

Matching

Write the letter of the choice in the second column that best matches each item in the first column.

5. engraving illustrates Babylonian king who goes mad and acts like beast _____ A

6. school where Blake enrolled to study art _____ C

7. engraving depicts figures of mother, child, and angel encircled by partly opened bud _____ D

8. important characteristic of Blake's engravings _____ B

9. favorite subjects of Blake's _____ E

10. two sides of Blake _____ F
    A. "Nebuchadnezzar"
    B. Art should be created from imagination.
    C. Royal Academy of Art
    D. "Infant Joy"
    E. Milton's *Paradise Lost* and Dante's *Divine Comedy*
    F. poetic and artistic creation

How can you better remember and understand the material in this Literary History? *Recite* your notes, *Reflect* on them, and *Review* them. You can also use your notes to review your understanding of the poetry in this unit by Blake.

IN PATAGONIA

Building Background

In the 1500s, traveling could be just uncomfortable, or it could be disastrous. In 1591, Captain-General Thomas Cavendish led a British fleet on a voyage from Plymouth, England to the Pacific Ocean. His captain, John Davis, was considered the best navigator of his day.

Their trip was a disaster. Bad weather, serious errors, and bad luck cost them the lives of many of the fleet's crew, including Cavendish.

Centuries later, British travel writer Bruce Chatwin wrote *In Patagonia* about the disaster. In the following selection from *In Patagonia* Chatwin describes the awful voyage of 1591–1592. He also discusses the connections between the famous disaster and Samuel Taylor Coleridge's classic poem *The Rime of the Ancient Mariner.*

Setting Purposes for Reading

Have you ever taken a trip and been surprised along the way? With a classmate discuss the following questions:

- What do you know about sailing in the 1500s?
- What do you need to be safe on a long trip?

Read to discover the historical basis for Coleridge's *The Rime of the Ancient Mariner.*

Reading Strategy | Evaluating Historical Influences

When you **evaluate historical influences,** you gather and examine the background information related to the writing of a literary work. Background information may include such categories as transportation, technology, scientific advancements, politics, social rules and customs, religion, and even diet.

Active Reading Focus | Responding to Characters

When you **respond to characters,** you analyze the characters' actions and words and decide how you feel about them. As you read the selection, pause to ask yourself if you like, admire, or respect the characters, and why.

Literary Element | Atmosphere

Atmosphere is the overall mood or emotional feeling of a literary work. Atmosphere is established mainly—but not only—by physical qualities that contribute to a mood, such as time, place, and weather.

Big Idea | Nature and the Imagination

Nature plays a big role in this excerpt from *In Patagonia,* helping the characters as well as hindering them. Aspects of nature in this excerpt include weather, climate, animal and plant life, the landscape, and also ailments for which they had no cure out at sea in the 1500s.

Vocabulary

Read the definitions of these words from *In Patagonia.* The origin of each word, or its *etymology,* can be found in a dictionary. A word's origin reflects the history and development of the word. Discovering the *etymology* of a word can help you unlock its meaning.

mutiny (mū′ tə nē) *n.* a rebellion against legal authority, such as sailors refusing to obey their commander's orders, and then attacking the officers; p. 134 *The sailors hated their Captain, disagreed with every command he made, and decided to stage a mutiny.*

skirmish (skər′ mish) *n.* a brief fight between small groups of troops; p. 134 *Ten people were wounded in the skirmish, two of them seriously.*

forage (for′ ij) *v.* to search for something, as for food or supplies; p. 134 *Mary and Josie would forage in the forest for berries and wood.*

scurvy (skər′ vē) *n.* a disease marked by swollen and bleeding gums and great physical weakness, caused by a lack of vitamin C in the diet; p. 135 *To prevent scurvy, the sailors ate citrus fruit every day.*

nemesis (ne′ mə səs) *n.* just punishment or vengeance; p. 135 *Carl's nemesis for his poor treatment of his friends was that he was shunned.*

In Patagonia
By Bruce Chatwin

On October 30th 1592, the ship *Desire,* of 120 tons, limping home to England, dropped anchor in the river at Port Desire, this being her fourth visit since Thomas Cavendish[1] named the place in her, his flagship's, honor, seven years before.

The captain was now John Davis, a Devon man, the most skilled navigator of his generation. Behind him were three Arctic voyages in search of the North-West Passage. Before him were two books of seamanship and six fatal cuts of a Japanese pirate's sword.

Davis had sailed on Cavendish's Second Voyage "intended for the South Sea." The fleet left Plymouth on August 26th 1591, the Captain-General in the galleon *Leicester;* the other ships were the *Roebuck,* the *Desire,* the *Daintie,* and the *Black Pinnace,* the last so named for having carried the corpse of Sir Philip Sydney.[2]

Cavendish was puffed up with early success, hating his officers and crew. On the coast of Brazil, he stopped to sack[3] the town of Santos. A gale scattered the ships off the Patagonian coast, but they met up, as arranged, at Port Desire.

The fleet entered the Magellan Strait[4] with the southern winter already begun. A sailor's frostbitten nose fell off when he blew it. Beyond Cape Froward, they ran into north-westerly gales and sheltered in a tight cove with the wind howling over their mastheads. Reluctantly, Cavendish agreed to revictual[5] in Brazil and return the following spring.

On the night of May 20th, off Port Desire, the Captain-General changed tack[6] without warning. At dawn, the *Desire* and the *Black Pinnace* were alone on the sea. Davis made for port, thinking his commander would join him as before, but Cavendish set course for Brazil and thence to St. Helena.[7] One day he lay down in his cabin and died, perhaps of apoplexy,[8] cursing Davis for desertion: "This villain that hath been the death of me."

Davis disliked the man but was no traitor. The worst of the winter over, he went south again to look for the Captain-General.

---

1. *Thomas Cavendish* (1555–1592) was a famed explorer who led the third circumnavigation of the globe.
2. A *pinnace* is a small sailing ship. *Sir Philip Sydney* (1554–1586) was an Elizabethan poet, courtier, and soldier.
3. Here, *sack* means "pillage."
4. The *Magellan Strait* connects the Atlantic and Pacific Oceans near the southern tip of South America.
5. *Revictual* means to "re-supply with food."
6. Here, *tack* means "course."
7. *St. Helena,* first discovered in 1502, was a British island colony and port of call off the southwestern coast of Africa.
8. *Apoplexy* is a stroke.

Active Reading Focus

Responding to Characters When you **respond to characters**, you look at their words and actions and decide how you feel about them. Is Cavendish the type of person you would like to know? Explain.

Most students will say that they would *not* like to know Cavendish because he seems like a selfish, careless person who does not think he needs to take care of those in his command.

Literary Element

Atmosphere The general mood or emotional feeling of a literary work or passage is its **atmosphere**.

- Describe the atmosphere in this passage.
- What images contribute to this atmosphere?

Students may describe the atmosphere as cold, horrifying, and alarming. Images contributing to this atmosphere are the sailor's frostbitten nose falling off, and the howling wind.

Big Idea

Nature and the Imagination How do you think the power of nature affected the imagination of Davis and his crew?

<u>The crew was probably amazed and</u>

<u>scared by the power of nature, which</u>

<u>first destroys one of the ships and</u>

<u>then seems to protect the other ship.</u>

<u>They may have imagined that nature</u>

<u>had a character and personality just</u>

<u>like a very powerful human being.</u>

Reading Strategy

Evaluating Historical Influences Recall that **historical influences** include background information related to the writing of a literary work.

- Why do you think Davis had the penguins dried, salted, and stowed in the hold?

  <u>Davis had the penguins dried,</u>

  <u>salted, and stowed in the hold</u>

  <u>because, they had no refrigeration</u>

  <u>and needed to preserve the food</u>

  <u>for his crew.</u>

Vocabulary

mutiny (mū′tə nē) *n.* a rebellion against legal authority, such as sailors refusing to obey their commander's orders, and then attacking the officers

skirmish (skər′ mish) *n.* a brief fight between small groups of troops

forage (for′ ij) *v.* to search about for something, as for food or supplies

Gales blew the two ships in among some undiscovered islands, now known as the Falklands.

This time, they passed the Strait and out into the Pacific. <u>In a storm off Cape Pilar, the *Desire* lost the *Pinnace*, which went down with all hands. Davis was alone at the helm, praying for a speedy end, when the sun broke through the clouds.</u> He took bearings, fixed his position, and so regained the calmer water of the Strait.

He sailed back to Port Desire, the crew scurvied and **mutinous** and the lice lying in their flesh, "clusters of lice as big as peason, yea, and some as big as beanes." He repaired the ship as best he could. The men lived off eggs, gulls, baby seals, scurvy grass and the fish called *pejerrey*. On this diet they were restored to health.

Ten miles down the coast, there was an island, the original Penguin Island, where the sailors clubbed twenty thousand birds to death. They had no natural enemies and were unafraid of their murderers. John Davis ordered the penguins dried and salted and stowed fourteen thousand in the hold.

On November 11th a war-party of Tehuelche Indians[9] attacked "throwing dust in the ayre, leaping and running like brute beasts, having vizzards on their faces like dogs' faces, or else their faces are dogs' faces indeed." Nine men died in the **skirmish**, among them the chief mutineers, Parker and Smith. Their deaths were seen as the just judgment of God.

The *Desire* sailed at nightfall on December 22nd and set course for Brazil where the Captain hoped to provision with cassava[10] flour. On January 30th he made land at the Isle of Plasencia, off Rio de Janeiro. The men **foraged** for fruit and vegetables in gardens belonging to the Indians.

Six days later, the coopers[11] went with a landing party to gather hoops for barrels. The day was hot and the men were bathing, unguarded, when a mob of Indians and Portuguese attacked. The Captain sent a boat crew ashore and they found the thirteen men, faces upturned to heaven, laid in a rank with a cross set by them.

John Davis saw pinnaces sailing out of Rio harbor. He made for open sea. He had no other choice. He had eight casks of water and they were fouled.

As they came up to the Equator, the penguins took their revenge. In them bred a "loathsome worme" about an inch long. The worms ate everything, iron only excepted—clothes, bedding, boots, hats, leather lashings, and live human flesh. The worms gnawed through the ship's side and threatened to sink her. The more worms the men killed, the more they multiplied.

---

9. The *Tehuelche Indians* were a nomadic group that inhabited Patagonia.
10. *Cassava* is a tuber, or a plant with bulky, underground stems, that can be dried and milled into flour.
11. *Coopers* repair and build wooden barrels or casks.

Around the Tropic of Cancer, the crew came down with <u>scurvy</u>. Their ankles swelled and their chests, and their parts swelled so horribly that "they could neither stand nor lie nor go."

The Captain could scarcely speak for sorrow. Again he prayed for a speedy end. He asked the men to be patient; to give thanks to God and accept his chastisement. But the men were raging mad and the ship howled with the groans and curses of the dying.

Only Davis and a ship's boy were in health, of the seventy-six who left Plymouth. By the end there were five men who could move and work the ship.

And so, lost and wandering on the sea, with topsails and spritsails torn, the rotten hulk drifted, rather than sailed, into the harbor of Berehaven on Bantry Bay[12] on June 11th 1593. The smell disgusted the people of that quiet fishing village. . . .

"The Southern Voyage of John Davis" appeared in Hakluyt's[13] edition of 1600. Two centuries passed and another Devon man, Samuel Taylor Coleridge, set down the 625 controversial lines of *The Ancient Mariner,* with its hammering repetitions and story of crime, wandering, and expiation.[14]

John Davis and the Mariner have these in common: a voyage to the Black South, the murder of a bird or birds, the <u>nemesis</u> which follows, the drift through the tropics, the rotting ship, the curses of dying men. Lines 236–9 are particularly resonant of the Elizabethan voyage:

> The many men so beautiful!
> And they all dead did lie:
> And a thousand, thousand slimy things
> Lived on and so did I.

In *The Road to Xanadu,* the American scholar John Livingston Lowes traced the Mariner's victim to a "disconsolate Black Albitross" shot by one Hatley, the mate of Captain George Shelvocke's privateer in the eighteenth century. Wordsworth had a copy of this voyage and showed it to Coleridge when the two men tried to write the poem together. . . .

Lowes demonstrated how the voyages in Hakluyt and Purchas[15] fuelled Coleridge's imagination. "The mighty great roaring of ice" that John Davis witnessed on an earlier voyage off Greenland reappears in line 61: "It cracked and growled and roared and howled." But he did not, apparently, consider the likelihood that Davis's voyage to the Strait gave Coleridge the backbone for his poem.

---

12. *Bantry Bay* is in southwest Ireland.
13. Richard *Hakluyt* (1552–1616) was a British geographer and chronicler of British exploration. The second edition of his nautical record was completed and released between 1598–1600.
14. *Expiation* is the act of making atonement.
15. Samuel *Purchas* (1577–1626) chronicled British nautical discoveries, continuing the work of Hakluyt. His work was a favorite of Coleridge.

Literary Element

Atmosphere In your own words, describe the atmosphere here.

�»» Underline the details in the excerpt that create that atmosphere for you.

The atmosphere is awful, full of horror and disgust. Students may underline details including the "torn sails", the "rotten hulk", and the "terrible smell".

✔ Reading Check

1. What finally happened to the ship John Davis was sailing?

   He brought it, with torn sails and rotting, into Bantry Bay on June 11, 1593.

2. Name three qualities that John Davis and the Mariner in *The Rime of the Ancient Mariner* have in common.

   Three things John Davis and the Mariner have in common may include any of the following: a voyage to the Black South, the murder of a bird or birds, the nemesis that followed, the drift through the tropics, the rotting ship, and the sounds of dying men.

Vocabulary

<u>scurvy</u> (skər′ vē) *n.* a disease marked by swollen and bleeding gums and great physical weakness, caused by a lack of vitamin C in the diet

<u>nemesis</u> (ne′ mə səs) *n.* just punishment or vengeance

AFTER YOU READ

Graphic Organizer

What were the differences between Thomas Cavendish and John Davis? Use a **Venn diagram** to compare and contrast their characters. In the diagram below, record information that is unique to each person in his section. Then record information that is common to both in the center section. If you prefer, construct a Foldable™ to display the information.

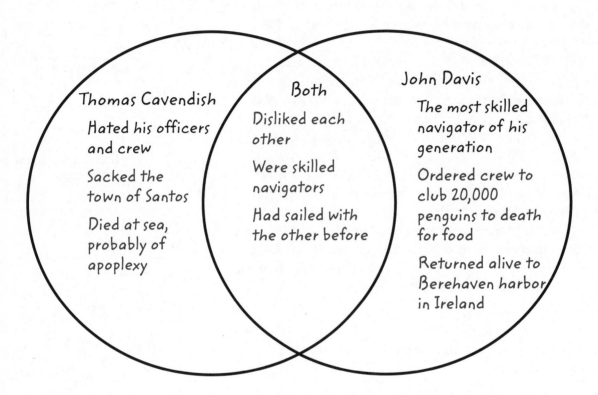

Thomas Cavendish

Hated his officers and crew

Sacked the town of Santos

Died at sea, probably of apoplexy

Both

Disliked each other

Were skilled navigators

Had sailed with the other before

John Davis

The most skilled navigator of his generation

Ordered crew to club 20,000 penguins to death for food

Returned alive to Berehaven harbor in Ireland

Active Reading Focus

Responding to Characters We can respond to characters in literature in the same way that we respond to people in real life. We can think about their behavior and words and decide whether or not we like them or dislike them. In a brief paragraph, explain your response to the character of John Davis. As you write, consider these questions: Do you approve of his actions? Do you admire his skills? Do you have sympathy for him?

Most students will approve of John Davis's actions. They may admire John Davis for his skill as a navigator. They may express sympathy for him, as someone who had a lot of bad luck. They may also sympathize with Davis for the terrible position Thomas Cavendish put him in.

Reading Strategy

Evaluating Historical Influences An account of John Davis's voyage, "The Southern Voyage of John Davis," was included in a book on exploration published in 1600. How do you think that account may have influenced Coleridge to write *The Rime of the Ancient Mariner?* Write a short paragraph in which you discuss this possible historical influence on Coleridge's poem.

Students should see how Coleridge may have been

influenced by details of Davis's voyage, such as the

killing of birds, the bad weather, the voyage to the

South Seas, the rotting ship, the lack of fresh water

or good food, and the toll the voyage took on

Davis's men.

Literary Element

Atmosphere How do the setting and the weather affect the atmosphere of this excerpt from *In Patagonia?* Give examples to support your answer.

Students should note that the setting and the weather

contribute to an atmosphere of scariness, depression,

and despair. Examples to support their answers may

include: problems caused by the storm; devastating

cold; the rotting ship; the heat that led to the rotting

and stench.

Vocabulary Practice

Using Word Origins Word origins, or *etymology,* reflect the history and development of words. Use the clues to the word origins to determine the correct word from the choices.

1. This word comes from the name of the Greek goddess of vengeance or just punishment.
    (a) skirmish
    (b) nemesis

2. This word comes from a Medieval Latin word for a skin disease.
    (a) mutiny
    (b) scurvy

3. This word comes from an Old English word, *fodor,* which means "fodder" (food for animals).
    (a) forage
    (c) skirmish

4. This word's origins include an Italian word, *schermire,* meaning "to fight."
    (a) forage
    (b) skirmish

1. (b) nemesis

2. (b) scurvy

3. (a) forage

4. (b) skirmish

Literary History: The Byronic Hero (p. 848)

Preview

- How is a Byronic hero different from a traditional hero?

- In what ways is this archetype still in literature and movies?

This article discusses a remarkable character in literature—the Byronic hero. The Byronic hero is the archetype of the moody, unhappy hero—the opposite of a traditional hero. This archetype appears in a range of literature, music, and movies, and is part of our literary history.

As you read the article, use the Cornell Note Taking System to record important points and to remember what you have read.

Reduce

TO THE POINT *Note key words and phrases. For example:*

cantos

"Childe Harold's

Pilgrimage"

Byronic hero

Record

➡ *Briefly note the details about George Gordon, Lord Byron. One detail has been listed for you.*

died young, at 36

led a bold, daring, sensual life

became famous overnight in 1812 for "Childe Harold's

Pilgrimage"

Characteristics of the Byronic Hero

➡ *Run-in heads are boldfaced headings that run on the same line as information, and introduce specific topics within a section. List the run-in heads that organize this section. Under each, note the key traits and influences that describe the Byronic hero. The first head and a key trait have been written for you.*

Rebellious

rejects society's laws, conventions, and morality

models: Melmoth the Wanderer and Napoleon

Alienated

hates society and the upper class

outcast or outlaw who believes in democracy

Gloomy

darkly handsome man with mysterious past

Bold

arrogant, confident, effective leader

Dangerous

self-destructive but charming; appealing to women

Literary History: The Byronic Hero *(p. 849)*

Reduce

ANY QUESTIONS? *Ask questions as you read, and use them to organize your notes. Then answer them when you reread your notes.*

_____

_____

_____

_____

Record

The Legacy of the Byronic Hero

➡ *How has Byron the person and the Byronic hero influenced art, literature, and culture? Organize this information into the classification chart below. The chart has been started for you.*

Lifestyle and Travel	Russian poet Alexander Pushkin: had himself painted the way Byron dressed. Many artists: traveled to Europe, the Middle East, and North Africa, copying Byron's travels.
Painting	French painter Eugène Delacroix: based many works on Byron's poems.
Music	Berlioz, Schumann, and Tchaikovsky: composed ballets and symphonies based on Byronic heroes.
Novels	Many 19th-century novels: have brooding characters similar to the Byronic hero: —Mr. Rochester in Charlotte Brontë's <u>Jane Eyre</u> —Heathcliff in Emily Brontë's <u>Wuthering Heights</u>
Popular Culture	Harlequin romances comic books detective stories
Movies	"Spaghetti westerns": Clint Eastwood, outlaw but does the right thing James Dean in <u>Rebel Without a Cause</u>— loner, sad

Literary History: The Byronic Hero

Summarize

➡ *Review your notes on this article. Then write a brief essay explaining the Byronic hero. Write your summary as a letter, to a friend who has been cast in a school play as a "rebellious, mysterious outsider." You friend wants to learn as much as he can about the tradition and development of this type of character in literature, music, movies, and pop culture. Your goal is to provide information to help him learn all about the Byronic hero.*

Students' responses should cover at least some of the characteristics of the

Byronic hero, such as the confident leader or the self-destructive wanderer. Students

should write about this type of hero's influence on different forms of expression—from

Mr. Rochester in *Jane Eyre* to James Dean. They might also identify key inspirations

for this character, and the beliefs associated with this archetype—such as Napoleon's

rise to power and the belief in democracy instead of privilege.

Literary History: The Byronic Hero

Apply

Multiple Choice

Circle the letter of the best choice for the following questions.

1. Who was George Gordon, Lord Byron? C
   A. a pirate
   B. a French revolutionary
   C. a famous Romantic poet
   D. two famous Romantic poets

2. What is *not* a quality of the Byronic hero? C
   A. gloomy
   B. confident
   C. generous
   D. rebellious

3. What did the Byronic hero think of the privileged upper class? C
   A. they wanted to be in that class
   B. they believed in society based on wealth and rank
   C. they rejected the notion that upper class should have advantages based on rank and wealth
   D. they had no opinions on the upper class

4. Where was Byron's influence *most* felt? C
   A. in the movies
   B. in ballets
   C. in literature
   D. in classical music

Matching

Write the letter(s) of the choice in the second column that best matches each item in the first column.

5. adapted the Byronic hero to music
   _____ C, E

6. key poem with a Byronic hero
   _____ B

7. character in a novel with the qualities of a Byronic hero _____ F

8. a main character in Byron's poetry
   _____ G

9. movie actor who plays Byronic-type characters in westerns _____ D

10. name of ballet based on Byronic hero
    _____ A
    A. "Corsair Overture"
    B. "Childe Harold's Pilgrimage"
    C. Hector Berlioz
    D. Clint Eastwood
    E. Peter Ilich Tchaikovsky
    F. Mr. Rochester
    G. Manfred

How can you better remember and understand the material in this Literary History? *Recite* your notes, *Reflect* on them, and *Review* them. You can also use your notes as to reconsider the selections by Byron, particularly *Childe Harold's Pilgrimage.* Your notes will also prove useful for literature you read that has a character based on this archetype.

Introductory Text: The Victorian Age 1837–1901

Looking Ahead (p. 907)

Preview

- What were Victorian values?

- How were Victorian social change and literary realism connected?

- What caused the decline of Victorian optimism?

This introduction prepares you for the literature you will read in a unit of your textbook. It explains the historical, social, and cultural forces of the Victorian age. It explains how Britain led much of the world politically and culturally during this period. The introduction includes information about the period and about its literature.

As you read the introduction, use the Cornell Note Taking System to record important points and to remember what you have read.

Reduce

TO THE POINT *Note key words and phrases. For example:*

social consciousness

Victorian optimism

_____

_____

Record

Looking Ahead

➡ *What historical and cultural forces shaped Victorian literature? One sample has been given.*

Britain became "workshop of the world"

quarter of world's people lived in the British Empire

social consciousness stirred reforms

_____

_____

_____

ANY QUESTIONS? *Write them now; answer them as you reread your notes. For example: "What is optimism?"*

_____

_____

_____

_____

Keep the following questions in mind as you read

➡ *What historical or cultural element is being asked about in each question? One sample has been given.*

changes in Britain and British Empire

Victorian optimism

mood of later Victorian writers

_____

_____

Introductory Text: The Victorian Age 1837–1901

Timeline *(pp. 908–909)*

Reduce

TO THE POINT *Note kinds of writing. For example:*

humor magazine

novel

children's book

poetry

science

dictionary

science fiction

ANY QUESTIONS? *Use them to organize your notes. For example: "What kind of reforms do the Chartists demand?"*

Record

British Literature

➡ *Which kinds of writing were being created during the Victorian Age? List kinds of writing and titles of publications. Two samples have been given.*

humor magazine—Punch

novel—Emily Brontë, Wuthering Heights

Other possible responses:

children's book—Lewis Carroll, Alice's Adventures in Wonderland

poetry—Matthew Arnold, New Poems

science—Charles Darwin, On the Origin of Species

dictionary—Oxford English Dictionary

horror fiction—Bram Stoker, Dracula

science fiction—H. G. Wells, The War of the Worlds

British Events

➡ *What are some general categories of British events? List one or more events in each category. Use wording that makes the event clear to you. Two samples have been given.*

Queen Victoria

political reform

Other possible categories might include science and technology, British Empire, disasters, war, exploration.

Introductory Text: The Victorian Age 1837–1901

Timeline *(pp. 908–909)*

Reduce

TO THE POINT *Note key words, phrases, and titles. For example:*

<u>Communist Manifesto</u>

<u>The Interpretation of</u>

<u>   Dreams</u>

<u>science</u>

<u>inventions</u>

Record

World Events

➡ *What are the general categories of world events? List one or two events in each category. Use wording that makes the event clear to you. Two samples have been given.*

<u>technology</u>

<u>revolution</u>

Other possible categories might include science, reform, war, colonies, rulers, art, and awards.

Recap

➡ *Review your notes on the Timeline. Then recap by creating a specific timeline of entries connecting to one of the major features of the Victorian age such as Queen Victoria, political reform, or technology. A sample major feature and two entries have been given.*

<u>Queen Victoria</u>

1837—Victoria is crowned queen

1840—Queen Victoria marries Prince Albert

Other possible responses:

1861—Prince Albert dies

1876—Queen Victoria is proclaimed Empress of India

1897—Queen Victoria celebrates her Diamond Jubilee

1901—Queen Victoria dies; Edward VII becomes king

Introductory Text: The Victorian Age 1837–1901

By the Numbers *(p. 910)*

Reduce

TO THE POINT *Note key words and phrases for the heads on this page. For example:*

Great Exhibition of
the Works of Industry
of All Nations
compulsory education
life-size models
iron frame
Crystal Palace

Record

Growth in the British Electorate, 1832–1884

➡ *Summarize the information on this graph.* Possible response: A series of reform bills greatly increased the number of male voters during the Victorian age .

The Great Exhibition of 1851

➡ *What are the main ideas? The first has been listed for you.*
The Great Exhibition was the first world's fair.

Possible responses:
The huge Crystal Palace was a prefabricated building of iron and glass.
Millions of people attended the Great Exhibition, and it made a large profit.

Introductory Text: The Victorian Age 1837–1901

By the Numbers *(p. 910)*

Reduce

TO THE POINT *Note key words and phrases for the heads on this page.*

convicts

candles

education

mortality

compulsory

Record

➥ *List the remaining heads on this page. For each, note what the statistics tell you about the period. One has been listed for you.*

Settling Australia

Many of Australia's first settlers were British convicts.

Possible responses:

Home Lighting

Candles and oil lamps needed constant attention in Victorian homes.

Child Mortality

Child mortality was very high.

Servants

Servants were common in many middle class Victorian homes.

Education

Compulsory education increased people's ability to write.

Hunting

Hunting was a major pastime for the Victorian upper class

Introductory Text: The Victorian Age 1837–1901

Being There *(p. 911)*

Reduce

ANY QUESTIONS? *Ask questions about illustrations.*

_____

_____

_____

_____

_____

TO THE POINT *Note key words and phrases. For example:*

"the Jewel in the

Crown"

annexation

British Empire

African colonies

Record

➡ *Illustrations are part of the information in this introduction. What do these illustrations show about life in the British Empire in the Victorian age?* Possible response:

The British colonized the Caribbean; British emigrants

were often sad to leave home; the British built a

railway system in India.

_____

_____

➡ *What were some world regions with many British colonies?* Possible response:

the Caribbean, Africa, Southeast Asia

_____

_____

_____

Recap

➡ *Review your notes on By the Numbers and Being There. Then recap by using the information to draw several conclusions about Britain or the British Empire in the Victorian age. One has been listed for you.*

The success of the Great Exhibition started the trend for world's

fairs.

Students' conclusions might relate to political reform,

Australia, home life, children, servants, education, and the

upper class.

_____

_____

Introductory Text: The Victorian Age 1837–1901

Historical, Social, and Cultural Forces (*p. 912*)

Reduce

TO THE POINT *Note key words and phrases. For example:*

Queen Victoria

technological advances

Karl Marx

Charles Darwin

empire

Record

Queen Victoria and Her Empire

➡ *What are the main ideas?* Possible response:

Queen Victoria played a major symbolic role in unifying Britain's widespread colonies.

Britain began to settle Australia in 1788.

Britain was a major player in the scramble to colonize Africa.

Britain consolidated and expanded its rule in India.

Technological Advances

➡ *Use a chart to organize this information.* Possible responses:

Advances	Results
• faster trains and steamships	• better transportation
• cast iron and elevators	• taller buildings
• telegraphs and telephones	• quicker communication
• aniline dyes	• brighter clothing
• electric light	• safer streets
• vaccines and pasteurization	• improved health
• canned food	• more varied diet
• photographs	• memories preserved

Marxism and Darwinism

➡ *What problem did many Victorians see? How did Karl Marx address this problem?* Possible response:

Victorian material progress was not matched by social progress.

Karl Marx wrote <u>Das Kapital</u> ("Capital").

He believed class warfare was inevitable.

He believed all property and the means of production should be held in common.

Introductory Text: The Victorian Age 1837–1901

Historical, Social, and Cultural Forces *(p. 913)*

Reduce

TO THE POINT *Note key words and phrases.*

Blue Books

Social Darwinism

"the survival of the fittest"

evolution

On the Origin of Species

Record

Marxism and Darwinism (continued)

➡ *Use a chart to organize the information about Charles Darwin and Social Darwinism.* Possible responses:

Charles Darwin	Social Darwinism
• He published <u>On the Origin of Species by Means of Natural Selection</u> in 1859. • He developed his ideas on an expedition to gather biological specimens. • All living organisms are governed by the same natural laws. • Evolution is controlled by blind chance; there is no agent behind the changes and no intended goal.	• Late 19th-century interpreters of Darwin claimed evolution implied progress. • Biological notions of "survival of the fittest" justified the power of the rich. • Darwin was not involved in Social Darwinism and didn't apply his theories to social policy.

Introductory Text: The Victorian Age 1837–1901

Historical, Social, and Cultural Forces (p. 913)

Reduce

TO THE POINT *Note key words and phrases. For example:*

Realism

Naturalism

empire

advances

technology

Record

Preview Big Ideas of the Victorian Age

➡ *Restate each of the Big Ideas to make them easier to remember.* Possible responses:

The British Empire, wealth, improved technology, and social reforms made Victorian Britain and its literature optimistic.

Realism was a reaction to Romanticism that explored contemporary life and ordinary experience. Victorian realist writers wanted to reform society.

Naturalism developed from Realism and tried to present life very accurately. Naturalists were often very pessimistic and believed that life was predetermined and had no meaning.

Recap

➡ *Review your notes on the Historical, Social, and Cultural Forces. Then recap using summary notes to help you remember the main points.* Possible response:

Topic: The Victorian Age

Main Points:

Queen Victoria played a major symbolic role in unifying Britain's widespread colonies.

Britain settled Australia, colonized Africa, and expanded its rule in India.

Technological advances improved Victorian life, but were not matched by social progress.

Karl Marx believed class warfare was inevitable.

Marx believed all property and the means of production should be held in common.

Charles Darwin believed evolution is controlled by blind chance; there is no agent behind the changes and no intended goal.

Social Darwinists claimed evolution implied progress and "survival of the fittest" justified the power of the rich.

Introductory Text: The Victorian Age 1837–1901

Big Idea 1: Optimism and the Belief in Progress *(p. 914)*

Reduce

TO THE POINT *Note key words and phrases.*

self-improvement

moral earnestness

value of hard work

thrift

patience

Record

Victorian Values

➡ *What is the main idea? What are some supporting details? One has been listed.* Possible responses:

Main idea

Victorians valued self-improvement, moral earnestness, and value of work.

Supporting details

Samuel Smiles's Self-Help preached gospel of thrift, hard work, and patience.

Moral earnestness defined work of poet laureate Tennyson.

The Middle-Class Public

➡ *Complete this sentence: For the Victorian middle-class, reading . . .*
was a major way of self-improvement.

The Expansion of Democracy

➡ *How did the British electorate change during the Victorian Age?*
Possible response:
Reform bills expanded the electorate to include middle-class men and working-class men.

Imperialism

➡ *What are the main ideas? One has been listed.* Possible response:
Britain gained its empire more through commercial expansion than military conquest.
British colonial rule did not aim at centralized control.
British institutions offered some inclusion and mobility to colonials.
Victorians believed the British Empire was bringing the colonial subjects the benefits of western civilization.

Introductory Text: The Victorian Age 1837–1901

Big Idea 1: Optimism and the Belief in Progress *(p. 915)*

Reduce

TO THE POINT *Note key words and phrases. For example:*

Band of the Immortals

Bodyguard of the

Empire of Mankind

"All true Work is

sacred"

"Complain not"

Record

from *Past and Present* by Thomas Carlyle

➡ *Write down some phrases that show Victorian values. One has been listed.* Possible response:

"All true Work is sacred"

"Labor, wide as the earth, has its true summit in

Heaven."

"Complain not."

Recap

➡ *Review your notes on Big Idea 1: Optimism and the Belief in Progress. Then recap using a web to help you remember the main points.* Responses will vary.

self-improvement, moral earnestness, and hard work

increase in electorate and social mobility

Victorian Values

middle-class— reading for self-improvement

empire seen as benefiting colonial subjects

Introductory Text: The Victorian Age 1837–1901

Big Idea 2: The Emergence of Realism *(p. 916)*

Reduce

TO THE POINT *Note key words and phrases.*

free-market policy

reform

socially realistic novels

Adam Smith

Utilitarianism

Record

The Road to Wealth

➡ *What was Adam Smith's free-market idea? What is Utilitarianism?* Possible responses:

Adam Smith argued that individuals free to pursue economic self-interest without government interference produce a wealthier nation.

Utilitarianism is the view that the ethical value of an activity is measured by the extent of its usefulness.

Voices of Reform

➡ *Note examples of Victorian reform. One has been listed.*

Carlyle inspired writers and reformers such as Karl Marx and Charles Dickens.

Possible responses:

Doctors, ministers, journalists, and private philanthropists formed charitable organizations.

Reformers within Parliament issued Blue Book reports to educate the middle class about the poor.

The Novel and the Condition of England

➡ *What are the characteristics of Victorian novels about the "Condition of England"?*

Possible responses:

set in factory towns

Characters are working-class mill-hands, clerks, seamstresses, or lower-class, such as paupers.

Plots include riots among workers and meetings to discuss working conditions.

Introductory Text: The Victorian Age 1837–1901

Big Idea 2: The Emergence of Realism (p. 917)

Reduce

TO THE POINT *Note key words and phrases.*

square

emphasis

facts

dictatorial teacher

Record

from *Hard Times* by Charles Dickens

➡ *How does the speaker's insistence on facts reflect the ideas of Utilitarianism?* Possible response:

The speaker feels that nothing else will ever be of any use to a child but facts. This reflects the idea of Utilitarianism that the value of an activity is measured by its usefulness.

Recap

➡ *Review your notes on Big Idea 2: The Emergence of Realism. Then recap using a chart to help you organize the forces for and against reform in Victorian Britain. One sample has been listed.* Possible responses:

Forces Against Reform	Forces for Reform
• free-market policy • Utilitarianism • Social Darwinism	• writers and reformers such as Carlyle, Karl Marx, and Charles Dickens • charitable organizations • reformers in Parliament • writers who wrote realistic novels about the "Condition of England"

Introductory Text: The Victorian Age 1837–1901

Big Idea 3: Disillusionment and Darker Visions *(p. 918)*

Reduce

TO THE POINT *Note key words and phrases.*

Naturalism: grim view
of the world
Decadent literature:
embraced life's
futility pessimism

Record

Pessimism and Naturalism

➡ *What are the main ideas? One has been listed.* Possible responses:
Writers such as Thomas Carlyle and John Ruskin
questioned Victorian concerns with technology and
money.
New writers were influenced by Darwinism to look for
inevitable natural forces guiding human life.
French writer Émile Zola wrote novels according to a
set of beliefs called Naturalism.
Naturalistic literature presents a grim, fatalistic view
of working-class characters trapped in circumstances
beyond their control.
Even writers who did not identify with Naturalism,
such as Thomas Hardy, shared its somber realization
of life's randomness.

Decadent Literature

➡ *Ask yourself questions about this information; then answer them.
One question and answer has been written for you.* Possible responses:
Q: What does <u>decadence</u> mean?
A: to "decline" or "decay."
Q: When did Decadent literature appear?
A: at the close of the 19th century
Q: What was it a reaction to?
A: the prevailing optimism of the Victorian age
Q: What were the characteristics of Decadent writers?
A: They rejected the idea that works of art had to
   serve any useful purpose; disdained and despised the
   consolations of religion and bourgeois life; and
   embraced life's futility through extremes of style.

Introductory Text: The Victorian Age 1837–1901

Big Idea 3: Disillusionment and Darker Visions (p. 919)

Reduce

TO THE POINT *Note key words and phrases.*

"I did not will a grave
Should end thy
pilgrimage to-day"
Thomas Hardy

Record

"The Subalterns" by Thomas Hardy

➥ *How does Hardy's poem express the views of Naturalism?*

Possible response:

It presents human beings as the helpless victims of
natural forces.

Recap

➥ *Review your notes on Big Idea 3: Disillusionment and Darker Visions.*
Then recap using a web to help you remember the main points about Naturalism.
Responses will vary.

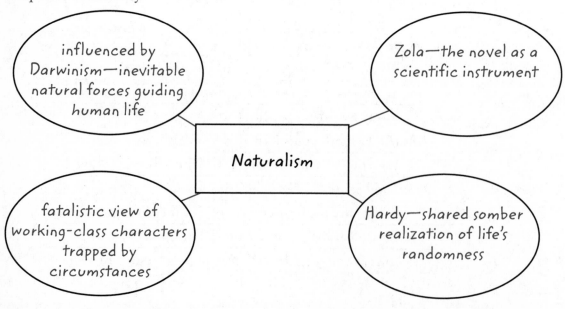

influenced by
Darwinism—inevitable
natural forces guiding
human life

Zola—the novel as a
scientific instrument

Naturalism

fatalistic view of
working-class characters
trapped by
circumstances

Hardy—shared somber
realization of life's
randomness

Introductory Text: The Victorian Age 1837–1901

Wrap-Up *(p. 920)*

Reduce

TO THE POINT *Note key words and phrases.*

material goods

social reform

uneasy faith

_____

_____

MY VIEW *Which of these cultural links do you find the most interesting?*

_____

_____

_____

_____

Record

Why It Matters

➡ *What is the main idea of each paragraph?*

paragraph 1—Victorian problems and solutions still affect us. Victorian city planning and appetite for material goods are still around.

paragraph 2—Education, social reform, democratization, government's role, and Darwinism are still issues.

paragraph 3—Victorian faith and doubt about progress remain.

Cultural Links

➡ *What link is described in each paragragh?*

paragraph 1—Gerard Manley Hopkins and modern literature

paragraph 2—Victorian novels and modern retellings

paragraph 3—Lewis Carroll and modern English and literature

Recap

➡ *Review your notes on the Wrap-Up. Then recap by writing a paragraph in which you explain which of the Victorian traits and issues mentioned you feel is most in evidence today.*

Students' paragraphs should have a clearly expressed topic sentence, well-organized supporting sentences drawn from their notes, and an effective conclusion.

_____

_____

Introductory Text: The Victorian Age 1837–1901

Summarize

➥ *Review your notes on this introduction. Then recap by making several generalizations about the events of this period. A sample generalization has been given.*

The Victorian concern with self-improvement is reflected in compulsory education, the Great Exhibition, and middle-class reading habits.

Students' generalizations might be based on information drawn from any part of the introduction.

Introductory Text: The Victorian Age 1837–1901

Apply

Multiple Choice

Circle the letters of the best choice(s) for the following questions.

1. What did the Victorians value? B, C, D
   A. fatalism
   B. value of work
   C. self-improvement
   D. moral earnestness

2. Which of the following does *not* describe Naturalism? D
   A. influenced by Darwinism
   B. reaction against Victorian optimism
   C. characters trapped by circumstances
   D. rejected idea that art has a useful purpose

3. Which of the following made Victorian society more democratic? C
   A. Victorian individualism
   B. British imperialism
   C. reform bills that expanded electorate
   D. commercial expansion

4. Utilitarianism is the view that the value of an activity is measured by its _____. C
   A. factualness
   B. uselessness
   C. usefulness
   D. emphasis

Matching

Write the letters of the choice in the second column that best matches each item in the first column.

5. symbolically unified the British empire _____ B

6. wrote *Self-Help* _____ D

7. shared Naturalism's realization of life's randomness _____ F

8. wrote *Das Kapital* _____ E

9. wrote about the Victorians' value of work _____ C

10. wrote novels in a socially realistic way _____ A
    A. Charles Dickens
    B. Queen Victoria
    C. Thomas Carlyle
    D. Samuel Smiles
    E. Karl Marx
    F. Thomas Hardy

How can you better remember and understand the material in this introduction? *Recite* your notes, *Reflect* on them, and *Review* them. You can also use your notes for a quick review of the historical period or the Big Ideas of this unit. As you learn more about the ideas in the unit, add to your notes.

JABBERWOCKY

Building Background

In *Jabberwocky*, poet and novelist Wanda Coleman describes her experiences as a young person during the 1950s and 1960s in South Central Los Angeles. The selection is from her collection of essays *First Loves*. Coleman describes her childhood love of literature and her frustration at not being able to find positive representations of African Americans in books. She also tells how Lewis Carroll's famous poem "Jabberwocky" gave her a metaphor for her own experiences as an African American, during a period of intense racial discrimination.

Setting Purposes for Reading

As soon as a child learns to read, a whole new world opens up. With a classmate, discuss the following questions:

- What was the first book you read that you found really exciting?
- What effect did that book—and others like it—have on your awareness of the world and your place in it?

Read to discover how reading a literary classic influences a future writer.

| Reading Strategy | **Analyzing Literary Influences**

Analyzing literary influences involves examining the ways that literary works affect writers.

| Active Reading Focus | **Connecting to Personal Experience**

When you **connect to personal experience,** you find connections between what you are reading and what you have experienced or observed in your own life. As you read, stop to ask yourself if you have had experiences like those the author is describing.

| Literary Element | Memoir

A **memoir** is a kind of narrative nonfiction that presents the story of a period in the writer's life. It is usually written from the first-person point of view and emphasizes the narrator's own experience of this period.

Big Idea Optimism and the Belief in Progress

The Victorian Era, with its military and economic successes, encouraged optimism and the ideals of hard work, self-improvement, and moral earnestness.

Vocabulary

Read the definitions of these words from "Jabberwocky." The dictionary definition of a word is its **denotation.** As you read the selection, use the word's denotation and its context to help figure out its **connotation,** or suggested meaning. A word's connotation can be positive, negative, or neutral.

glowered (glou´ərd) *intr. v.* looked or stared at with anger; p. 161 *Reggie glowered at Emil when he arrived late to the rehearsal.*

onerous (on´ər əs) *adj.* unpleasant, unwanted; difficult to bear; p. 161 *Tara's summer school classes forced her to keep an onerous schedule.*

enclaves (en´klāvz) *n.* small areas where minority groups live surrounded by another culture; p. 162 *Amit searched for an apartment in the Indian enclaves of Philadelphia, where he could feel more at home.*

engrossing (en grō´sing) *adj.* engaging a person's full attention; fascinating, gripping; p. 162 *The fisherman's engrossing story about the great white shark kept everyone spellbound.*

belated (bi lā´tid) *adj.* too late, tardy; p. 162 *Corey missed his cousin's party, but to make up for it, he sent her a belated birthday card.*

Jabberwocky
By Wanda Coleman

The stultifying[1] intellectual loneliness of my Watts upbringing was dictated by my looks—dark skin and unconkable kinky hair. Being **glowered** at was a constant state of being. The eyes of adults and children alike immediately informed me that some unpleasant *ugliness* had entered their sphere and spoiled their pleasure because of its close and **onerous** proximity. I recall one such moment very strongly: a white man was standing in front of me at such an angle that I was momentarily uncertain what he was frowning at. I turned to look behind me and saw nothing.

I have come to mark such moments—as they have recurred throughout my life—as indicative of the significance of physical likeness, beyond the issue of physical beauty: of the importance of "mirror image" (a phrase that recurs in one form or another in my poetry); in the ongoing dialogue of race, as I've struggled to grasp and respond to what others *assume* when their eyes are directed at or on me. I find the shifts in visual context as infuriating now as they were in childhood. The act of wading through stereotypes, in order to become clearly visible in the larger society, corresponds exactly to that moment when Lewis Carroll's Alice steps through that looking glass.

Incapable of imagining my world, removed from it by gender and race as well as by time and place, Lewis Carroll had nevertheless provided me with a means (and an attitude) with which to assess, evaluate, and interpret my own journey through this bizarre actuality of late-twentieth-century America, where nothing is ever as it seems. I was a *Negro* child—yet this book, and its poem "Jabberwocky," served singularly to buoy my self-esteem, constantly under assault by my Black peers, family members, and the world outside.

I found the rejection unbearable and—encouraged by my parents to read—sought an escape in books, which were usually hard to come by. In the South Central Los Angeles of the 1950s and 1960s, there were only three Black-owned bookstores, and I would not discover them until early adulthood. In my childhood there was no Harlem Renaissance, no Black arts movement; I did not encounter the poems of Paul Laurence Dunbar and James Weldon

---

1. *Stultifying* means "negating" or "dulling."

Active Reading Focus

Connecting to Personal Experience When you **connect to personal experience**, you recall similar events in your own life. Describe a time you experienced the disapproval of someone you did not know. How did it make you feel?

Students' answers will vary. Make sure they describe a time they experienced the disapproval of someone they did not know.

Reading Strategy

Analyzing Literary Influences Recall that when you **analyze literary influences**, you examine the ways that literary works affect writers. Based on what you have read so far, how do you think Lewis Carroll's work helped the author cope with her problems? Search the text around the passage to find information.

Students should recognize that Coleman treated literature as a "buoy" and as a method of escape. They should also realize that the slaying of the Jabberwocky could be interpreted as a metaphor for Coleman's attempts to overcome racial discrimination.

Vocabulary

glowered (glou′ ərd) *intr. v.* looked or stared at with anger

onerous (on′ ər əs) *adj.* unpleasant, unwanted; difficult to bear

Memoir A **memoir** often reveals the impact of significant events in the writer's life. Based on this passage, what can you conclude was most important to Wanda Coleman when she was young?

Students should conclude that

access to literature was most

important to her.

Vocabulary

Denotation and Connotation A *tome* is "a large thick scholarly book." Do you think the connotation of this word is positive, negative, or neutral?

➥ Underline the words and phrases that give the connotation of *tomes*. The connotation of this word is

positive. Students should

underline the phrase *immediately*

enthralled.

Big Idea

Optimism and the Belief in Progress How does Coleman's use of the word *nourishing* contribute to the feeling of optimism in this sentence?

Students should realize that

nourishing has a positive connotation

and implies an optimistic future, as

well as progress.

Vocabulary

enclaves (en′klāvz) *n.* small areas where minority groups live surrounded by another culture

engrossing (en grō′sing) *adj.* engaging a person's full attention; fascinating, gripping

belated (bi lā′tid) *adj.* too late, tardy

Johnson[2] except at church socials and in the early 1960s, during Negro History "week" celebrations. There were no images of Black children *of any age* in the American literature I encountered. The sole exception was "Little Black Sambo," whom I immediately rejected upon finding the book on my desk in the first grade—along with equally boring books featuring Dick, Jane, and Spot. There was no way in which I could "identify" with these strange images of children. I was born and raised in the white world of Southern California; it gave birth to me, but excluded me. Even the postwar Watts of the poet Arna Bontemps,[3] and the South Central Los Angeles that would riot in 1965, were predominantly working-class white neighborhoods with small Black **enclaves**.

Whenever my father visited public libraries, he allowed me to roam the stacks. This was my Wonderland. I was immediately enthralled with the forbidden world of adult literature, hidden away in leather-bound **tomes** I was neither able to reach nor allowed to touch. I hungered to enter, and my appetite had no limits. I plowed through Papa's dull issues of *National Geographic* and Mama's tepid copies of *Reader's Digest* and *Family Circle* in desperation, starved. At age ten I consumed the household copy of the complete works of Shakespeare. Although the violence was striking, and *Hamlet* **engrossing** (particularly Ophelia), I was too immature to appreciate the Bard until frequent rereadings in my mid-teens.

On Christmas, thereabouts, I received Johanna Spyri's[4] *Heidi* as a well-intended gift. I had exhausted our teensy library, and my father's collections of *Knight* and *Esquire*. . . . Between my raids on the adults-only stuff, there was nothing but *Heidi*, reread in desperation until I could quote chunks of the text, mentally squeezing it for what I imagined to be hidden underneath. One early spring day, my adult cousin Rubyline came by the house with a nourishing **belated** Christmas gift: an illustrated collection of *Alice's Adventures in Wonderland* and *Through the Looking-Glass*. (She also gave me my first *Roget's*—which I still use—on my twelfth birthday in 1958.) In love with poetry since kindergarten, my "uffish" vows were startlingly renewed. I promptly retired *Heidi* and steeped myself in Alice to an iambic spazz.

---

2. *Paul Lawrence Dunbar* (1872–1906) was an African American poet and novelist. *James Weldon Johnson* (1871–1938) was an African American poet and leading member of the National Association for the Advancement of Colored People.
3. *Arna Bontemps* (1902–1973) was an African American novelist, historian, and poet.
4. *Johanna Spyri* (1829–1901) was a Swiss writer.

In the real world I was an outsider, but in the stories and poems of Carroll I *belonged*. Why? Perhaps because when he freed Alice in the mirror, he also freed my imagination and permitted me to imagine myself living in an adventure, sans[5] the constraints of a racist society. If a drink or a slice of cake could transform her, alter her shape and size, the next leap for me was the most illogically logical of all: *Why not a transformation of her skin color?* In my frequent rereadings of Alice, I rewrote her as me.

"Jabberwocky" was and remains one of only a dozen poems I've ever loved enough to memorize. It heads the very long list of my favorite childhood poems, along with Poe's "Raven," Service's "Cremation of Sam McGee," Byron's "Prisoner of Chillon," Coleridge's "Rime of the Ancient Mariner," Henley's "Invictus," and E. A. Robinson's "Richard Cory."[6] To the astute reader, Carroll's lasting influence on my poetry is easily discerned. Many have referred to "Jabberwocky" as nonsense, but in my Los Angeles childhood, it made absolutely one hundred percent perfect sense. And within the context of Los Angeles today, that "nonsense" is dangerously and exhilaratingly profound.

---

5. *Sans* is a French word that means "without."
6. Edgar Allan *Poe* (1809–1849) was an American poet and fiction writer; Robert *Service* (1874–1958) was a Canadian poet; Lord *Byron* (1788–1824) and Samuel Taylor *Coleridge* (1772–1834) were British Romantic poets; William Ernest *Henley* (1849–1903) was a British critic and poet; and Edwin Arlington *Robinson* (1869–1935) was an American poet.

Graphic Organizer

A **cause-effect organizer** can help you understand the relationship between effects and their causes. The boxes to the left are causes. The box to the right contains an effect of those causes. Complete the organizer by filling in the remaining boxes. If you prefer, construct a Foldable™ to display the information.

Active Reading Focus

Connecting to Personal Experience Recall that when you **connect to personal experience**, you find connections between what you are reading and what you have experienced or observed in your own life. In a brief paragraph, describe the feelings and experiences that you share with Wanda Coleman.

Students' answers will vary. Make sure students

describe the similarities between their feelings and

experiences and those of Wanda Coleman.

Cause
As a result of racism, Coleman felt like an outsider.

Cause
Coleman could not find images of African Americans in literature.

Effect
Coleman reads "Jabberwocky" and has an exhilarating, transformative experience.

Cause
Coleman was disappointed in the literature available to her. She found it dull, tepid, or too difficult.

Cause
Coleman receives "Jabberwocky" as a belated Christmas present.

Reading Strategy

Analyzing Literary Influences How was the author's experience reading Lewis Carroll's works different from her earlier reading experiences? Write a short paragraph that includes references to the other authors she read.

Students should recognize that Coleman's earlier

experiences reading various magazines, Shakespeare's

plays, and *Heidi* were boring, frustrating, and

disappointing. She found Lewis Carroll enthralling.

Literary Element

Memoir Recall that a **memoir** is a kind of narrative nonfiction that presents the story of a period in the writer's life. How do you know that this piece can be described as a memoir? Give examples to support your answer.

Students should note that the piece is written in the

first person and tells of personal experiences that were

significant in the writer's life. Check to make sure

students give examples to support their answers.

Vocabulary Practice

Using Connotation and Denotation Recall that the **denotation** of a word is its dictionary definition. Its **connotation** is its suggested meaning, or the feelings, ideas, and attitudes associated with it. Choose the connotation of each word based on its context in the sentence.

1. "The eyes of adults and children alike informed me that some unpleasant *ugliness* had entered their sphere . . . because of its close and **onerous** proximity."
   - (a) positive
   - (b) negative
   - (c) neutral

2. "Although the violence was striking, and *Hamlet* **engrossing** . . . I was too immature to appreciate the Bard until frequent rereadings in my mid-teens."
   - (a) positive
   - (b) negative
   - (c) neutral

3. "One early spring day, my adult cousin Rubyline came by the house with a nourishing **belated** Christmas gift. . . ."
   - (a) positive
   - (b) negative
   - (c) neutral

1. (b) negative

2. (c) neutral

3. (a) positive

Literary History: The Age of the Novel (p. 964)

(p. 964)

Preview

- What factors caused an increase in the novel's popularity?

- What are social-problem novels?

- What are Regionalist novels?

This article presents a literary history of the factors that led to the increasing popularity of the novel in nineteenth-century England. It examines some of the main types of Victorian novels. It will help you better understand the novel excerpts you will read in your textbook.

As you read the article, use the Cornell Note Taking System to record important points and to remember what you have read.

Reduce

ANY QUESTIONS? *Use them to organize your notes. For example: "What is the difference between a 'triple decker' novel and a serial novel?"*

_____
_____
_____
_____
_____
_____
_____
_____

TO THE POINT *Note key words and phrases.*

Charles Dickens
social-problem novels
Elizabeth Gaskell
"Condition of England"
novels

Record

➡ *List the social factors that encouraged the rise of the novel. One has been listed for you.*

literacy rates in England's growing middle class rose, increasing readership and creating new markets for literature

the emergence of libraries

Charles Edward Mudie's "triple-decker" novels

innovations in publishing such as literary magazines and serial novels

new literary genres

Social-Problem Novels

➡ *How did social-problem novels trigger reform throughout England?*

Social-problem novelists opposed blind optimism and presented a realistic account of the negative effects of the Industrial Revolution. Novels such as Charles Dickens's <u>Oliver Twist</u> and Elizabeth Gaskell's <u>Mary Barton</u> revealed the poverty and exploitation of the working class in order to raise public consciousness and trigger social reform.

Literary History: The Age of the Novel (p. 965)

Reduce

TO THE POINT *Note key words and phrases.*

dialect

landmarks

social values

regionalist novels

Thomas Hardy

Charlotte Brontë

Emily Brontë

Record

Regionalist Novels

➡️ *Complete the web below with characteristics of Regionalist Novels. The web has been started for you.*

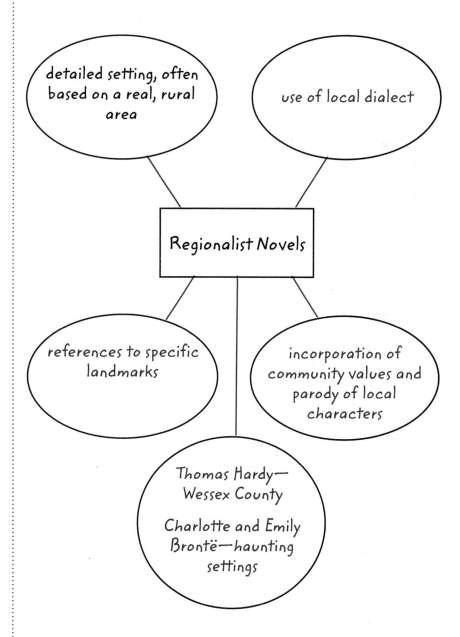

detailed setting, often based on a real, rural area

use of local dialect

Regionalist Novels

references to specific landmarks

incorporation of community values and parody of local characters

Thomas Hardy—Wessex County

Charlotte and Emily Brontë—haunting settings

Literary History: The Age of the Novel

Summarize

➥   *Review your notes on this article. Then complete the web below to describe The Age of the Novel. The chart has been started for you.*

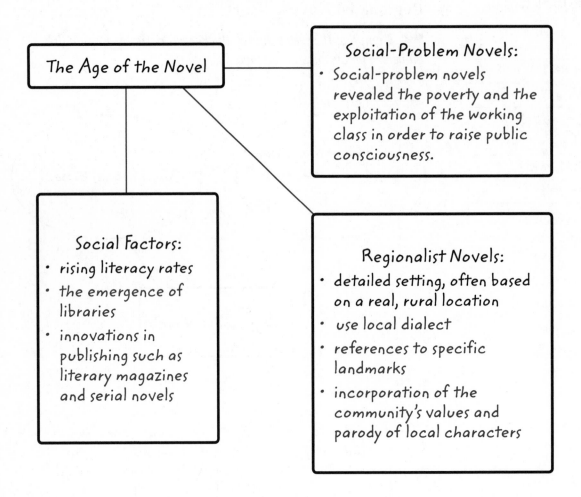

The Age of the Novel

Social-Problem Novels:
- Social-problem novels revealed the poverty and the exploitation of the working class in order to raise public consciousness.

Social Factors:
- rising literacy rates
- the emergence of libraries
- innovations in publishing such as literary magazines and serial novels

Regionalist Novels:
- detailed setting, often based on a real, rural location
- use local dialect
- references to specific landmarks
- incorporation of the community's values and parody of local characters

Literary History: The Age of the Novel

Apply

Multiple Choice

Circle the letter(s) of the best choice(s) for the following questions.

1. _____ did *not* propel the novel to the forefront of the literary world. B
   A. Rising literary rates
   B. "Anxiety of influence"
   C. Emergence of subscription libraries
   D. Innovations in the publishing industry

2. Which of the following were new genres explored by novelists of this period? B, C, D
   A. gothic novel
   B. sporting novel
   C. social-problem novel
   D. comic novel

3. Social-problem novelists opposed _____. C
   A. uses of local dialect
   B. parodies of local characters
   C. blind optimism in progress
   D. inexpensive literary magazines

4. Which of the following were *not* writers of Regionalist fiction? B, D
   A. Charlotte Brontë
   B. Jane Austen
   C. Thomas Hardy
   D. Charles Edward Mudie

Matching

Write the letter of the choice in the second column that best matches each item in the first column.

5. created so subscription libraries could charge readers for each volume _____ B

6. establishment that charged customers a fee to borrow one book at a time _____ F

7. invented the "triple-decker" novel _____ E

8. innovation that published complete novels in short monthly installments _____ A

9. wrote social-problem novels _____ C

10. novels used a detailed, rural setting _____ D

   A. literary magazine
   B. "triple-decker" novel
   C. Charles Dickens
   D. Regionalist novels
   E. Charles Edward Mudie
   F. subscription library

How can you better remember and understand the material in this Literary History? *Recite* **your notes,** *Reflect* **on them, and** *Review* **them. You can also use your notes to help you read the fiction in this unit.**

Introductory Text: The Modern Age 1901–1950

Looking Ahead *(p. 1029)*

- What is Modernism?
- How did Modernist writers respond to the two world wars?
- How did Modernism affect English society and culture?

This introduction prepares you for the literature you will read in a unit of your textbook. It explains Modernism, a literary movement that developed during the first half of the twentieth century. This period includes both World War I and World War II. The introduction includes information about the period and about its literature.

As you read the introduction, use the Cornell Note Taking System to record important points and to remember what you have read.

Reduce

TO THE POINT *Note key words and phrases.*

class conflict, war,

economic depression,

demands for

independence

Record

Looking Ahead

class conflict

two world wars

global economic depression

colonial peoples demanding independence

Keep the following questions in mind as you read

➡ *Organize this information into a web.*

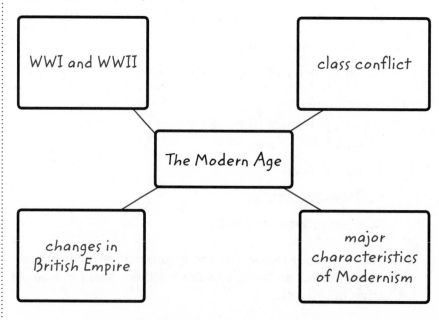

Introductory Text: The Modern Age 1901–1950

Timeline *(pp. 1030–1031)*

Reduce

TO THE POINT *Note key names, works, dates, and events.*

1913—<u>Pygmalion</u> produced

1920—Owen's <u>Collected Poems</u>

1922—Eliot's <u>The Wasteland</u>

Record

British Literature

➡ *Organize the information about Nobel Prize winners and their works. One sample has been done for you.*

Rudyard Kipling:

won the Nobel Prize in 1907

wrote <u>Kim</u>

George Bernard Shaw:

won the Nobel Prize in 1925

wrote <u>Pygmalion</u>

T. S. Eliot:

won the Nobel Prize in 1948

wrote "The Waste Land"

British Events

Possible notes:

<u>Monarchy and Government</u>

1901—Queen Victoria dies; Edward VII becomes king

1918—Women over 30 gain right to vote

1924—First Labour government formed

1936—George VI replaces Edward VIII as king

1940—Churchill becomes prime minister

<u>War and Catastrophe</u>

1902—Boer War ends

1912—Titanic sinks

1915—Germans sink <u>Lusitania</u>

1940—Battle of Britain begins

<u>Technology and Medicine</u>

1922—BBC begins radio broadcasts

1928—penicillin discovered

1946—National Health Service established

Introductory Text: The Modern Age 1901–1950

Timeline *(pp. 1030–1031)*

Timeline *(pp. 1030–1031)*

Reduce

ANY QUESTIONS? *Ask them now; answer them as you reread your notes. For example: "What conditions led to two world wars in this period?"*

_____

_____

_____

_____

_____

Record

World Events

➡ *What are the general categories of world events? List several events in each category. Use wording that makes the events clear to you.*

<u>Science and technology</u>

1903—Wright brothers' flight

1905—Einstein's theory of relativity

1914—Panama Canal

<u>World Wars</u>

1914—WWI begins

1917—United States enters WWI

1918—WWI ends

1933—Hitler becomes German chancellor

1939—WWII begins

1945—U.S. drops atomic bombs on Japan; WWII ends

Recap

➡ *Review your notes on the Timeline. Then use this classification chart to sum up the main ideas of this period.*

War	Science and Technology	Political Leaders and the Monarchy	Protest and Civil Rights
1902—Boer War ends	1928—penicillin	1901—Queen Victoria dies	1918—Women over 30 gain right to vote
1914—WWI begins	1946—National Health Service	1924 first Labour government	1926—general strike
1918—WWI ends	1903—Wright brothers' flight	1933 Hitler becomes German chancellor	1930—Gandhi leads Salt March
1939—WWII begins	1905—Einstein's theory of relativity	1940 Churchill becomes prime minister	
1945—U.S. drops atomic bombs; WWII ends	1914—Panama Canal		

Introductory Text: The Modern Age 1901–1950

By the Numbers *(p. 1032)*

Reduce

MY VIEW *What do you find most interesting or surprising about these statistics?*

_____

_____

_____

_____

Record

World War I Casualties

➡ *Summarize the information in this chart. Use compare-and-contrast statements. One sample has been done for you.*

The Allied Powers had more forces than the Central Powers.

Russia, France, and Austria-Hungary had high numbers of casualties compared with the other countries.

The Evacuation of Dunkirk

British and French forces joined forces during World War II.

Pandemic

A flu epidemic killed many people in 1918 and 1919. It actually killed more people than died in World War I.

Introductory Text: The Modern Age 1901–1950

By the Numbers *(p. 1032)*

Reduce

MY VIEW *What do you find most interesting about the information under these heads?*

_____

_____

_____

_____

➡ *List the remaining heads on this page. For each note, list what the statistics tell you about the period.*

<u>Sinking of the Titanic</u>

The <u>Titanic</u> sunk in 1912. More than half of the ship's passengers and crew died in the water.

<u>Packages from Home</u>

British troops received support from civilians at home.

<u>Vacation Time</u>

British workers who had paid vacation days increased more than five times during this period, largely because of a law.

<u>Class and Diet</u>

A middle-class family could afford much better food than a working-class family.

Introductory Text: The Modern Age 1901–1950

Being There *(p. 1033)*

Reduce

TO THE POINT *Note key words and phrases. For example:*

Western Front

Record

➡ *Summarize the key information provided by the map and the illustrations.*

There was terrible bomb damage in London in 1941.

There was still an upper-class social life in London during this period, in spite of the wars.

In World War I, many English troops fought on the Western Front in trenches that ran along much of France.

The Battle of Somme was fought in France.

Recap

➡ *Review your notes on By The Numbers and Being There. Then recap by making several generalizations about this period. One sample has been done for you.*

Students should mention the prevalence of war during this period.

Sample generalization:

World Wars I and II greatly affected people throughout Europe and took many lives.

There was also a terrible flu epidemic that killed more than twice as many people as WWI.

Introductory Text: The Modern Age 1901–1950

Historical, Social, and Cultural Forces (p. 1034)

ANY QUESTIONS? *Use them to organize your notes. For example: "How did the British Empire lose power?"*

_____

_____

_____

_____

The British Empire

➥ *What is the main idea and the supporting details?*

<u>Main idea</u>: The British Empire lost power after reaching its peak in the early 20th century.

<u>Supporting details</u>: Parts of Ireland became independent in 1922.

Indian and Pakistan became independent after WWII.

World War I

➥ *Group information related to World War I: causes of the war, sides in the war, methods of warfare, and effects of the war. One sample has been done.*

<u>Causes:</u> political crises and an arms race

<u>Sides:</u> Allied Powers—Britain, France, and Russia

Central Powers—Germany, Austria-Hungary, and Turkey

<u>Methods:</u> new tanks, machine guns, flamethrowers, poison gas

<u>Effects:</u> brought a violent end to an era of progress

The 1920s and the Great Depression

WWI hurt British industry. In the 1920s, Britain lost many markets to U.S. and Japan.

The 1929 stock market crash in the U.S. led to the financial ruin of thousands of British companies and millions of British people.

World War II

➥ *Take sequence notes on the period between the wars.*

<u>First:</u> Dictatorships rise due to postwar problems.

<u>Second:</u> Hitler and the Nazis gain power in Germany.

<u>Third:</u> Nazi Germany expanded by taking over other countries.

Introductory Text: The Modern Age 1901–1950

Historical, Social, and Cultural Forces *(p. 1035)*

Reduce

ANY QUESTIONS? *Use them to organize your notes: Ask Who, What, When, Where, Why, and How. Then briefly answer some or all of those questions.*

Record

World War II (continued)

➡ *What were the key characteristics of British and German warfare during World War II?*

<u>German warfare:</u>

Nazi forces attacked multiple countries in Europe.

The Luftwaffe bombed civilian targets nightly.

<u>British warfare:</u>

Prime Minister Winston Churchill gave speeches that showed British heroism.

British morale remained high even though German bombing was heavy.

Britain won the war when Germany and Japan surrendered in 1945.

Postwar Britain: New Priorities

➡ *What are the main ideas? Show them as cause-and-effect diagrams.*

Causes		Effects
The end of WWII left huge economic problems and bitter class conflict.	→	The Labour Party won the postwar election by promising economic reform.
The Labour Party passed legislation to help the unemployed, sick, and aged—including a national system of healthcare.	→	The cost of welfare meant that Britain couldn't afford the cost of being a world power.

Introductory Text: The Modern Age 1901–1950

Historical, Social, and Cultural Forces (p. 1035)

Reduce

ANY QUESTIONS? *Use them to organize your notes.*

_____

_____

_____

_____

Record

Preview Big Ideas of the Modern Age

Class, Colonialism, and the Great War—British writers responded to conflict between classes, resistance to colonialism, and the outbreak of World War I.

Modernism—After WWI, writers attempted to find meaning in new literary movement known as Modernism.

World War II and Its Aftermath—Dictatorships in the 1920s and 1930s led to WWII. Even though Britain and its Allies defeated the Axis powers, postwar Britain had to dismantle its colonial empire. This was a period of disillusionment that affected British writing.

Recap

➡ *Review your notes on the Historical, Social, and Cultural Forces. Then use a Venn diagram to recap the main ideas of Britain's involvement in World War I and World War II.*

WWI
- caused by political crises and arms race
- fought against Austria-Hungary and Turkey
- devastated the economic, social, and political order of Europe, which led to rise of Hitler

Both
- against Germany
- on side with France
- massive numbers of people killed
- caused economic problems and bitter class conflict
- led many people to question traditional values

WWII
- dictatorships
- Winston Churchill
- Hitler's Nazi forces
- German bombing of British cities
- end of war led to Labour Party victory and economic reform
- forced Britain to dismantle its empire

Introductory Text: The Modern Age 1901–1950

Big Idea 1: Class, Colonialism, and the Great War (p. 1036)

Reduce

ANY QUESTIONS? *Ask questions about heads. For example: "What were the causes of class conflict in Britain?"*

Record

Class Conflict

huge gap between the upper and lower classes—to the point that they lived in different worlds

labor unions form and agitate for economic change

Labour Party forms in 1900 to represent working class

Angry Young Men—writers who attacked British manners, snobbery, and hypocrisy

Women's Rights

➡ *Summarize the main ideas of the women's rights movement.*
Emmeline Pankhurst founded the Women and Social Political Union.

WSPU used stunts to call attention to demands— throwing eggs at government officials and smashing store windows.

Women over 30 were granted right to vote in 1918.

In 1928 the voting age for women was lowered to 21.

British Imperialism

➡ *Group information: writers supporting colonialism; writers criticizing imperialism.*
<u>Kipling:</u> for colonialism—wrote "Take up the White Man's burden"

<u>Orwell:</u> against imperialism—witnessed abuse of colonial power that left him "with an intolerable sense of guilt"

The Great War

WWI known as the Great War because it was unprecedented

Western Front—chief area of combat, hundreds of miles of trenches across northern France

Battle of the Somme, 1916—more than 400,000 British deaths

Introductory Text: The Modern Age 1901–1950

Big Idea 1: Class, Colonialism, and the Great War (p. 1037)

Reduce	Record

Reduce

TO THE POINT *Note key words and phrases from the excerpt. For example:*

<u>detached</u>

<u>youth departed</u>

<u>deeper darkness</u>

Record

from *Testament of Youth*

➡ *How does Brittain say she felt at the end of the war?*
Brittain feels "detached" from others. She realizes all the life and youthful spirit that were lost because of the war would never return. She doesn't express happiness that the war is finally over; instead she expresses deep sadness over the people she had loved who died in the war.

Recap

➡ *Review your notes on Big Idea 1: Class, Colonialism, and the Great War. Then organize the information about the key topics using this classification chart.*

Class Conflict	Women's Rights	Imperialism	The Great War
Class conflict was a problem for years in Britain. Trade unions, the Labour party, and writers loudly criticized it.	Women gained the right to vote in 1918 after years of bold protesting.	Some writers thought Britain had a duty to colonize weaker countries. Others felt guilty because they believed Britain abused its colonial power.	WWI was an unprecedented war. Many, like Vera Brittain, couldn't feel happiness when it ended because so many young people had died.

Introductory Text: The Modern Age 1901–1950

Big Idea 2: Modernism *(p. 1038)*

Reduce

TO THE POINT *Note key words, phrases, and people.*

art influenced
    literature
stream of
    consciousness
new subjects

Record

➡ *Summarize the definition in the opening paragraph.*

Modernism—a literary and artistic movement from the early 1900s to the 1940s that emerged just before and after WWI

Groundbreaking Ideas

New ideas in science—biology, psychology, and physics—influenced Modernism.

Darwin—theory of evolution

Freud—role of the unconscious in human personality

Einstein—theory of relativity: space, time, and energy

Modern Art

➡ *Organize this information in a chart.*

Cubism	Surrealism
Georges Braque Pablo Picasso angular, geometric, fragmented shapes different sides of the same subject	Freud's theories—role of subconscious and dreams in human behavior René Magritte and Salvador Dali—dreamlike images Salvador Dalí—"The Persistence of Memory" (melting watches)

Modernist Literature

➡ *Group information: styles, themes, subjects, and key works*

Styles: several perspectives, free verse, stream of consciousness

Themes: alienation, despair, disillusionment

Subjects: anything goes

Key works: T. S. Eliot's poem "The Waste Land", James Joyce's experimental novel Ulysses

Introductory Text: The Modern Age 1901–1950

Big Idea 2: Modernism (p. 1039)

MY VIEW *Indicate what you find most interesting, surprising, or confusing about this excerpt.*

_____

_____

_____

_____

Record

from *Ulysses*

➡ *A headnote—text that explains something that follows—can help you understand difficult sections. How does the headnote before the excerpt by James Joyce help you point out its Modernist qualities? Which passages in the excerpt most stimulate your curiosity?*

The speaker expresses his thoughts and feelings as they happen. This is more like the way people actually think.

His interior monologue includes many quick, short sentences that break the rules of grammar. Joyce is expressing something in a new, interesting way rather than in polished sentences.

I wonder what he means about "Purse" and "Potato," and by the "tepid paper stuck." Maybe he is describing Bloom finding his library card.

Recap

➡ *Review your notes on Big Idea 2: Modernism. Then create an outline to recap the main ideas.*

I. Influence of Science	II. Influence of Modern Art	III. Characteristics of Modernism
A. Darwin—theory of evolution B. Freud—dreams and unconscious C. Einstein—theory of relativity: space, time, and energy	A. Cubism Braque and Picasso: angular, geometric, fragmented shapes different sides of same subject B. Surrealism Magritte and Dalí influenced by Freud's theories about the role of subconscious and dreams in human behavior	A. <u>Styles:</u> several perspectives, free verse, stream of consciousness B. <u>Themes:</u> alienation, despair, and disillusionment C. <u>Subjects:</u> anything can be the subject of literature D. <u>Key works:</u> T. S. Eliot's poem "The Waste Land" James Joyce's experimental novel <u>Ulysses</u>

Introductory Text: The Modern Age 1901–1950

Big Idea 3: World War II and Its Aftermath *(p. 1040)*

Wartime Britain

 Display quotes—quotes set in large type apart from the rest of the text—provide important information. What conclusions can you draw from the quote by Churchill?

Churchill encouraged the British by saying they had a

great opportunity to stand up against ruthless dictators.

 Take sequence notes on the progression from World War II to the Cold War. Here is a start.

First—early WWII France falls in 1940 and only Britain left standing in Europe to stop the Nazi's takeover of Europe.
Second—mid WWII Nazis began massive bombing campaign; British remain defiant under Churchill's leadership and the RAF defends Britain.
Third—end of WWII By end of 1941 the United States and the Soviet Union join Britain—the Allies defeat Germany and Japan in 1945.
Fourth—Cold War Americans and Soviets become rivals and the Cold War begins. Both nations have atomic weapons; many are worried after seeing the effects of the atomic bombs dropped by the U.S. on Japan in WWII.

Postwar Britain

slow economic recovery after WWI—Britain bankrupt

India and Pakistan become independent in 1947

Ceylon (Sri Lanka), Burma (Myanmar), and Palestine

(Israel) also become independent

Labour party welfare reforms—National Insurance

Act and National Health Service Act (1946)

Introductory Text: The Modern Age 1901–1950

Big Idea 3: World War II and Its Aftermath *(p. 1041)*

Reduce

TO THE POINT *Note key words, phrases, and ideas.*

disorganization

public shelters

Record

from *George Orwell's Wartime Diary*

➡ *List key words and phrases from the excerpt that capture Orwell's main idea. Then paraphrase them in a sentence.*

"wear one out and turn life into a constant scramble to catch up lost time" — The bombing campaign made people exhausted.

"little groups of disconsolate-looking people wandering about with suitcases and bundles" — Unexploded bombs caused a hazard for many people in South London.

"grousing bitterly about the hardness of the seats and the longness of the night, but no defeatist talk." — People were uncomfortable but no one despaired

---

Recap

➡ *Review your notes on Big Idea 3: World War II and Its Aftermath. Then create a storyboard to recap your understanding. Write a short summary in each panel to summarize the key ideas and events. Then create a descriptive title below the summary. Here is a start.*

1. Wartime Britain	2. Emergence of Cold War	3. Postwar Britain
France is defeated in 1940 and Britain must save Europe from the Nazis. Churchill encourages the British and the RAF fights back while the Nazis begin a massive bombing campaign. People are forced to live in shelters though they refuse to feel defeated. By the end of 1941 the U.S. and the Soviet Union join Britain—the Allies defeat Germany and Japan in 1945.	After World War II the Americans and Soviets become rivals. A Cold War begins because both nations possess the threat of nuclear weapons. Many people become worried of global annihilation after seeing the effects of the atomic bombs dropped by the U.S. on Japan in WWII.	Britain bankrupt after the war and recovery is slow. Food and coal have to be rationed. Colonies India and Pakistan became independent in 1947—others follow. This is a blow to British pride and is the end of the empire. The Labour party makes important welfare reforms following WWII.
Title: Backs Against the Wall	Title: Nuclear Fear	Title: Challenge of Recovery

Introductory Text: The Modern Age 1901–1950

Wrap-Up *(p. 1042)*

Reduce

TO THE POINT *Note key words and phrases. For example:*

cultural watershed

_____

_____

_____

_____

_____

_____

Record

Why It Matters

WWI was a cultural watershed

many young men died, many haunted by the Western Front

loss of innocence

Modernism: familiar objects made exotic

T. S. Eliot and James Joyce create new literature classics

reality defined by patterns of myth and flow of subconscious mind

Cultural Links

➡ *What links are described here?*

Joyce's "Finnegans Wake"—word "quark" for subatomic particle

Woolf's A Room of One's Own—feminism and the idea that women artists need independence

George Orwell—"newspeak" (misleading language) and "Orwellian" (totalitarian government)

Churchill—used "iron curtain" to describe Soviet Union control

Recap

➡ *Review your notes on the Wrap-Up. Then write a brief paragraph to recap the significance of the events of this period and the innovations of Modernism.*

Students should mention the effects of World War I and World War II, the rise of women's rights, the criticism of totalitarian regimes, and the experimentation of form and theme associated with Modernism in their recap of the Modern Age's relevance.

Introductory Text: The Modern Age 1901–1950

Summarize

➡ *Review your notes on this introduction. Then organize the information about key influences on Modernist literature by using this classification chart. Sort information by topic and note how the influence of each is reflected in literature of the period. Here is a start.*

Category	Influence	Effect on Modern Literature
War	WWI was called the "Great War" because it was so unprecedented. Britain suffered from massive bombing attacks by the Nazis during World War II.	Writers shocked and disillusioned by the war and loss of life. Winston Churchill wrote influential speeches that encouraged the British to fight.
Class Conflict	Post-WWII economic problems and class conflict got even worse.	Writers such as the Angry Young Men criticized British snobbery.
Women's Rights	Emmeline Pankhurst's protest movement helped women over 30 gain the right to vote.	Writers such as Virginia Woolf gained attention in Modernism—Woolf says women artists need more independence.
Technology and Science	psychological theories of Freud about the power of dreams and the unconscious mind Einstein's theory of relativity and Darwin's theory of evolution	Writers used stream of consciousness technique to portray thoughts of characters Modernist writers inspired to write about anything in life.
Art	fragmented art of Picasso and Cubism Surrealist art—distortion of reality	Writers portrayed several perspectives at the same time. Writers experimented with free verse, stream of consciousness.
British Empire	Economic losses following WWII led to the end of the British empire.	Writers such as Kipling defended colonialism; writers such as Orwell argued imperialism led to abuse of power.

Introductory Text: The Modern Age 1901–1950

Apply

Multiple Choice

Circle the letter of the best choice for the following questions.

1. What led to World War I? A, D
   A. multiple political crises
   B. nuclear weapons
   C. Nazi attacks
   D. an arms race

2. What artists and scientists influenced Modernist writing? A, B, D
   A. Einstein
   B. Freud
   C. Shakespeare
   D. Dali

3. Which of the following *best* describes Modernist writers? C
   A. use of angular shapes
   B. interest in traditional forms
   C. use of free verse
   D. interest in colonialism

4. _____ were rivals during the Cold War. B
   A. Soviets and Germans
   B. Americans and Soviets
   C. Germans and British
   D. French and British

Matching

Write the letter of the choice in the second column that best matches each item in the first column.

5. attacked British snobbery and hypocrisy _____ E

6. encouraged British with heroic speeches _____ F

7. wrote *Ulysses* _____ B

8. inspired the feminist movement _____ A

9. main area of combat in WWI _____ D

10. Labor Party reform _____ C

   A. Virginia Woolf
   B. James Joyce
   C. National Health Service Act
   D. Western Front
   E. Angry Young Men
   F. Winston Churchill

How can you better remember and understand the material in this introduction? *Recite* your notes, *Reflect* on them, and *Review* them. You can also use your notes for a quick review of the historical period or the Big Ideas of this unit. As you learn more about the ideas in the unit, add to your notes.

Literary History: The Modern British Short Story

(pp. 1066–1067)

Preview

- What are the characteristics of the modern British short story?

- Who are the major writers in the genre?

- How did the British short story change in the twentieth century?

This article presents a literary history of the development of the modern British short story and the major writers of the genre. It will help you better understand the short stories you will read in your textbook.

As you read the article, use the Cornell Note Taking System to record important points and to remember what you have read.

Reduce

TO THE POINT *Note key words, phrases, and ideas. For example:*

around 1800, British
began to question
Victorian values and
conventions
historical continuity

ANY QUESTIONS? *Use them to organize your notes. For example:*

What was the main
criticism of the short
story in the late
1800s?

Record

➡ *Why was the novel more relevant than the short story in nineteenth-century England? Why did this change?*

The novel focused on society and historical continuity.
When society began to question Victorian values, the
form of the short story made more sense. As the
Victorian world fell apart, writers focused on the
individual and the present moment.

Toward Realism

➡ *What are some characteristics of the Realist writers mentioned in this section? One sample has been done for you.*

Thomas Hardy's short stories reflect a melancholy
attitude and a shift toward Realism. He also used
artificial Victorian language.
Rudyard Kipling stories focus on brief episodes and use
of literary "tricks."
Joseph Conrad united Realism and Romanticism by
using concrete, realistic details to suggest deeper
symbolic and philosophical meaning.

Literary History: The Modern British Short Story

(pp. 1066–1067)

Reduce

TO THE POINT *Note key words, phrases, and ideas. For example:*

short stories are
known for "slices of
life" that depend on
important moments

TO THE POINT *Note the boldfaced term.*

epiphany

TO THE POINT *Note key words and ideas.*

psychological and
moral struggle

Record

Modernism

➡ *How did the alienation between audience and writer lead to the development of Modernism? List key modernist writers who wrote short stories. One writer has been listed for you.*

During the 1890s, many modernist writers deliberately
opposed popular tastes and trends.

After the turn of the century, prevailing assumptions
about the individual, faith, history, materialism, and
knowledge shattered. Writers no longer saw reality as
a recognizable constant. Therefore, they began to
focus on the individual rather than society.

Key Modernist writers who wrote short stories:

Virginia Woolf

Katherine Mansfield

James Joyce

D. H. Lawrence

Mid-Twentieth-Century Style

Mid-twentieth century writers, such as Elizabeth
Bowen and Graham Greene, focused on the internal
psychological and moral struggles within characters.
However, these writers often linked their characters
to contemporary political and social settings.

Literary History: The Modern British Short Story

Summarize

➥   *Review your notes on this article. Then create a graphic organizer to summarize your notes.*

Students' graphic organizers should show the dominant trends and styles in Realism, Modernism, and mid-twentieth century writing. Possible organizers include classification notes or a web diagram.

Literary History: The Modern British Short Story

Apply

Multiple Choice

Circle the letter of the best choice for the following questions.

1. Why was the novel more popular in Victorian England than the short story? A, C, D
   A. the short story could not express a large amount of moral teaching
   B. there were fewer working authors
   C. Victorians focused on society and historical continuity
   D. the form of the short story did not make sense to a unified society

2. Which of the following Modernist writers united Realism and Romanticism? C
   A. Thomas Hardy
   B. H.E. Bates
   C. Joseph Conrad
   D. Virginia Woolf

3. What is *epiphany*? D
   A. concrete, realistic details
   B. an object in a story that stands for something else
   C. the mental consciousness of a character
   D. a revelation in which something commonplace is seen in new light

4. Which of the following is a *main* characteristic of mid-twentieth-century writers? B
   A. opposes popular tastes and trends
   B. focuses on moral struggles within characters
   C. tolerates "a weight of moral teaching"
   D. uses epiphany to close short stories

Matching

Write the letter of the choice in the second column that best matches each item in the first column.

5. stories reflected melancholy attitude and shift toward realism _____ D

6. broadened reading public in nineteenth-century England _____ F

7. focused on "slices of life" about important moments _____ B

8. every detail must contribute to overall meaning _____ A

9. suggested other writers "look within" _____ C

10. continued Modernist tradition in mid-twentieth century _____ E

   A. short story
   B. Modernism
   C. Virginia Woolf
   D. Thomas Hardy
   E. Graham Greene
   F. public literacy

How can you better remember and understand the material in this Literary History? *Recite* your notes, *Reflect* on them, and *Review* them. You can also use your notes to help you read the literature in this unit.

THE GREAT WAR AND MODERN MEMORY

Building Background

Paul Fussell was born in California in 1924. He fought as an infantryman in World War II. His experiences had a profound influence on his beliefs about war, its causes, and its relationship to literature and the arts. Fussell is well known for his works of historical and social criticism. He is also well known for his exploration of techniques in poetry. These works include *Poetic Meter and Poetic Form*. Fussell won a National Book Award for *The Great War and Modern Memory*. In the following excerpt, he describes the trenches that spanned the Western Front during World War I.

Setting Purposes for Reading

Writers often present war in a ridiculous light. In war, circumstances are not what they seem. The logic, or common sense, of the peacetime world does not apply. With a classmate discuss the following questions:

- How do people—both soldiers and civilians—respond to war?
- What do you imagine life was like in the trenches?

Read to learn about the experiences of soldiers and the trenches in which they lived and fought during World War I.

Reading Strategy | Synthesizing Information

To **synthesize** means to draw information from multiple sources in order to come to a conclusion.

Active Reading Focus | Recognizing Author's Purpose

An **author's purpose** is an author's aim in writing a literary work. Authors often write for one or a combination of the following reasons: to persuade, to inform, to explain, to entertain, or to describe. To **recognize author's purpose** pay attention to the **tone**, or the attitude that the author expresses toward his or her subject, as well as the **language**, **structure**, and **content** of the selection.

Literary Element | Description

Description is writing that creates a clear image of a feeling, an action, or a scene in the reader's mind. Good descriptive writing appeals to the senses through **imagery**. The use of **figurative language** makes a description more vivid. It helps to use precise verbs, nouns, adjectives, and adverbs.

Big Idea Class, Colonialism, and the Great War

During World War I, the main battlefield for British troops, known as the Western Front, stretched for hundreds of miles across northern France. The front was basically a series of muddy and dangerous trenches that were shelled daily. This was the first time trenches were used in warfare.

Vocabulary

Read the definitions of these words from *The Great War and Modern Memory*. When you come across an unfamiliar word, you can often break it down into parts—prefix, root, and suffix—for clues to its meaning.

wastage (wās′tij) *n.* something lost by wear, decay, or waste; p. 194 *Disease caused greater wastage of troops than battle during the war.*

repelling (ri pel′ing) *tr. v.* driving away or forcing back; p. 194 *Repelling the flames took every bit of the firefighters' strength.*

perpetually (pur pech′o͞o ə lē) *adv.* continuing without stop; constantly; p. 195 *The group of children playing on the playground were perpetually in motion.*

entanglements (en tang′gəl mənts) *n.* things that entangle; traps that catch a victim; p. 195 *A park ranger pointed out the spider web entanglements in the bushes that surrounded the campground.*

brainchild (brān′child) *n.* someone's original idea or invention; a product of creative thinking and work; p. 195 *A bicycle path that weaves through the city was the brainchild of the mayor.*

The Great War and Modern Memory
By Paul Fussell

Henri Barbusse[1] estimates that the French front alone contained about 6250 miles of trenches. Since the French occupied a little more than half the line, the total length of the numerous trenches occupied by the British must come to about 6000 miles. We thus find over 12,000 miles of trenches on the Allied side alone. When we add the trenches of the Central Powers, we arrive at a figure of about 25,000 miles, equal to a trench sufficient to circle the earth. Theoretically it would have been possible to walk from Belgium to Switzerland entirely below ground, but although the lines were "continuous," they were not entirely seamless: occasionally mere shell holes or fortified strong-points would serve as a connecting link. Not a few survivors have performed the heady imaginative exercise of envisioning the whole line at once. Stanley Casson is one who, imagining the whole line from his position on the ground, implicitly submits the whole preposterous conception to the criterion of the "normally" rational and intelligible. As he remembers, looking back from 1935,

> Our trenches stood on a faint slope, just overlooking German ground, with a vista of vague plainland below. Away to right and left stretched the great lines of defense as far as eye and imagination could stretch them. I used to wonder how long it would take for me to walk from the beaches of the North Sea to that curious end of all fighting against the Swiss boundary; to try to guess what each end looked like; to imagine what would happen if I passed a verbal message, in the manner of the parlor game, along to the next man on my right to be delivered to the end man of all up against the Alps. Would anything intelligible at all emerge?

Another imagination has contemplated a similar absurd transmission of sound all the way from north to south. Alexander Aitken[2] remembers the Germans opposite him celebrating some happy public event in early June, 1916, presumably either the (ambiguous) German success at the naval battle of Jutland (May 31–June 1) or the drowning of Lord Kitchener, lost on June 5 when the cruiser *Hampshire* struck a mine and sank off the

---

1. *Henri Barbusse* (1873–1935) was a French infantryman and novelist.
2. *Alexander Aitken* (1895–1967) was a soldier, war memoirist, and famed mathematician.

Active Reading Focus

Recognizing Author's Purpose
Recall that an **author's purpose** is an author's aim in writing a literary work. In this passage, Fussell writes specific details about the trenches. Why do you think he included this information? What does it suggest about his purpose for writing?

Most students will argue that this

information helps demonstrate the

size and the importance of the

trenches and World War I. Most will

argue that it suggests his purpose is to

persuade the reader of the absurdity

of both the trenches and the war.

Active Reading Focus

Recognizing Author's Purpose For what purpose might have Casson described this daydream? Based on what you have read so far, is his purpose for writing the same as Fussell's? Explain.

➥ Underline words or phrases that most suggest the author's purpose.

Most students will argue that Casson

is trying to describe his feelings of

confusion when he imagines the

length of the trenches. Most will

agree that their purposes are similar.

Many students will underline "curious

end of all fighting" and "try to guess

what each end looked like" and

"anything intelligible."

Big Idea

Class, Colonialism, and the Great War In what way does this story influence your perception of the war?

Students will likely claim that this story makes the war seem more absurd.

Reading Strategy

Synthesizing Recall that **synthesizing** means to draw information from multiple sources in order to come to a conclusion. How does Sassoon's statement in this passage compare and contrast with descriptions found in the works of the Trench Poets?

This grim opinion does seem to match the mood and tone of Wilfred Owen's work and Sassoon's own poetry. Rupert Brooke's poem seems less cynical.

✔ Reading Check

1. What event does Fussell mention that is "impossible to believe," but plausible "in this mad setting"?

He mentions the tin-canning and beating of shell-gongs that passed from one end of the German trenches to the other.

2. What did the British staff call those who were killed and wounded daily?

They referred to these people as *wastage*.

Vocabulary

wastage (wās′tij) *n.* something lost by wear, decay, or waste

repelling (ri pel′ing) *tr. v.* driving away or forcing back

Orkney Islands.[3] Aitken writes, "There had been a morning in early June when a tremendous tin-canning and beating of shell-gongs had begun in the north and run south down their lines to end, without doubt, at Belfort and Mulhausen[4] on the Swiss frontier." Impossible to believe, really, but in this mad setting, somehow plausible.

"When all is said and done," Sassoon[5] notes, "the war was mainly a matter of holes and ditches." And in these holes and ditches extending for ninety miles, continually, even in the quietest times, some 7000 British men and officers were killed and wounded daily, just as a matter of course. "**Wastage**," the Staff called it.

There were normally three lines of trenches. The front-line trench was anywhere from fifty yards or so to a mile from its enemy counterpart. Several hundred yards behind it was the support trench line. And several hundred yards behind that was the reserve line. There were three kinds of trenches: firing trenches, like these; communication trenches, running roughly perpendicular to the line and connecting the three lines; and "saps," shallower ditches thrust out into No Man's Land, providing access to forward observation posts, listening posts, grenade-throwing posts, and machine gun positions. The end of a sap was usually not manned all the time: night was the favorite time for going out. Coming up from the rear, one reached the trenches by following a communication trench sometimes a mile or more long. It often began in a town and gradually deepened. By the time pedestrians reached the reserve line, they were well below ground level.

A firing trench was supposed to be six to eight feet deep and four or five feet wide. On the enemy side a parapet[6] of earth or sandbags rose about two or three feet above the ground. A corresponding "parados"[7] a foot or so high was often found on top of the friendly side. Into the sides of trenches were dug one- or two-man holes ("funk-holes"), and there were deeper dugouts, reached by dirt stairs, for use as command posts and officers' quarters. On the enemy side of a trench was a fire-step two feet high on which the defenders were supposed to stand, firing and throwing grenades, when **repelling** attack. A well-built trench did not run straight for any distance: that would have been to invite

---

3. The *naval battle of Jutland*, which took place off the coast of Denmark, was the only major naval battle of the war. It ended without a decisive victor. *Lord Kitchener* (1850–1916) was a British field marshal and secretary of state for war. The *Orkney Islands* sit off the northeast coast of Scotland.
4. *Belfort*, the capital of the Territoire de Belfort in eastern France, was successfully defended by the allies during World War I. *Mulhausen* is an industrial town in northeastern France.
5. Siegfried *Sassoon* was one of the Trench Poets (see page 1093).
6. A *parapet* is a wall used to protect soldiers.
7. The *parados* was the side of the trench that faced away from the enemy.

enfilade[8] fire. Every few yards a good trench zig-zagged. It had frequent traverses designed to contain damage within a limited space. Moving along a trench thus involved a great deal of weaving and turning. The floor of a proper trench was covered with wooden duckboards, beneath which were sumps a few feet deep designed to collect water. The walls, perpetually crumbling, were supported by sandbags, corrugated iron, or bundles of sticks or rushes. Except at night and in half-light, there was of course no looking over the top except through periscopes, which could be purchased in the "Trench Requisites" section of the main London department stores. The few snipers on duty during the day observed No Man's Land through loopholes cut in sheets of armor plate.

The entanglements of barbed wire had to be positioned far enough out in front of the trench to keep the enemy from sneaking up to grenade-throwing distance. Interestingly, the two novelties that contributed most to the personal menace of the war could be said to be American inventions. Barbed wire had first appeared on the American frontier in the late nineteenth century for use in restraining animals. And the machine gun was the brainchild of Hiram Stevens Maxim (1840–1916), an American who, disillusioned with native patent law, established his Maxim Gun Company in England and began manufacturing his guns in 1889. He was finally knighted for his efforts. At first the British regard for barbed wire was on a par with Sir Douglas Haig's[9] understanding of the machine gun. In the autumn of 1914, the first wire Private Frank Richards saw emplaced before the British positions was a single strand of agricultural wire found in the vicinity. Only later did the manufactured article begin to arrive from England in sufficient quantity to create the thickets of mock-organic rusty brown that helped give a look of eternal autumn to the front.

The whole British line was numbered by sections, neatly, from right to left. A section, normally occupied by a company, was roughly 300 yards wide. One might be occupying front-line trench section 51; or support trench S 51, behind it; or reserve trench SS 51, behind both. But a less formal way of identifying sections of trench was by place or street names with a distinctly London flavor. *Piccadilly* was a favorite; popular also were *Regent Street* and *Strand*; junctions were *Hyde Park Corner* and *Marble Arch*. Directional and traffic control signs were everywhere in the trenches, giving the whole system the air of a parody modern city, although one literally "underground."

---

8. *Enfilade* is gunfire directed at a position from that position's flank.
9. *Sir Douglas Haig* (1861–1928) was a British field marshal and commander in chief of British forces in France.

Literary Element

Description Writing that creates a clear image of a feeling, an action, or a scene in the reader's mind is referred to as **description**. Why is this an effective use of description? Is this how you imagined the trenches? Explain.

This is an effective description because of its use of precise and vivid detail. Students' answers will vary. Many will say that this description does fit with how they imagined the trenches.

Active Reading Focus

Recognizing Author's Purpose Remember that to figure out an **author's purpose** it helps to pay attention to the use of **language**, **structure**, and **content**. What image does Fussell create of the trenches? What does this statement suggest to you about his purpose for writing this selection?

Students should understand that Fussell compares the trenches to a parody of an underground city. His purpose is to persuade his readers that the situation in the trenches was strange, absurd, and sad.

Vocabulary

perpetually (pur pech′ o͞o ə lē) *adv.* continuing without stop; constantly

entanglements (en tang′gəl mənts) *n.* things that entangle; traps that catch a victim

brainchild (brān′child) *n.* someone's original idea or invention; a product of creative thinking and work

AFTER YOU READ

(Graphic Organizer)

A **main idea organizer** can help you figure out and better understand the main idea and supporting details of a selection. Begin by filling in the top row with what you believe to be the main idea of this excerpt from *The Great War and Modern Memory*.

Then, add details from the selection that supports the main idea. Lastly, add the conclusion reached in the selection. If you prefer, construct a Foldable™ to display the information.

Main Idea:
The trenches of World War I were huge and confusing.

Supporting Details:

The length of the trenches is mind-boggling. When trying to imagine the whole line, people often come to absurd conclusions.

There were three lines of trenches, and three kinds of trenches; each kind of trench had its own design and purpose.

The trenches were like mazes, dangerous, uncomfortable, and always crumbling.

The trenches were like entire cities below ground; soldiers even named sections of the trench after London streets and places.

Conclusion:
The trenches were strange, dangerous, and unpleasant places from which to fight the war.

:::: Active Reading Focus :::: ## Recognizing Author's Purpose

An author may write for one or more of the following reasons: to persuade, to inform, to explain, to entertain, or to describe. In your opinion, what was Fussell's main purpose for writing this selection? Explain. What other purposes for writing might have Fussell had? Support your answer with evidence from the text.

Most students will argue that Fussell's main purpose for writing this selection was to describe the trenches. Fussell may have also been writing to persuade readers that World War I was absurd and terrible. Students might point to numerous examples of description throughout this selection to support their claim. They might also indicate Fussell's inclusion of the passage by Stanley Casson as evidence that he was trying to persuade readers.

Reading Strategy Synthesizing Information

Synthesize information from multiple sources cited within this selection. What conclusions can you draw about trench life based on these sources? Write a brief paragraph in which you explain your conclusions.

Students' answers will vary. Make sure that they depict

trench life in a way that is consistent with these

sources. Most will argue that trench life was

exceedingly unpleasant.

_____

_____

_____

_____

Literary Element Description

Locate a particularly effective example of description in this selection. What makes it effective? How does the description contribute to the main idea?

". . . the thickets of mock-organic rusty brown that

helped give a look of eternal autumn to the front." This

is an effective use of description because it uses a

precise and vivid image. Fussell's phrase "eternal

autumn" suggests a sad feeling, which supports his

underlying claim that World War I was terrible.

_____

_____

_____

_____

Vocabulary Practice

Understanding Word Parts Words are made up of different parts. There are three main word parts: *prefixes*, *roots*, and *suffixes*.

- A **root** is the most basic part of a word. For example, the word *myth* is the root of the word *mythology.*
- A **prefix** is a word part that can be added to the beginnings of other words. The prefix *re-* can mean "again." When added to the word *state*, the word becomes *restate* and means to "state again."
- A **suffix** is a word part that can be added to the ends of other words. The suffix *-ly*, for example, can be added to the ends of some words to turn them into adverbs. When *-ly* is added to the adjective *bold*, it becomes the adverb *boldly.*

Use your knowledge of word parts to answer the following questions.

1. Which of the following words has a suffix that can be used to form nouns?
   - (a) **wastage**
   - (b) **perpetually**
   - (c) **repelling**

2. Which of the following words has a prefix that implies a repetition?
   - (a) **brainchild**
   - (b) **repelling**
   - (c) **wastage**

3. Which of the following words has a suffix that can be used to form adverbs?
   - (a) **entanglements**
   - (b) **perpetually**
   - (c) **brainchild**

1. (a) wastage

2. (b) repelling

3. (b) perpetually

Introductory Text: An International Literature 1950–Present

Looking Ahead *(p. 1227)*

- What forces shaped contemporary British literature?

- How did the end of the British Empire affect literature in English?

- How has literature in English become part of global culture?

This introduction prepares you for the literature you will read in a unit of your textbook. It explains the historical, social, and cultural forces of the present period, during which the English language and literature in English have spread around the world. The introduction includes information about the period and about its literature.

As you read the introduction, use the Cornell Note Taking System to record important points and to remember what you have read.

Reduce

TO THE POINT *Note key words and phrases. For example:*

dismantled

declining status abroad

adjust to home rule

economy sputtered

outpouring of literature

Record

Looking Ahead

➡ *What historical and cultural forces are shaping literature in English today? One example has been listed for you.*

The British Empire was dismantled.

The British economy declined and Britain's class system no longer seemed secure.

Writers in Britain and its former colonies produced a great amount of literature.

Keep the following questions in mind as you read

➡ *What historical or cultural element is being asked about in each question? One element is listed.*

characteristics of contemporary British literature

collapse of the British Empire

English as a global language

Introductory Text: An International Literature 1950–Present

Timeline *(pp. 1228–1229)*

Reduce

TO THE POINT *Note kinds of events.*

Nobel prizes

theater openings

books published

Record

British Literature

➡ *What are some kinds of literary events during this period?*
Possible kinds of events might include theater openings
and Nobel prizes.

British Events

➡ *What are some general categories of British events? One has
been listed for you.*

Science

Other possible categories of events might include the
royal family, transportation, popular culture, politics,
war, and terrorism.

Introductory Text: An International Literature 1950–Present

Timeline *(pp. 1228–1229)*

Reduce

TO THE POINT *Note key words and phrases.*

exploration

wars

science discoveries

_____

_____

Record

World Events

➡ *What are the general categories of world events? One has been listed for you.*

Politics

Other possible categories might include exploration,

British Empire, technology, war, medicine, economics,

terrorism, and disasters.

_____

_____

Recap

➡ *Review your notes on the Timeline. Then recap by creating a specific timeline of entries that relate to one of the major features of the present period, such as terrorism or science.*

Terrorism

1988—Terrorists blow up an airline over Lockerbie, Scotland.

2001—Terrorist attacks destroy the World Trade Center in New
    York City.

2005—Terrorist bombings in London claim more than fifty lives.

Introductory Text: An International Literature 1950–Present

By the Numbers *(p. 1230)*

Reduce

TO THE POINT *For the heads on this page, note key words and phrases.*

North Sea oil

independence for

colonies

consumer spending

Americanized

Record

British Oil Production, 1975–2000

➡ *Summarize the information on this graph.* Possible response: British North Sea oil production peaked in the 1980s and 1990s and is declining.

End of Empire

➡ *What is the main idea of this list?* Possible response: Since World War II, a large number of former British colonies have become independent.

Introductory Text: An International Literature 1950–Present

By the Numbers *(p. 1230)*

Reduce

TO THE POINT *For the heads on this page, note key words and phrases.*

ethnic change

appliances

supermarkets

comprehensive schools

rapid inflation

English-global language

Record

➡ *List the remaining heads on this page. For each, note what the statistics tell you about the period. One has been listed for you.*

<u>Immigration</u>

Immigration is changing the ethnic make-up of
   Britain.

Possible responses:

<u>Consumer Spending</u>

In postwar Britain, more people own appliances and
   cars and shop in supermarkets.

<u>Education</u>

Today, Most British public schools admit children from
   all ability levels.

<u>Inflation</u>

Inflation was very high in postwar Britain.

<u>English Speakers</u>

English has become a global language.

Introductory Text: An International Literature 1950–Present

Being There *(p. 1231)*

Reduce

ANY QUESTIONS? *Ask questions about illustrations. For example: "What changes do these illustrations show about life in the former British Empire?"*

_____

_____

_____

_____

_____

Record

➡ *Illustrations are part of the information in this introduction. What do these illustrations show about life in Britain and the former British Empire today? One example is listed.*

Immigration has changed the ethnic make-up of
contemporary Britain.

Possible response:

City life in former British colonies mixes contemporary
and traditional cultures.

_____

_____

_____

Introductory Text: An International Literature 1950–Present

Being There *(p. 1231)*

Reduce

TO THE POINT *Note key words and phrases. For example:*

Commonwealth of

  Nations

Caribbean

Africa

Pacific

Record

➡ *What are some world regions with many Commonwealth nations?*

  Possible responses:
  the Caribbean, Africa, and Pacific islands

Recap

➡ *Review your notes on By the Numbers and Being There. Then recap by using the information to draw several conclusions about Britain or the former British Empire today. One sample conclusion has been listed for you.*

The independence of Ghana encouraged many other African nations to

  seek independence.

Other possible conclusions might relate to British oil production, the end of

the British Empire, immigration, consumer spending, education, inflation,

English as a global language, and the Commonwealth of Nations.

Introductory Text: An International Literature 1950–Present

Historical, Social, and Cultural Forces *(p. 1232)*

Reduce	Record

Reduce

TO THE POINT *Note key words and phrases.*

weak economy

welfare state

Northern Ireland

violence

IRA terrorists

Record

Domestic and Foreign Problems

➡ *What are the main ideas? One response has been listed for you.* Postwar Britain had serious economic problems.

Other possible responses:

To strengthen the economy, the Labour government established a welfare state that became a model for other European countries.

Violence broke out between Protestants and Catholics in Northern Ireland.

IRA terrorists carried out bombings in Britain.

Introductory Text: An International Literature 1950–Present

Historical, Social, and Cultural Forces *(p. 1232)*

Reduce	Record
TO THE POINT *Note key words and phrases.*	**End of the Empire**

TO THE POINT *Note key words and phrases.*

independence

overpopulation

capitalism or

   community ownership

apartheid

End of the Empire

Possible notes:

To save money, Britain agreed to its colonies' demands for home rule and dismantled its empire.

New nations in Asia and Africa faced problems of overpopulation, poverty, and ethnic and religious strife.

Some African leaders followed Western-style capitalism.

Others followed traditional African socialism based on community ownership rights.

Black South Africans struggled to end apartheid.

Introductory Text: An International Literature 1950–Present

Historical, Social, and Cultural Forces *(p. 1233)*

Reduce

TO THE POINT *Note key words and phrases.*

ties to Europe
NATO
EEC becomes European Union
free-trade zone

Record

Joining Europe

Possible notes:

After the loss of its colonial empire, Britain sought closer security and economic ties to Europe.

Security—Britain joined NATO (North Atlantic Treaty Organization) in 1949.

Economy—Britain joined EEC (European Economic Community) in 1973.

EEC became European Union in 1994.

Introductory Text: An International Literature 1950–Present

Historical, Social, and Cultural Forces *(pp. 1232–1233)*

Reduce

TO THE POINT *Note key words and phrases.*

cultural questioning

colonial literature

global language—
   multicultural

Record

Preview Big Ideas of an International Literature

Possible notes:

Postwar Britain questioned its cultural identity. In response, British writers reshaped traditional literary themes and forms.

In the postwar period, many of Britain's former colonies declared independence. Writers in these new nations brought new styles and subject matter to English literature.

The British Empire spread the English language around the world. As a result, contemporary literature in English has been enriched by writers from many different cultures.

Recap

➡ *Review your notes on the Historical, Social, and Cultural Forces. Then recap using summary notes to help you remember the main points.*

Topic: Britain Today

Main Points:

Possible responses:

Postwar Britain had serious economic problems.

Labour government established the welfare state.

Violence in Northern Ireland led to IRA bombings in Britain.

To save money, Britain dismantled its empire.

New nations in Asia and Africa faced problems of overpopulation, poverty, and ethnic and religious strife.

Black South Africans struggled to end apartheid.

Britain established security and economic ties to Europe.

Security—Britain joined NATO (North Atlantic Treaty Organization).

Economy—Britain joined EEC (European Economic Community); EEC later became European Union.

Introductory Text: An International Literature 1950–Present

Big Idea 1: Making and Remaking Traditions *(p. 1234)*

Reduce

ANY QUESTIONS? *Use them to organize your notes.*

_____

_____

_____

_____

_____

TO THE POINT *Note key words and phrases.*

economic decline

youth culture

literary

experimentation

"permissiveness" in

mass media

Record

An Identity Crisis

➡ *What contributed to the British identity crisis? One example has been listed for you.*
Loss of the empire symbolized British decline.

Other possible responses:
After WWII, economic recovery was very slow.
Persistent unemployment and high inflation were
problems. Today, terrorist threats are causing rising
security costs.

Shift in Values

➡ *What are the main ideas?* Possible responses:
Youth rebellion and permissiveness disturbed older
people. Long-established classes of society began to
break down.

Contemporary British Literature

Possible notes:
Poetry
Postwar British poets reexamined literary tradition.
Ted Hughes's poetry—beauty and brutality of nature
Prose (novelists)
Salman Rushdie's Midnight's Children—postmodern
    take on Indian history
Zadie Smith's White Teeth—postmodern narrative
    about immigrant communities in London
Kazuo Ishiguro's The Remains of the Day and Never
    Let Me Go—more straightforward narratives
Other novelists—J. M. Coetzee, Ian McEwen, Julian
Barnes

Introductory Text: An International Literature 1950–Present

Big Idea 1: Making and Remaking Traditions *(p. 1234–1235)*

Reduce

ANY QUESTIONS? *Use them to organize your notes. For example: "How does Hughes describe the thistles?"*

_____

_____

_____

_____

_____

Record

"Thistles" by Ted Hughes

➡ *What are some phrases or lines from this poem that show the qualities of Ted Hughes's poetry?* Possible responses:

"Thistles spike the summer air"

"a revengeful burst"

"a grasped fistful / Of splintered weapons"

"a plume of blood"

"Then they grow grey, like men."

"Stiff with weapons"

Recap

➡ *Review your notes on Big Idea 1: Making and Remaking Traditions. Then recap using a web to help you remember the main points. It has been started for you.* Possible responses:

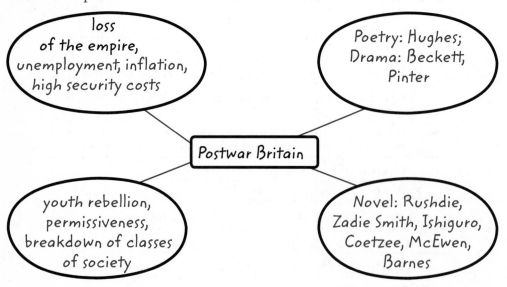

loss of the empire, unemployment, inflation, high security costs

Poetry: Hughes; Drama: Beckett, Pinter

Postwar Britain

youth rebellion, permissiveness, breakdown of classes of society

Novel: Rushdie, Zadie Smith, Ishiguro, Coetzee, McEwen, Barnes

Introductory Text: An International Literature 1950–Present

Big Idea 2: Colonialism and Postcolonialism (p. 1236)

Reduce

ANY QUESTIONS? *Use them to organize your notes.*

_____

_____

_____

_____

_____

TO THE POINT *Note key words and phrases.*

imperialism

exploitation and
    development

postcolonial struggles

native vs. colonial
    culture

Record

British Colonial Rule

➡ *How did Britain's "new imperialism" differ from earlier colonization? What good and bad sides did it have?* Possible responses:

less limited than earlier colonization; new imperialism
    aimed at control over vast territories

<u>Good side</u>

built railroads, telegraphs, schools, and hospitals

<u>Bad side</u>

based on economic exploitation, racist attitudes

devastating effect of colonialism and Christianity on
    traditional African way of life

Problems of Independence

➡ *What are the main ideas?* Possible responses:

Independence brought problems to former colonies.

When India and Pakistan became independent, millions
    died in violence between Hindus and Muslims.

New African nations had civil wars because colonial
    boundaries had not reflected ethnic diversity.

Non-whites in South Africa fought apartheid.

Postcolonial Literature Possible notes:

Achebe, Soyinka, Walcott, and Naipaul addressed
    problems of former British colonies.

deal with tension between native and colonial cultures

write in English because it is widely spoken

Introductory Text: An International Literature 1950–Present

Big Idea 2: Colonialism and Postcolonialism *(pp. 1236–1237)*

Reduce

ANY QUESTIONS? *Use them to organize your notes.*

_____

_____

_____

_____

_____

Record

"Homage to a Government" by Philip Larkin

➡ *What are some phrases or lines from this poem that show the good and bad sides of the "new imperialism"?*

Possible responses:

<u>Good side</u>

"Places they guard, or kept orderly."

<u>Bad side</u>

"The soldiers there only made trouble happen."

Recap

➡ *Review your notes on Big Idea 2: Colonialism and Postcolonialism. Then recap using a chart to help you remember the important points about colonialism and postcolonialism.* Possible responses:

Colonialism	Postcolonialism
• "new imperialism" aimed at control over vast territories	• violence between Hindus and Muslims after India and Pakistan became independent
• built railroads, telegraphs, schools, and hospitals	• civil warfare in new African nations
• based on economic exploitation	• apartheid in South Africa
• influenced by racist attitudes	• postcolonial literature—tension between native and colonial cultures
• devastating effect of colonialism and Christianity on traditional African way of life	• themes of identity, racism, and cultural dominance

Introductory Text: An International Literature 1950–Present

Big Idea 3: Globalization *(p. 1238)*

Reduce

TO THE POINT *Note key words and phrases.*

emigration and
migration
spread of English
Nobel prize to farmer
colony writers

Record

Movement of Peoples

➡ *What different movements are described here?*

Possible responses:

Emigrants left Britain to settle British colonies.

People moved within the British Empire in search of work.

Exporting English

➡ *Complete the following sentence: The growth of English as a global language was aided by . . .*

the British Empire and the emergence of the
United States as a superpower after World War II.

A Global Literature

Possible notes:

Spread of English language has given rise to
international literature in English.

Since WWII, Nobel laureates writing in English include
Patrick White from Australia, Nadine Gordimer and
J. M. Coetzee from South Africa, Wole Soyinka from
Nigeria, and Derek Walcott and V. S. Naipaul from the
Caribbean.

Introductory Text: An International Literature 1950–Present

Big Idea 3: Globalization (pp. 1238–1239)

Reduce

TO THE POINT *Note key words and phrases.*

colonialism

cultural identity

_____

_____

_____

Record

from *Midnight's Children* by Salman Rushdie

➡ *Note a line from this passage that shows the crossing of a boundary.* Possible response:

"at the precise moment of India's arrival at independence, I tumbled forth into the world."

_____

_____

_____

_____

Recap

➡ *Review your notes on Big Idea 3: Globalization. Then recap using summary notes to help you remember the main points.* Possible responses:

Topic: Globalization

Main Points:

Emigrants left Britain to settle British colonies.

People moved within the British Empire in search of work.

The growth of English as a global language was aided by the British Empire and the emergence of the United States as a superpower after World War II.

Spread of English language has given rise to international literature in English.

Since WWII, Nobel laureates writing in English come from around the globe.

Introductory Text: An International Literature 1950–Present

Wrap-Up *(p. 1240)*

Reduce

TO THE POINT *key words and phrases.*

global enriched

literature

postmodernism

innovation

MY VIEW *Which of these cultural links do you find the most interesting?*

_____

_____

_____

_____

Record

Why It Matters

➡ *What is the main idea of each paragraph?* Possible responses: paragraph 1—The spread of the English language has created a global audience for traditional British literature and given writers from around the world an opportunity to create modern classics in the English language.

paragraph 2—Postwar literature in Britain was influenced by postmodernism and British drama, which was the genre richest in innovation.

Cultural Links

➡ *What link is described in each paragragh?* Possible responses: paragraph 1—Seamus Heaney's translation of <u>Beowulf</u>

paragraph 2—Derek Walcott's <u>Omeros</u> and the Homeric epics

paragraph 2—V. S. Naipaul's <u>A Bend in the River</u> and Joseph Conrad's <u>Heart of Darkness</u>

Recap

➡ *Review your notes on the Wrap-Up. Then recap by creating a diagram to organize the information.*

Students' diagrams might include an outline, a web, or summary notes.

Introductory Text: An International Literature 1950–Present

Summarize

➥ *Review your notes on this introduction. Then recap by using a chart to organize information about contemporary British literature, postcolonial literature, and global literature in English.* Possible responses:

Contemporary British literature	Postcolonial literature	Global literature in English
• After WWII, British poets reexamined literary tradition. • Hughes's poetry—beauty and brutality of nature • Prose novelists—Salman Rushdie and Zadie Smith • other important novelists—Kazuo Ishiguro, J. M. Coetzee, Ian McEwen, and Julian Barnes • mid-1950s playwrights revolutionized British theater • Beckett's <u>Waiting for Godot</u>—classic of absurdist drama • Pinter's <u>The Caretaker</u> and <u>The Homecoming</u>—characters unable to communicate	• postcolonial writers—writers from former colonies • Achebe, Soyinka, Walcott, and Naipaul addressed problems of former British colonies. • They deal with tension between native and colonial cultures. • They address themes of identity, racism, and cultural dominance. • They write in English because it is widely spoken.	• Spread of English language has given rise to international literature in English. • Since WWII, Nobel laureates writing in English include global writers: Patrick White from Australia, Nadine Gordimer and J. M. Coetzee from South Africa, Wole Soyinka from Nigeria, and Derek Walcott and V. S. Naipaul from the Caribbean.

Introductory Text: An International Literature 1950–Present

Apply

Multiple Choice

Circle the letter of the best choices for the following questions.

1. What contributed to the postwar shift in British values? A, C
   A. breakdown of classes of society
   B. postmodernism
   C. youth rebellion and permissiveness
   D. inflation

2. Which of the following was *not* a result of Britain's "new imperialism"? B
   A. devastated African way of life
   B. violence in Northern Ireland
   C. building of railroads, schools, and hospitals
   D. total control of large territories

3. Which of the following does *not* describe postcolonial literature? B, C
   A. themes of racism and identity
   B. always written in native languages
   C. revolutionized British theater
   D. tension between native and colonial cultures

4. Which of the following contributed to English becoming a global language? B, D
   A. dismantling of colonialism
   B. emergence of U.S. as a superpower
   C. Britain's "identity crisis"
   D. spread of British Empire

Matching

Write the letter of the choice in the second column that best matches each item in the first column.

5. wrote about immigrants in London _____ F

6. wrote *Waiting for Godot* _____ A

7. created characters who were unable to communicate _____ D

8. wrote *The Remains of the Day* _____ E

9. wrote nature poetry combining beauty and brutality _____ B

10. wrote *Midnight's Children* _____ C

   A. Samuel Beckett
   B. Ted Hughes
   C. Salman Rushdie
   D. Harold Pinter
   E. Kazuo Ishiguro
   F. Zadie Smith

How can you better remember and understand the material in this introduction? *Recite* your notes, *Reflect* on them, and *Review* them. You can also use your notes for a quick review of the historical period or the Big Ideas of this unit. As you learn more about the ideas in the unit, add to your notes.

Literary History: British Drama—From the Drawing Room to the Kitchen Sink

(p. 1276)

Preview

- What are some characteristics of modern British drama?

- What is kitchen-sink drama?

- What is theater of the absurd?

This article presents a literary history of British drama during the late twentieth century. It was a period of revolutionary change and great creativity in British theater. This article will help you better understand the drama you will read in your textbook.

As you read the article, use the Cornell Note Taking System to record important points and to remember what you have read.

Reduce

TO THE POINT *Note key words and phrases.*

rationing

meaningless jobs

slow recovery

working-class dramas

_____

ANY QUESTIONS? *Write questions as you take notes.*

_____
_____
_____
_____
_____
_____

Record

➡ *What conditions following World War I influenced British theater? One example has been listed for you.*

wartime rationing of clothing, gasoline, and food
    caused frustration in England
college educations failed to lead to meaningful jobs
desire for social change intensified by slow postwar
    recovery

Kitchen-Sink Drama

➡ *Why are the plays mentioned in this section considered kitchen-sink dramas?*

<u>Look Back in Anger</u> by John Osborne featured a
    realistic setting that represented working-class life.
The main character is also angry with British society.
This led to the term "Angry Young Men."
<u>A Taste of Honey</u> by Shelagh Delaney presented the
experiences of a working-class girl struggling with
single motherhood.

Literary History: British Drama—From the Drawing Room to the Kitchen Sink

(p. 1277)

Reduce

TO THE POINT *Note key words and ideas.*

theater of the absurd

inexplicable universe

science and ethics

feminist

Record

Absurdists and Contemporaries

 *Describe the major playwrights mentioned in this section and the importance of their works.*

Samuel Beckett—his work is described as "theater of the absurd," or postwar plays that express the "bewilderment, anxiety, and wonder in the face of an inexplicable universe." His works also influenced the playwrights Tom Stoppard and Harold Pinter.

Tom Stoppard—his work shows an understanding of modern science and ethics. He uses puns and wordplay to provoke and amuse.

Harold Pinter—his writing explores the mysteries and underlying meanings in everyday dialogue. His plays have the appearance of Realism. His use of dialogue highlights the difficulties of communication. He won the Nobel Prize in 2005.

Caryl Churchhill—her political plays express feminist and socialist themes.

Literary History: British Drama—From the Drawing Room to the Kitchen Sink

Summarize

➡ *Review your notes on this article. Then summarize your notes by creating a graphic organizer.*

Students' graphic organizers should highlight the major characteristics of kitchen-sink drama, theater of the absurd, and contemporary dramatists. Possible answers include a classification chart, a web diagram, or a main idea organizer.

Literary History: British Drama—From the Drawing Room to the Kitchen Sink

Apply

Multiple Choice

Circle the letter of the best choice(s) for the following questions.

1. Which of the following was *not* a reason for frustration in Britain after World War I? B
   A. wartime rationing
   B. a lack of British theater
   C. slow postwar recovery
   D. college educations did not lead to meaningful work

2. Which drama influenced Tom Stoppard's *Rosencrantz and Guildenstern Are Dead*? D
   A. *Macbeth*
   B. *The Glass Menagerie*
   C. *A Doll's House*
   D. *Hamlet*

3. Which of the following describes a characteristic of "kitchen-sink drama"? B, D
   A. takes place in a drawing room
   B. deals with working-class life
   C. features upper-class characters
   D. features a realistic setting

4. The term "theater of the absurd" is drawn from the writings of   C
   A. Samuel Beckett.
   B. Martin Esslin.
   C. Albert Camus.
   D. Arnold Wesker.

Matching

Write the letter of the choice in the second column that best matches each item in the first column.

5. wrote play about a working-class girl struggling with single motherhood _____ F
6. postwar plays that express "bewilderment . . . in the face of an inexplicable universe" _____ C
7. wrote *Waiting for Godot* _____ D
8. works gave rise to the term "Angry Young Men" _____ B
9. explored the mysteries and underlying meanings in everyday dialogue _____ A
10. known for political plays with feminist themes _____ E
    A. Harold Pinter
    B. John Osborne
    C. theater of the absurd
    D. Samuel Beckett
    E. Caryl Churchill
    F. Shelagh Delaney

How can you better remember and understand the material in this Literary History? *Recite* your notes, *Reflect* on them, and *Review* them. You can also use your notes to help you read the drama in this unit.

IMAGINARY HOMELANDS

Building Background

- Salman Rushdie has written some of the most respected and controversial works of the past twenty-five years.
- The following passage from *Imaginary Homelands* is from a book of criticism and essays. It was written while Rushdie was living in hiding, under the threat of death.
- The threat was made as a result of his fourth novel, *The Satanic Verses*. In 1998, after nearly ten years, the threat was lifted.

Setting Purposes for Reading

Memory is easily confused by the passing of time and can often be misleading. As a result, it can be difficult to know the past truly and understand the world around us. With a classmate, discuss the following questions:

- Have you ever discovered that your memory of a childhood event was flawed? How did this make you feel?
- When we move away from a town, city, or country are we still capable of writing or speaking with complete understanding about our former home?

Read to understand a novelist's view on writing in this new global age.

Reading Strategy | ### Identifying Assumptions and Ambiguity

An **assumption** is an idea or belief that a person accepts as true without any actual proof. **Ambiguity** is the state of having more than one possible meaning. To **identify assumptions and ambiguity** pay attention to an author's use of opinion statements, figurative language, and tone.

Active Reading Focus | ### Evaluating Argument

Evaluating argument involves examining the parts of an argument to figure out if the main idea, supporting details, facts, and conclusions are logical, or make sense. As you read, pay attention to how effectively Rushdie uses rhetorical devices and literary elements to craft his argument.

Literary Element | ### Figurative Language

Figurative language is language used to write description, in order to express ideas or emotions. Figurative expressions are not literal but express some truth beyond the literal, or factual, level. Figurative language can include elements such as symbols, metaphors, similies, and personification

Big Idea | ### Globalization

The British Empire transformed the English language into a global language and English literature into a global literature. Since the collapse of the empire, writers from the former colonies have begun to explore the meaning of ethnic, or cultural, identity in a world without boundaries.

Vocabulary

Read the definitions of these words from *Imaginary Homelands*. As you read the selection, use your knowledge of antonyms—or words with opposite or nearly opposite meanings—to figure out the meanings of unfamiliar words.

continuity (kon´tə nōō´ə tē) *n.* a connected period of time and place; the quality of being continuous; p. 223 *The continuity of the comedy movie was broken when the story shifted to portray sad events from the past.*

conviction (kan vik´shən) *n.* a strongly held opinion or belief without need of proof; being convinced about something; p. 224 *All through the Civil War, Abraham Lincoln never abandoned his conviction that slavery was wrong.*

exiles (eg´zīls) *n.* people who are separated from their country; p. 224 *n. After five years of drought had dried up all his crops, the farmer was forced leave his African homeland and become an exile.*

alienation (āl´yə nā´shən) *n.* a feeling of being detached, or apart, from other people or familiar surroundings; p. 224 *The real cause of Rick's alienation from his family was that his hostile attitude had turned them all away.*

diaspora (dī as´pər a) *n.* a scattering of a people from their original homeland into other parts of the world; p. 225 *Hurricane Katrina caused the people of New Orleans to flee their city, and led to the diaspora of survivors in communities throughout the United States.*

Imaginary Homelands
By Salman Rushdie

An old photograph in a cheap frame hangs on a wall of the room where I work. It's a picture dating from 1946 of a house into which, at the time of its taking, I had not yet been born. The house is rather peculiar—a three-storeyed gable affair with tiled roofs and round towers in two corners, each wearing a pointy tiled hat. "The past is a foreign country," goes the famous opening sentence of L. P. Hartley's[1] novel *The Go-Between*, "they do things differently there." But the photograph tells me to invert this idea; it reminds me that it's my present that is foreign, and that the past is home, albeit a lost home in a lost city in the mists of lost time.

A few years ago I revisited Bombay, which is my lost city, after an absence of something like half my life. Shortly after arriving, acting on an impulse, I opened the telephone directory and looked for my father's name. And, amazingly, there it was; his name, our old address, the unchanged telephone number, as if we had never gone away to the unmentionable country across the border. It was an eerie discovery. I felt as if I were being claimed, or informed that the facts of my faraway life were illusions, and that this **continuity** was the reality. Then I went to visit the house in the photograph and stood outside it, neither daring nor wishing to announce myself to its new owners. (I didn't want to see how they'd ruined the interior.) I was overwhelmed. The photograph had naturally been taken in black and white; and my memory, feeding on such images as this, had begun to see my childhood in the same way, monochromatically. The colors of my history had seeped out of my mind's eye; now my other two eyes were assaulted by colors, by the vividness of the red tiles, the yellow-edged green of cactus-leaves, the brilliance of bougainvillea creeper.[2] It is probably not too romantic to say that that was when my novel *Midnight's Children* was really born; when I realized how much I wanted to restore the past to myself, not in the faded grays of old family-album snapshots, but whole, in CinemaScope and glorious Technicolor.

---

1. *L. P. Hartley* (1895–1972) was an English critic, novelist, and short story writer.
2. *Bougainvillea creeper* is a tropical ornamental plant.

Active Reading Focus

Evaluating Argument Recall that **evaluating argument** involves examining the parts of an argument to figure out if the main idea, supporting details, facts, and conclusions are logical, or make sense. Does Rushdie's claim in this passage seem logical? Explain.

Students' answers will vary. While most will feel that Rushdie's claim is logical, many will feel that Hartley's assessment is closer to their own perceptions of the past.

Active Reading Focus

Evaluating Argument How did the photograph influence Rushdie? How does this passage relate to Rushdie's claim that "the past is home"?

The black-and-white photograph had influenced Rushdie to see his childhood "monochromatically," and so Rushdie was surprised by the real colors of his old house. He discovered that the past is the place where the house exists as it actually is, in "CinemaScope and glorious Technicolor."

Vocabulary

continuity (kon´tə nōō´ə tē) *n.* a connected period of time; the quality of being continuous

Reading Strategy

Identifying Assumptions and Ambiguity Recall that an **assumption** is an idea or belief that a person accepts as true without any actual proof. What assumption(s) can you detect in this passage?

Students' answers will vary. Some will argue that Rushdie assumes that the history of Bombay's architecture influences the relationship between city and inhabitant.

Big Idea

Globalization In the context of globalization, what do you think Rushdie means by this?

Many students will claim that Rushdie is referring to the memories and imaginations of the many Indians living in foreign countries. Each individual is creating a personal India in his or her own mind.

Active Reading Focus

Evaluating Argument In this passage, Rushdie makes a point about writers who write from "outside India." How does his use of **rhetorical questions**, or questions to which no answer is expected, strengthen his argument?

These rhetorical questions serve to argue other points of view to Rushdie's claims. By offering these other points of view and then disproving them, Rushdie makes his argument appear stronger.

Bombay is a city built by foreigners upon reclaimed land; I, who had been away so long that I almost qualified for the title, was gripped by the **conviction** that I, too, had a city and a history to reclaim.

It may be that writers in my position, **exiles** or emigrants or expatriates, are haunted by some sense of loss, some urge to reclaim, to look back, even at the risk of being mutated into pillars of salt. But if we do look back, we must also do so in the knowledge—which gives rise to profound uncertainties—that our physical **alienation** from India almost inevitably means that we will not be capable of reclaiming precisely the thing that was lost; that we will, in short, create fictions, not actual cities or villages, but invisible ones, imaginary homelands, Indias of the mind.

Writing my book in North London, looking out through my window on to a city scene totally unlike the ones I was imagining on to paper, I was constantly plagued by this problem, until I felt obliged to face it in the text, to make clear that (in spite of my original . . . ambition to unlock the gates of lost time so that the past reappeared as it actually had been, unaffected by the distortions of memory) what I was actually doing was a novel of memory and about memory, so that my India was just that: "my" India, a version and no more than one version of all the hundreds of millions of possible versions. I tried to make it as imaginatively true as I could, but imaginative truth is simultaneously honorable and suspect, and I knew that my India may only have been one to which I (who am no longer what I was, and who by quitting Bombay never became what perhaps I was meant to be) was, let us say, willing to admit I belonged. . . .

So literature can, and perhaps must, give the lie to official facts. But is this a proper function of those of us who write from outside India? Or are we just dilettantes[3] in such affairs, because we are not involved in their day-to-day unfolding, because by speaking out we take no risks, because our personal safety is not threatened? What right do we have to speak at all?

My answer is very simple. Literature is self-validating. That is to say, a book is not justified by its author's worthiness to write it, but by the quality of what has been written. There are terrible books that arise directly out of experience, and extraordinary imaginative feats dealing with themes which the author has been obliged to approach from the outside.

---

3. Here, *dilettantes* means "amateurs" or "those with a superficial understanding."

Literature is not in the business of copyrighting certain themes for certain groups. And as for risk: the real risks of any artist are taken in the work, in pushing the work to the limits of what is possible, in the attempt to increase the sum of what it is possible to think. Books become good when they go to this edge and risk falling over it—when they endanger the artist by reason of what he has, or has not *artistically* dared.

So if I am to speak for Indian writers in England I would say this, paraphrasing G. V. Desani's[4] H. Hatterr: The migrations of the fifties and sixties happened. "We are. We are here." And we are not willing to be excluded from any part of our heritage; which heritage includes . . . the right of any member of this post-**diaspora** community to draw on its roots for its art, just as all the world's community of displaced writers has always done.

Let me override at once the faintly defensive note that has crept into these last few remarks. The Indian writer, looking back at India, does so through guilt-tinted spectacles. (I am of course, once more, talking about myself.) I am speaking now of those of us who emigrated . . . and I suspect that there are times when the move seems wrong to us all. . . . Sometimes we feel that we straddle two cultures; at other times, that we fall between two stools. But however ambiguous and shifting this ground may be, it is not an infertile territory for a writer to occupy. If literature is in part the business of finding new angles at which to enter reality, then once again our distance, our long geographical perspective, may provide us with such angles. Or it may be that that is simply what we must think in order to do our work. . . .

---

4. *G. V. Desani* (1909–2000) was an Indian novelist and journalist. His best-known work is the novel *All About H. Hatterr.*

Reading Strategy

Identifying Assumptions and Ambiguity What assumption(s) can you detect in this statement?

Rushdie assumes that some people question the claims made in the work of emigrants who write about their homelands.

Literary Element

Figurative Language Language used to create description, in order to express ideas or emotions, is known as **figurative language.** For what reasons might Rushdie use figurative language in this passage?

↦ Underline examples of figurative language in this passage.

Rushdie uses this figurative language to express his feelings about being an emigrant in a vivid and precise way. Students might underline "guilt-tinted spectacles," "fall between two stools," and "infertile territory."

Vocabulary

conviction (kən vik´shən) *n.* a strongly held opinion or belief without need of proof; being convinced about something

exiles (eg´zīls) *n.* people who are separated from their country

alienation (āl´yə nā´shən) *n.* a feeling of being detached, or apart, from other people or familiar surroundings

diaspora (dī as´pər a) *adj.* a scattering of a people from their original homeland into other parts of the world

Active Reading Focus

Evaluating Argument What point is Rushdie making about Indo-British fiction writers? How might this passage relate to his idea of "imaginary homelands"?

The writers of Indo-British fiction in the future will be creating their own "imaginary homelands," their own "Indias of the mind," because they will be living in places such as London, Birmingham, and Yorkshire.

Big Idea

Globalization Based on this passage, what is one effect that globalization has on families?

Families must learn to deal with the way in which their children will change as they adapt to new cultures.

Reading Strategy

Identifying Assumptions and Ambiguity What is ambiguous about Rushdie's claim in this passage?

The claim that people who have moved across the world have become "translated men" is ambiguous. This statement could be interpreted in different ways.

England's Indian writers are by no means all the same type of animal. Some of us, for instance, are Pakistani. Others Bangladeshi. Others West, or East, or even South African. And V. S. Naipaul, by now, is something else entirely. This word "Indian" is getting to be a pretty scattered concept. Indian writers in England include political exiles, first-generation migrants, affluent expatriates whose residence here is frequently temporary, naturalized Britons, and people born here who may never have laid eyes on the subcontinent. Clearly, nothing that I say can apply across all these categories. But one of the interesting things about this diverse community is that, as far as Indo-British fiction is concerned, its existence changes the ball game, because that fiction is in future going to come as much from addresses in London, Birmingham and Yorkshire as from Delhi or Bombay.

One of the changes has to do with attitudes towards the use of English. Many have referred to the argument about the appropriateness of this language to Indian themes. And I hope all of us share the view that we can't simply use the language in the way the British did; that it needs remaking for our own purposes. Those of us who do use English do so in spite of our ambiguity towards it, or perhaps because of that, perhaps because we can find in that linguistic struggle a reflection of other struggles taking place in the real world, struggles between the cultures within ourselves and the influences at work upon our societies. To conquer English may be to complete the process of making ourselves free.

But the British Indian writer simply does not have the option of rejecting English, anyway. His children, her children, will grow up speaking it, probably as a first language; and in the forging of a British Indian identity the English language is of central importance. It must, in spite of everything, be embraced. (The word "translation" comes, etymologically, from the Latin for "bearing across." Having been borne across the world, we are translated men. It is normally supposed that something always gets lost in translation; I cling, obstinately, to the notion that something can also be gained.)

To be an Indian writer in this society is to face, every day, problems of definition. What does it mean to be "Indian" outside India? How can culture be preserved without becoming ossified?[5]

---

5. Here, *ossified* means "rigidly conventional."

How should we discuss the need for change within ourselves and our community without seeming to play into the hands of our racial enemies? What are the consequences, both spiritual and practical, of refusing to make any concessions to Western ideas and practices? What are the consequences of embracing those ideas and practices and turning away from the ones that came here with us? These questions are all a single, existential question. How are we to live in the world?

I do not propose to offer, prescriptively, any answers to these questions; only to state that these are some of the issues with which each of us will have to come to terms.

To turn my eyes outwards now, and to say a little about the relationship between the Indian writer and the majority white culture in whose midst he lives, and with which his work will sooner or later have to deal:

In common with many Bombay-raised middle-class children of my generation, I grew up with an intimate knowledge of, and even sense of friendship with, a certain kind of England: a dream-England. . . . I wanted to come to England. I couldn't wait. And to be fair, England has done all right by me; but I find it a little difficult to be properly grateful. I can't escape the view that my relatively easy ride is not the result of the dream-England's famous sense of tolerance and fair play, but of my social class, my freak fair skin and my "English" English accent. Take away any of these, and the story would have been very different. Because of course the dream-England is no more than a dream. . . .

As Richard Wright[6] found long ago in America, black and white descriptions of society are no longer compatible. Fantasy, or the mingling of fantasy and naturalism, is one way of dealing with these problems. It offers a way of echoing in the form of our work the issues faced by all of us: how to build a new, "modern" world out of an old, legend-haunted civilization, an old culture which we have brought into the heart of a newer one. But whatever technical solutions we may find, Indian writers in these islands, like others who have migrated into the north from the south, are capable of writing from a kind of double perspective: because they, we, are at one and the same time insiders and outsiders in this society. This stereoscopic vision[7] is perhaps what we can offer in place of "whole sight."

---

6. *Richard Wright* (1908–1960) was an African American novelist.
7. *Stereoscopic vision* refers to the combining of two images—often photographs of the same thing taken at slightly different angles—into a single three-dimensional image, with the aid of a stereoscope.

| **Active Reading Focus** |

Evaluating Argument Do you agree with Rushdie's statement that he does not offer any "answers to these questions"? Explain. It may help you to review the main ideas, supporting details, and conclusions that Rushdie makes in the selection.

Students' answers will vary. Many will agree that he does not offer precise answers to these questions. Rather, he is simply pointing out issues faced by individuals of Indian descent no longer living in India.

✔ **Reading Check**

1. For what reason does Rushdie feel he had a "relatively easy ride" in England?

   He claims to have had an easy ride as a result of his social class, light skin, and English accent.

2. What kind of perspective does Rushdie claim Indian writers can write from?

   He claims they can write from a double perspective.

AFTER YOU READ

To understand and remember a writer's viewpoint and supporting details, use a **chart** to note the parts of his or her argument. Record the writer's viewpoint in the left column, the writer's supporting details in the middle column, and any opposing viewpoints the writer addresses in the right column. If you prefer, construct a Foldable™ to display the information.

Active Reading Focus

Evaluating Argument To evaluate an argument it is necessary to figure out the main idea of that argument. In this excerpt from *Imaginary Homelands*, Rushdie makes a complicated argument, with many parts. What is the main idea of this selection? Does Rushdie effectively support this argument? Explain.

Students' answers will vary. Many will claim that

Rushdie argues that it is necessary to see the world

from more than one perspective; to see the past and

the present, the imagined and the real, and the native

and the foreign at the same time. Most will agree that

he does effectively support his main idea.

Viewpoint:	Supporting Details:	Opposing Viewpoints:
Although our modern, global society poses many problems for emigrant Indian writers, and for all writers living away from their homelands, there are solutions to these problems. One such solution is to blend the past and the present, the imagined and the real.	• "...the past is home, albeit a lost home in a lost city in the mists of lost time." • While writing <u>Midnight's Children</u> in London, Rushdie realizes that he is creating an "India of the mind." • The migrations of the 1950s and 1960s are a part of the Indian experience, and emigrants have the right to draw on their roots for their art. • Geographic distance might create new angles at which to enter reality. • A stereoscopic vision of society can stand in for a "whole sight" of society.	• "The past is a foreign country, they do things differently there." • Emigrants should not write about their home countries because they risk nothing. • Because emigrants are not part of the day-to-day workings, they should not write about their home countries. • Indian writers who have emigrated straddle two cultures and so can speak with complete understanding about neither. • Black and white descriptions of society are no longer compatible.

Reading Strategy

Identifying Assumptions and Ambiguity Describe an assumption made by Rushdie in *Imaginary Homelands*. Where in the selection is this assumption revealed? Do you agree or disagree with this assumption? Explain.

Students' answers will vary. Make sure that students

support their answers with evidence from the text.

_____

_____

_____

Literary Element

Figurative Language Figurative language is used to write description, and to express ideas or emotions. Locate one particularly striking example of figurative language from this selection. What effect does this figurative language produce?

Possible answer: Rushdie's claim that he wished to

"unlock the gates of lost time" is an effective

metaphor. His use of this metaphor makes his

description of his goals in writing *Midnight's Children*

more vivid and precise.

_____

_____

_____

_____

Vocabulary Practice

Understanding Antonyms Recall that antonyms are words with opposite or nearly opposite meanings. Determine each word's antonym from the choices below.

1. After years of being a part, Ana welcomed the **closeness** with her family.
   (a) diaspora
   (b) conviction
   (c) alienation
   (d) continuity

2. The audience was moved by the speaker's **uncertainty**.
   (a) alienation
   (b) conviction
   (c) diaspora
   (d) continuity

3. The new employees kept up the **interruption** of the work flow.
   (a) alienation
   (b) diaspora
   (c) continuity
   (d) conviction

1. (c) alienation

2. (b) conviction

3. (c) continuity

_____